IMAGES
of America

HARRINGTON

I0805772

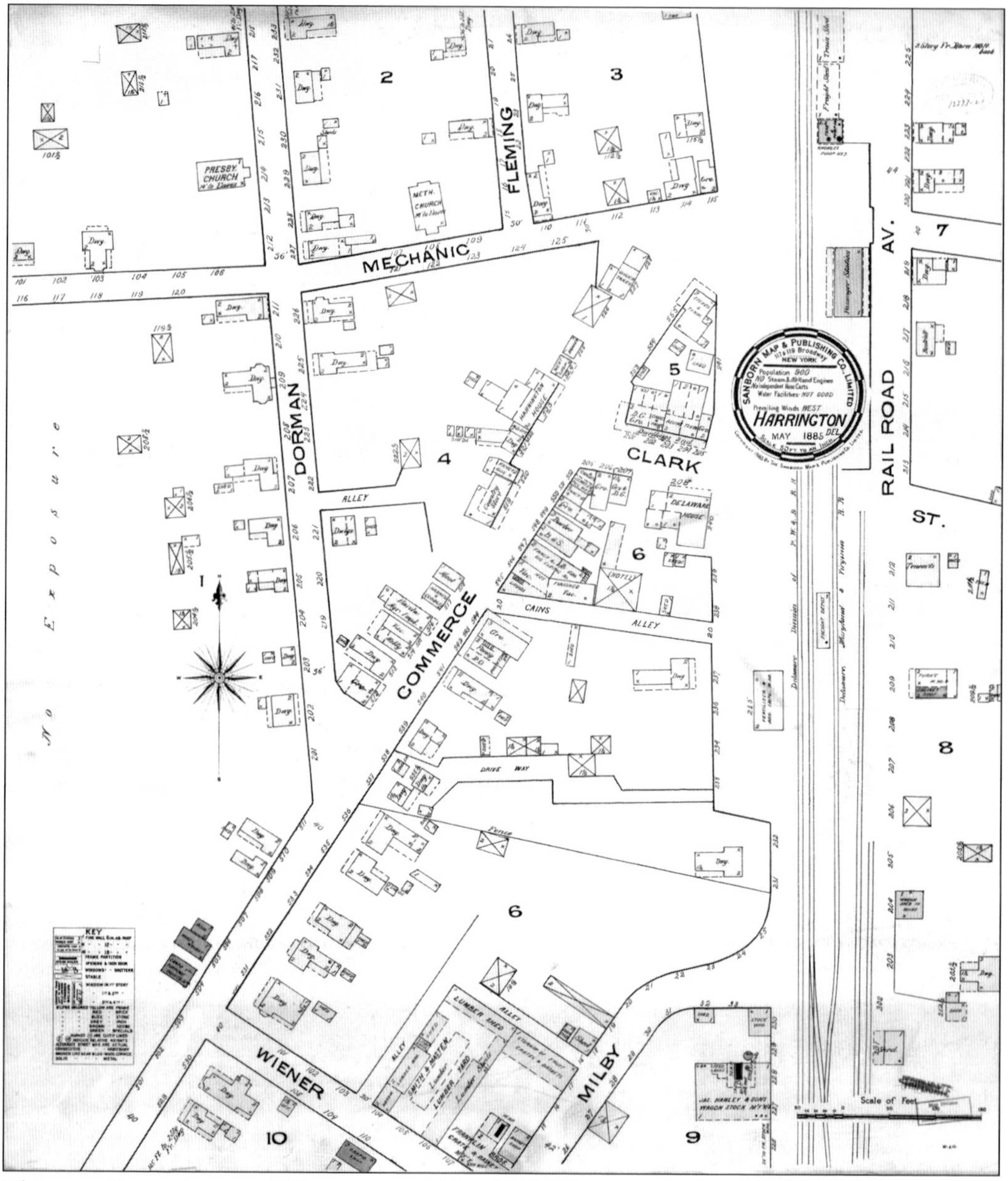

This map shows the city of Harrington in May 1885. The town had no water mains or electrical power. The streets were dirt, and sidewalks were just wooden planks. Only eight streets made up the town in those days. Large plots of timber still surrounded the outer streets. The town's population at the time was approximately 900 people. (Courtesy of the Greater Harrington Historical Society.)

On the Cover: Commerce Street is seen here looking northeast in the early 1920s. Paved streets and concrete sidewalks were signs of progress in this active business district at the heart of the town. (Courtesy of the Greater Harrington Historical Society.)

IMAGES
of America

HARRINGTON

Doug Poore for the
Greater Harrington Historical Society
Foreword by Arthur "Buck" Cahall

ARCADIA
PUBLISHING

ISBN 978-1-4671-0293-3

Published by Arcadia Publishing
Charleston, South Carolina

Printed in the United States of America

Library of Congress Control Number: 2018962702

For all general information, please contact Arcadia Publishing:
Telephone 843-853-2070
Fax 843-853-0044
E-mail sales@arcadiapublishing.com
For customer service and orders:
Toll-Free 1-888-313-2665

Visit us on the Internet at www.arcadiapublishing.com

This book is dedicated to every citizen who has played even a small role in creating the city we all call our home. And in memory of my son Brian.

Contents

Acknowledgments

This book could have never been possible without the foresight of a small group of citizens. In 1977, this group was having a casual lunch conversation, as happens in a number of small towns. This one involved a newly elected mayor of the city, Arthur "Buck" Cahall. He and this small group held two formal meetings, resulting in the formation of the Greater Harrington Historical Society. Pres. Kenny McKnatt, Vice Pres. Buck Cahall, Secretary Charlotte Hutson, and Treasurer Bernadine Butler were the first officers. Tommy and Bert Parsons offered their home for the meetings, and the first museum was housed in his insurance office. With hard work and dedication, guided by other leaders such as Grace Welch, Clarence Collins, and Jean Miller, this small group of determined citizens grew the organization to amass a collection of over 50,000 artifacts that are housed in three museums today. I wish to thank the Greater Harrington Historical Society for allowing me to use this vast archive to acquire the needed images for this endeavor. Finally, to all who have supported me, highest on this list my wife and photograph scanning partner, Lisa, I thank each of you from the bottom of my heart.

Unless otherwise noted, all images appear courtesy of the Greater Harrington Historical Society.

Foreword

Harrington, Delaware, has been in existence by one name or another since 1780, just four years after the Declaration of Independence was signed.

Harrington started out as a part of the vast forest covering Kent County. It was first called Clark's Corner after Benjamin Clark.

In 1856, the Delaware Railroad put a junction in what is now Harrington. Commercial and residential development naturally grew around that junction, and the town prospered. The railroad made possible easy access to Dover, Wilmington, and Philadelphia. Harrington also connected to points east and south. The railroad was the premier mode of transportation for passengers, agricultural commerce, logging, and all forms of trade in a bustling new country. In 1857, a post office was built in the railroad town.

The railroad acted as a magnet by transporting just about everything; it created growth in population, in agriculture, and in other industries in the town. In 1862, Clark's Corner changed its name to Harrington in honor of Samuel Maxwell Harrington, chancellor of the court in Delaware. The area around the railroad continued to grow, and in 1869, the city of Harrington was officially formed.

There have been many reasons for Harrington's prosperity, all beginning because of the railroad. Harrington's economic success began with agriculture and the businesses that support it. There was a demand for agricultural products in the large population centers to the north. Also, there was strong demand for passenger traffic. Harrington has been called "the Hub of Delmarva" for its railroad and later for its highways.

Over time, there would be numerous manufacturing facilities, producing many textile goods, wood products, canned goods, and more.

One very important and long-lasting asset for Harrington began in 1920. A group of forward-thinking men gathered to start the Kent and Sussex Fair. It was and is an agriculture-based fair that emphasized agricultural products and modern methods, showcasing animals, fruits and vegetables, and fun. In 1962, it became the Delaware State Fair, and it continues to this day. The fair celebrates its 100th anniversary in 2019.

The city of Harrington is governed by a mayor, city council, and city manager and provides excellent police protection and other city services. The Harrington Volunteer Fire Company provides excellent protection. The business community is growing and thriving. There are three museums provided by the Greater Harrington Historical Society. There are many churches in Harrington.

Harrington is a great place to live and call home!

—Arthur "Buck" Cahall

Introduction

Harrington started out as a part of the vast forest covering Mispillion Hundred in Kent County. William Clark received a land grant for this area from William Penn in 1681 and became the first European settler in the area. Prior to the Clark family's settlement, the area was home to the Kuskarawaoks, later known as the Nanticoke Indian tribe. Thomas Clark built his home on a portion of his family's land in the early 1700s and named it Clark's Folly. The first business was an inn and tavern constructed by Benjamin Clark, William's grandson, in the late 1700s. He renamed the crossroads Clark's Corner.

By the 1850s, small farms had grown up in the rural portions of the area, with fruits being common crops. But getting these sweet fruits to market before they spoiled was a transportation nightmare. While schooners and steamships traveled the Delaware River and Delaware Bay daily to the port of Philadelphia, a more cost effective and faster way was needed, and a group of local politicians began to lobby for just such a method.

Railroads had been in America since the early 1800s, most linking major cities or, as in the South, cities to shipping ports. Finally, after years of lobbying and failed attempts, the Delaware Railroad was born. Clark's Corner was for a time the end of the line, so anyone who wanted to ship goods by rail had to come to town.

In 1862, Clark's Corner changed its name to Harrington in honor of Samuel Maxwell Harrington, chancellor of the court in Delaware and the man who had championed the growth of the railroads south. The area around the railroad continued to grow rapidly, and in 1869, the city of Harrington was officially formed.

"The Hub of Delaware" became Harrington's nickname due to its role on the railroad. As Samuel Harrington predicted, opening Harrington and other areas of Delaware to rail traffic created a boom in all aspects of life. Trains full of freight and passengers traveled the lines multiple times a day. In the 1920s, the next major transportation route was installed. The DuPont Highway, so named because of its support from Coleman DuPont, ran almost parallel to the railroad, and utilizing the new mode of transportation, cars and trucks, the town took another step forward. But it came at a cost. As in the rest of America, train usage began to decline. The last passenger trains left the area in the 1940s, and the freight station closed soon after. Today, the railroad still plays a role in the community, as Harrington serves as a major switching point for rail traffic on the line, but gone is the golden era of the railroad.

Through the camera lens and the stories of its citizens, this book is a look back at Harrington's history as it prepares to celebrate its 150th anniversary in 2019.

One

From Clark's Corner to Harrington

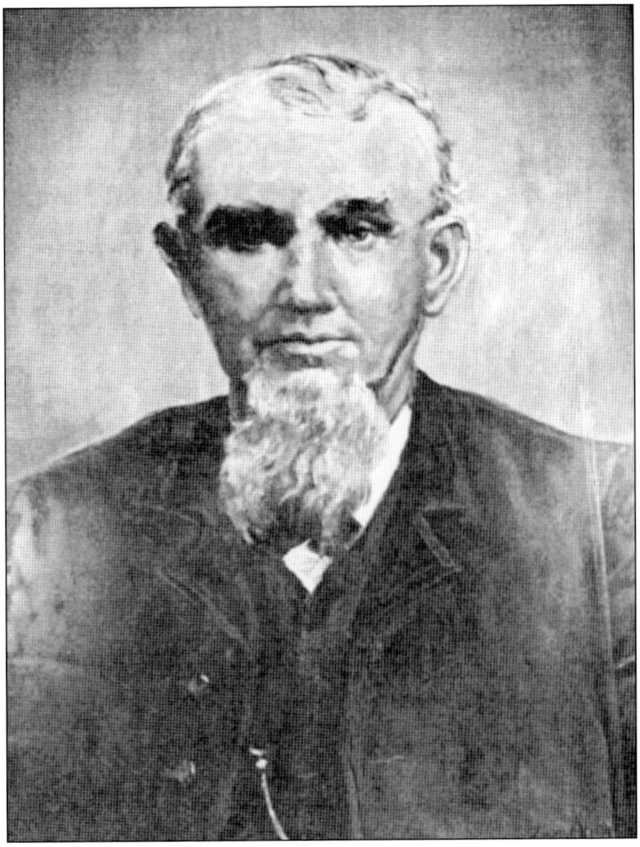

Matthew J. Clark was the founder of Clark's Corner, or Harrington as it is known today. Thomas Clark, his grandfather, was patented the land that was to become Clark's Corner on September 17, 1740. William Clark received a land grant for this area from William Penn in 1681. Benjamin Clark, Thomas Clark's son, built a stagecoach stop and tavern on the land in the late 1700s.

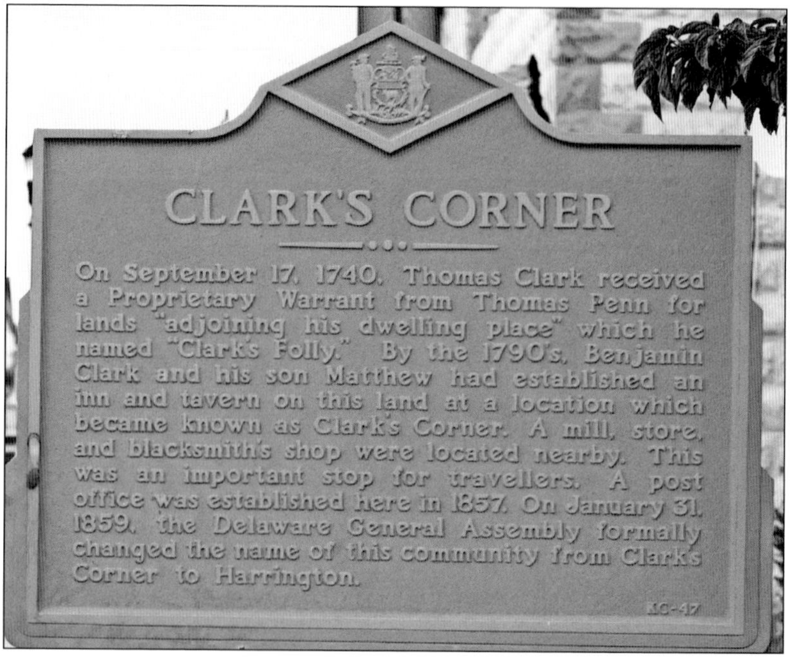

This sign marks the location of the Harrington House, the hotel that was built in the 1850s by Matthew J. Clark. Clark built the hotel in conjunction with the coming of the railroad to the area, laid out a townsite, and sold lots in the 1850s to begin Clark's Corner. Until that time, what had been originally named Clark's Folly was just a dot on the map.

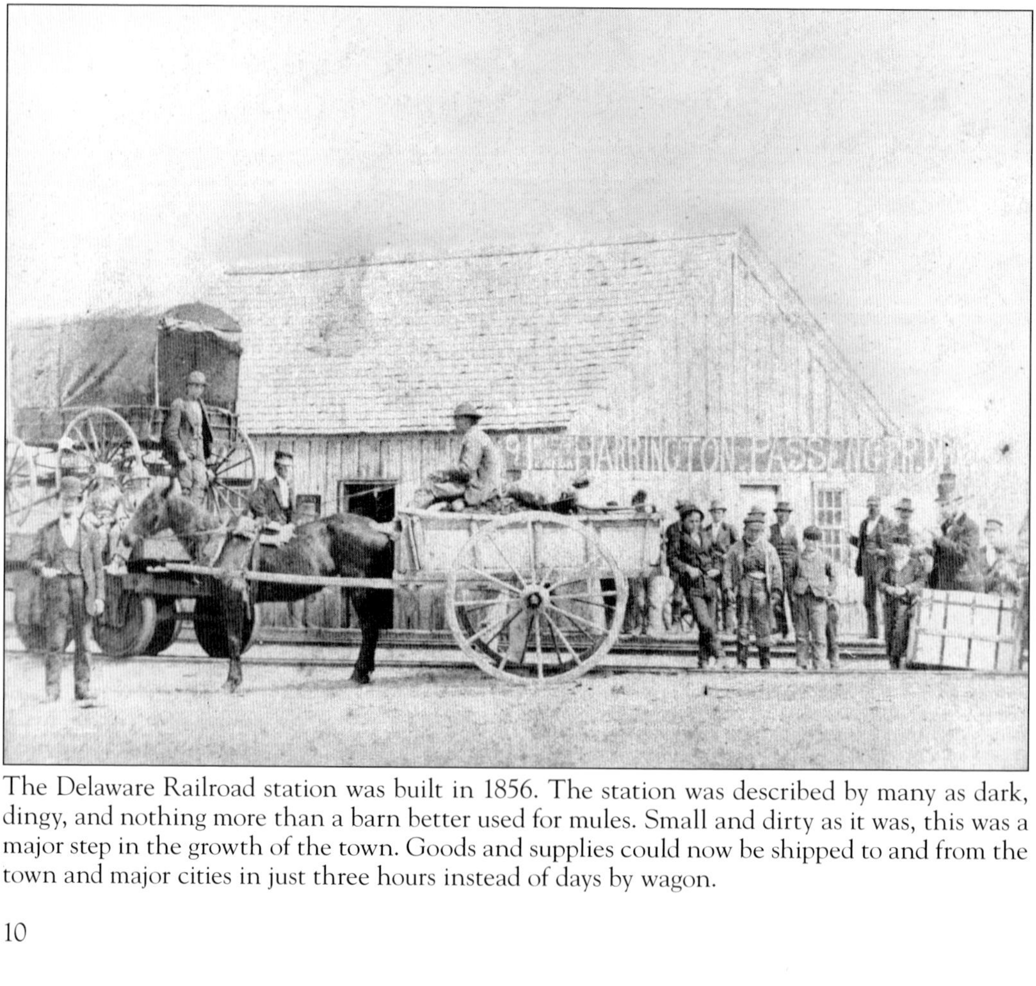

The Delaware Railroad station was built in 1856. The station was described by many as dark, dingy, and nothing more than a barn better used for mules. Small and dirty as it was, this was a major step in the growth of the town. Goods and supplies could now be shipped to and from the town and major cities in just three hours instead of days by wagon.

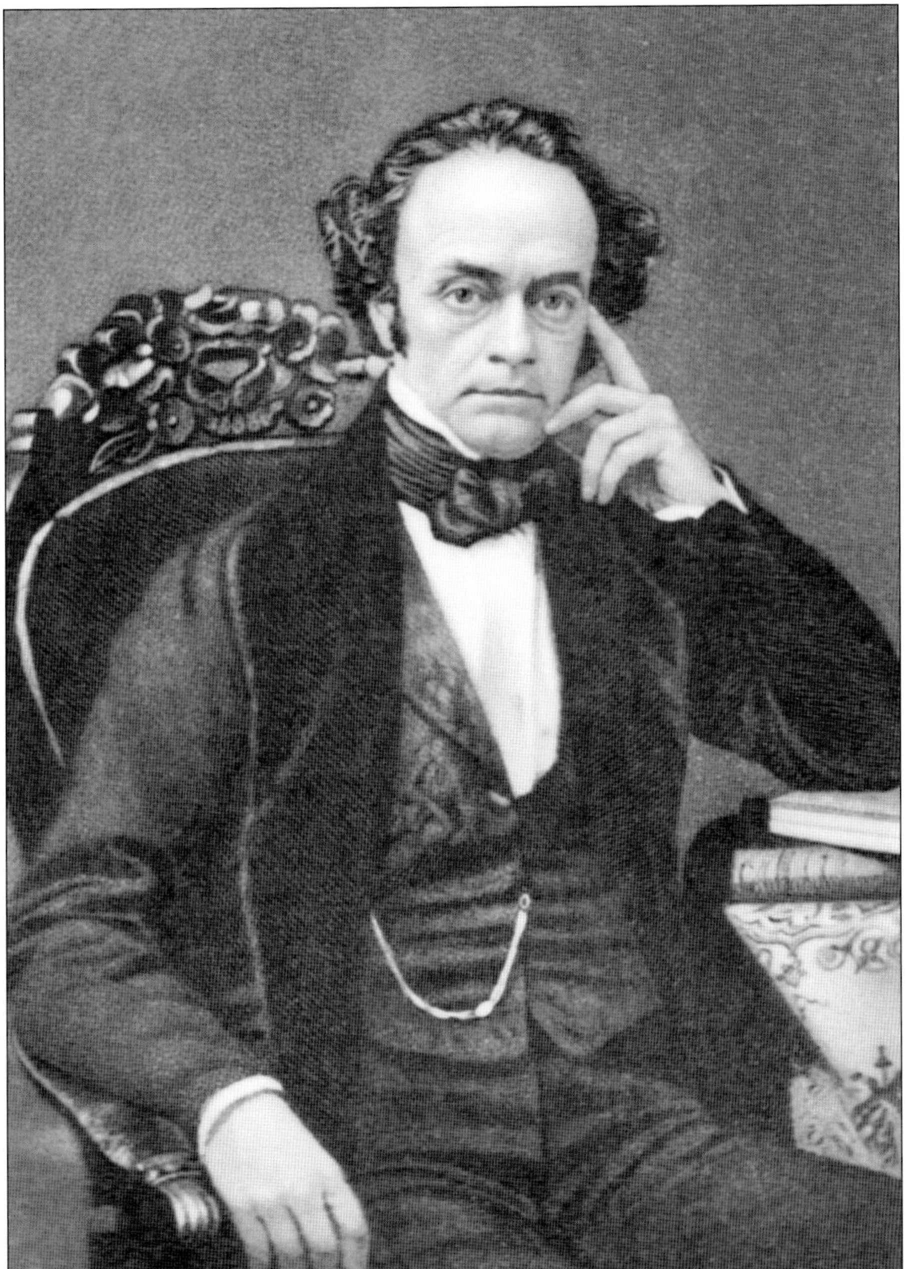

Judge Samuel Maxwell Harrington was born on February 3, 1803. By the time railroads had become major business ventures, he was the chief justice of the Delaware Supreme Court. He became an ardent supporter of and lobbied heavily for the building of a rail line to southern Delaware. He realized that growth in the lower part of the state had become stagnant. Farmers had no cheap way to get the goods they needed, nor did they have a method to bulk ship their crops to the major cities in the Northeast. These steps were needed in order for the region to prosper and grow. The population was so stagnant that, in the 1830 US Census, the lower two counties of Delaware were the only two areas of the country that showed zero growth in population. Due to his foresight and never wavering support, the town was renamed for Harrington on January 31, 1859.

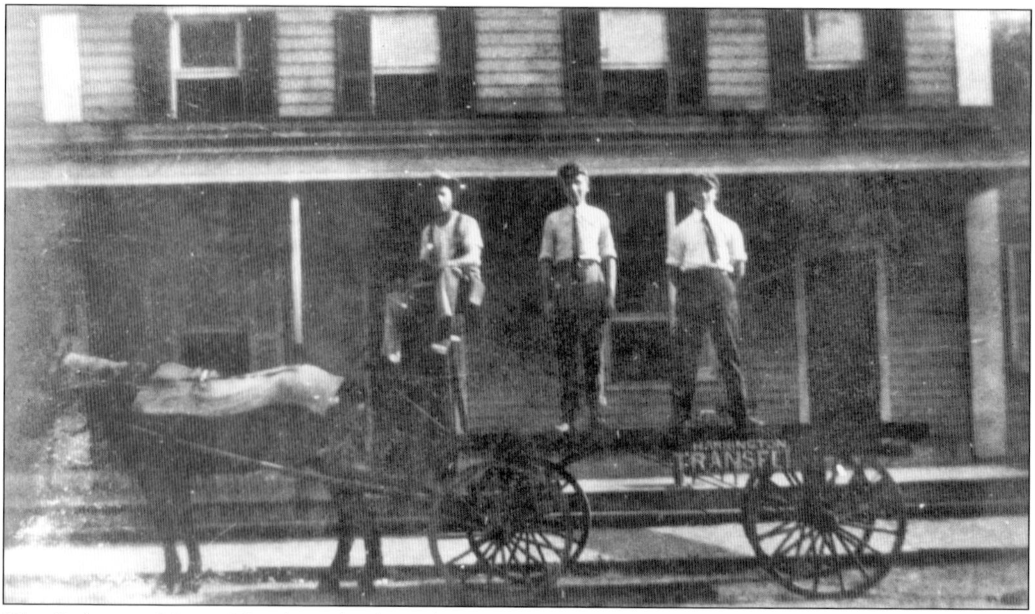

The Delaware House Hotel was built in the 1850s by Levi Cain as a warehouse for the railroad. In 1861, it was made into a hotel by William Sapp and Thomas Dorman. The hotel was sold in the 1920s and moved to Reese Avenue, where it was made into three houses. From left to right are Arlie Derrickson, Elmer Tee, and Gus Raughley. This photograph was taken in the early 1900s.

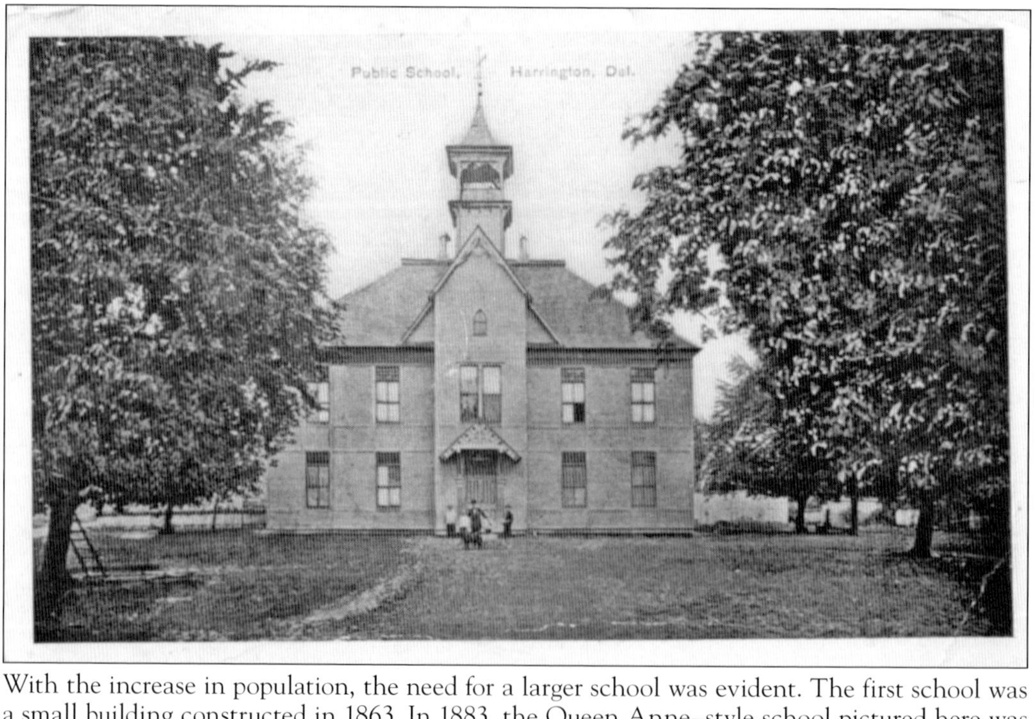

With the increase in population, the need for a larger school was evident. The first school was a small building constructed in 1863. In 1883, the Queen Anne–style school pictured here was constructed at a cost of $6,000. In just five years' time, the number of students grew from just over 100 to 296.

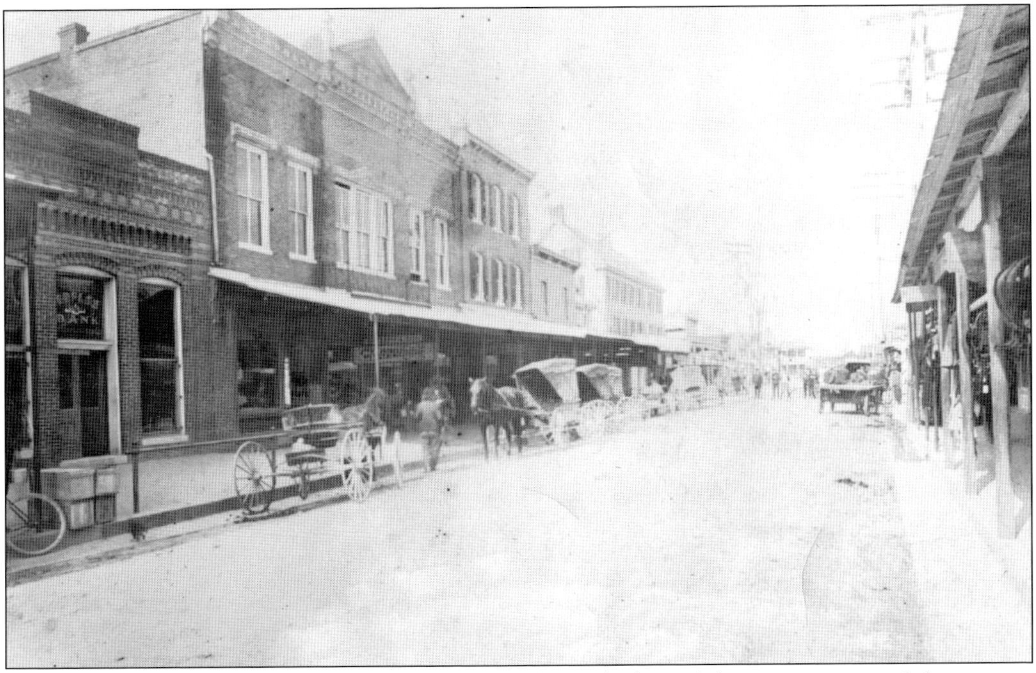

Commerce Street, also known as Main Street in the early days of the town, grew with businesses as more residents moved into the area. The Peoples Bank, the small brick building on the left, was incorporated in 1888. The Harrington Opera House, several restaurants, and mercantile shops now lined the dirt streets.

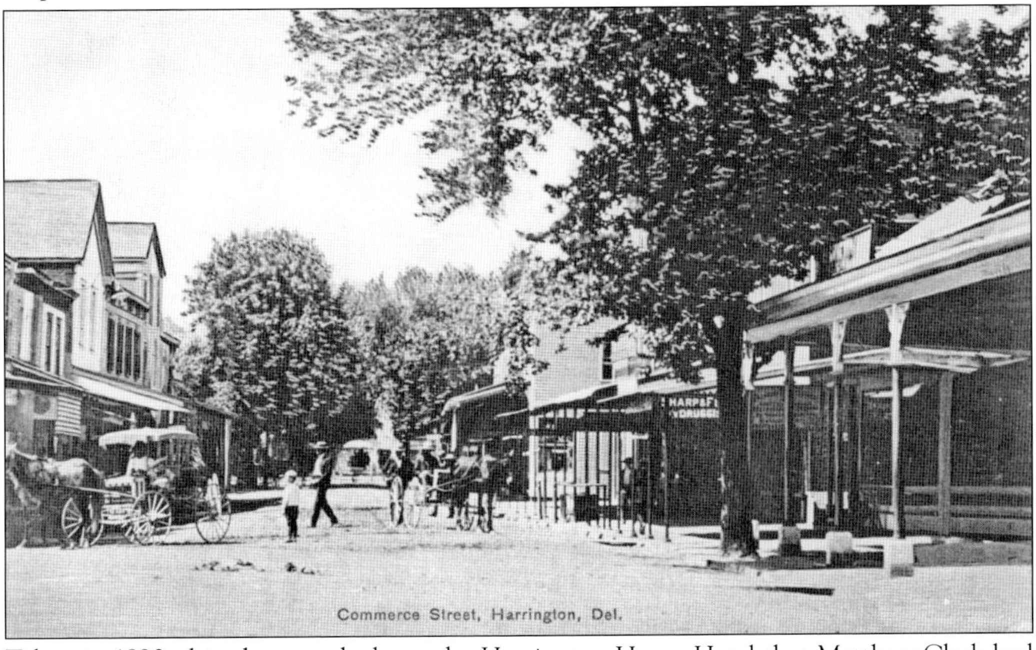

Taken in 1890, this photograph shows the Harrington House Hotel that Matthew Clark had constructed in the 1850s. Shown in the right foreground, the hotel remained in business until the late 1910s, when it was razed for the construction of a new bank. Also visible are several businesses, including a pharmacy, which had sprung up in just a few short years.

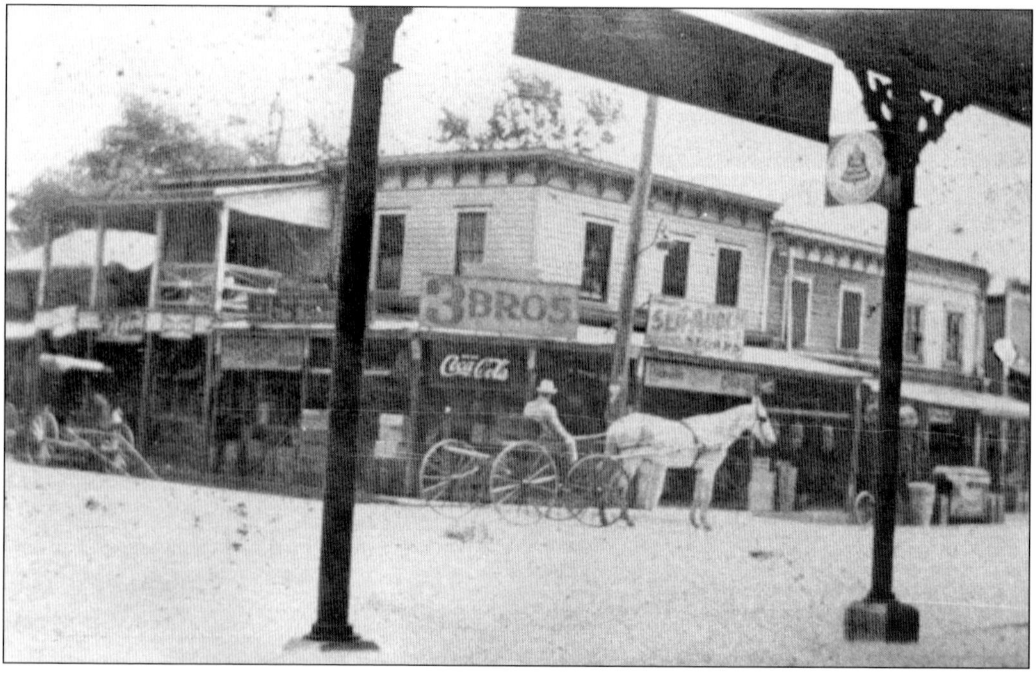

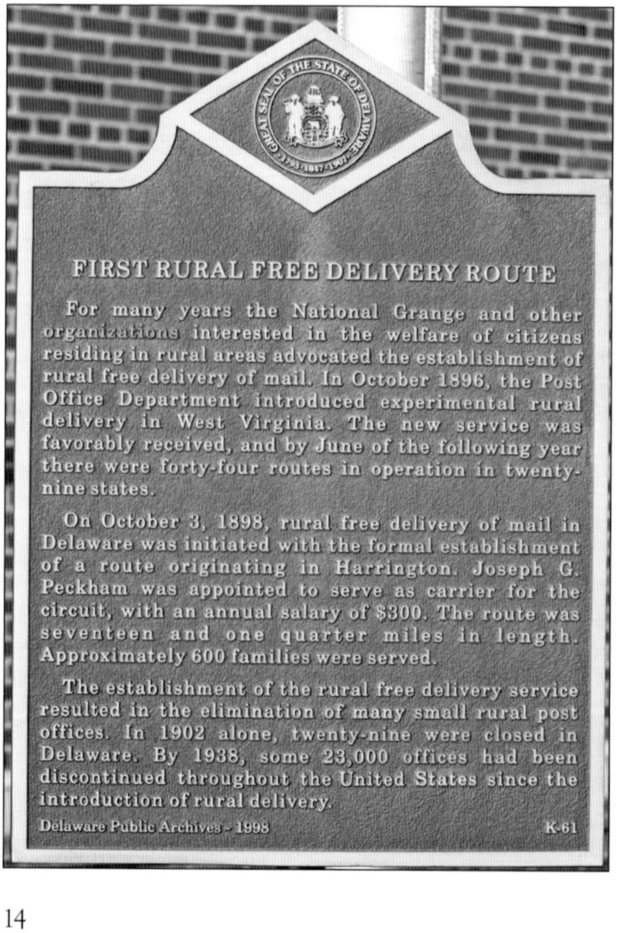

FIRST RURAL FREE DELIVERY ROUTE

For many years the National Grange and other organizations interested in the welfare of citizens residing in rural areas advocated the establishment of rural free delivery of mail. In October 1896, the Post Office Department introduced experimental rural delivery in West Virginia. The new service was favorably received, and by June of the following year there were forty-four routes in operation in twenty-nine states.

On October 3, 1898, rural free delivery of mail in Delaware was initiated with the formal establishment of a route originating in Harrington. Joseph G. Peckham was appointed to serve as carrier for the circuit, with an annual salary of $300. The route was seventeen and one quarter miles in length. Approximately 600 families were served.

The establishment of the rural free delivery service resulted in the elimination of many small rural post offices. In 1902 alone, twenty-nine were closed in Delaware. By 1938, some 23,000 offices had been discontinued throughout the United States since the introduction of rural delivery.

Delaware Public Archives - 1998 K-61

Looking from the front porch of the Harrington House, the growth of the town in the 1890s is apparent. A gentleman guides his horse past the expanding business district. At center is the store owned by John Harrington. To the right of the store was the building that housed the town's first post office, established on January 29, 1857.

Until the late 1890s, people who lived in rural areas had to travel to get their mail. This all changed in 1893, when Congress passed an act mandating new services. Rural Free Delivery (RFD) was first established in Delaware by the Town of Harrington on October 3, 1898, a major milestone for a growing community.

Two

New Life as the Hub of Delaware

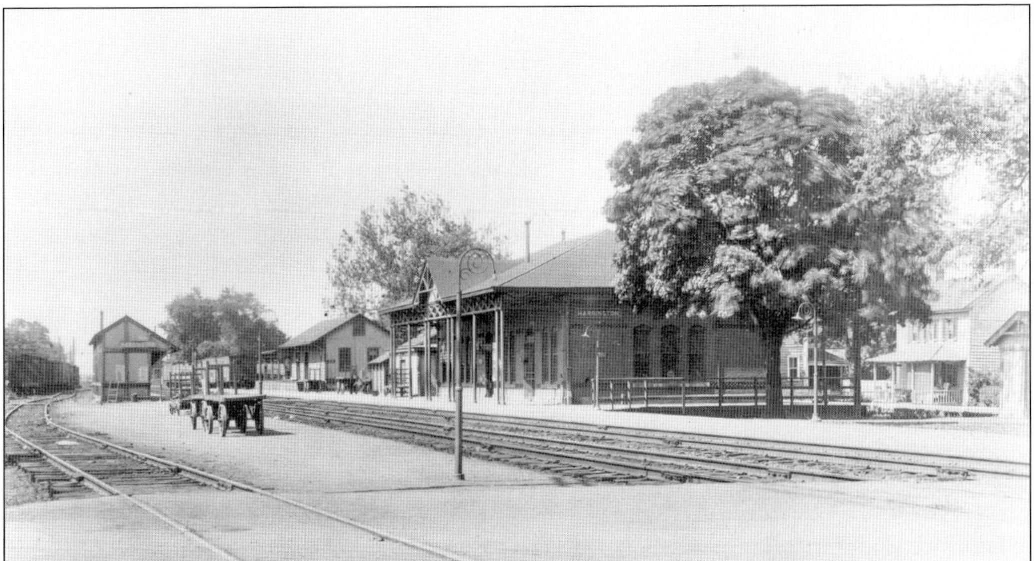

By 1859, the Delaware Railroad had reached Harrington. Initially, several large towns and cities lobbied against its construction. After seeing the boom the trains created, towns lined up to obtain rail service. The Junction & Breakwater Railroad was completed to Milford in late 1859, and by 1869, there was service all the way to Rehoboth Beach, Delaware. To the south, service was extended to Salisbury, Maryland, by 1861.

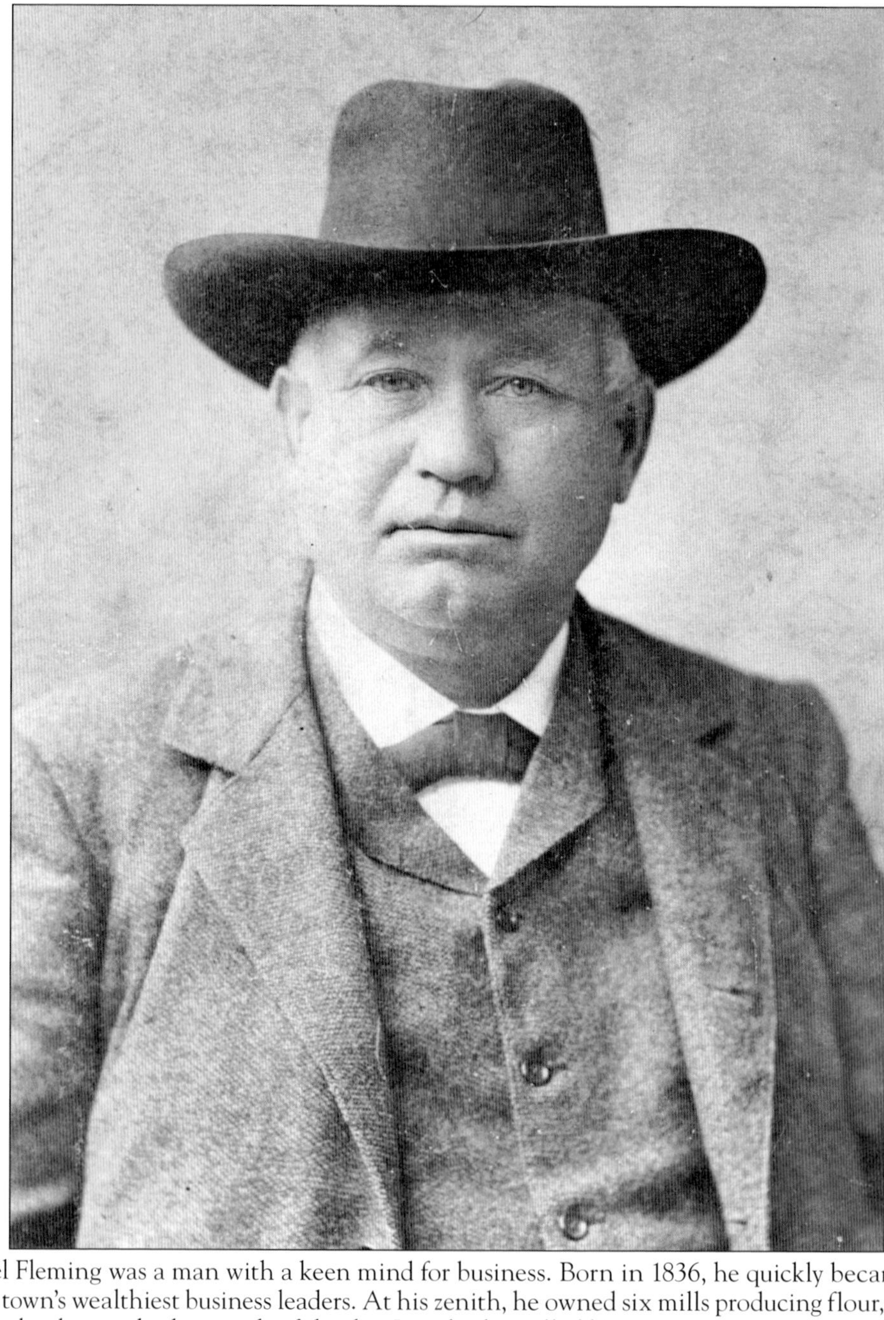

Ezekiel Fleming was a man with a keen mind for business. Born in 1836, he quickly became one of the town's wealthiest business leaders. At his zenith, he owned six mills producing flour, wagon wheels, lumber, and other goods of the day. Locals also called him a very generous man who paid his workers $1 per day, which at the time was above the average wage for this work. His mills employed over 50 men at their peak of production. Fleming was also known to extend company store credit to his employees at the various merchants in town. They could purchase goods and have their debt paid out of their next paycheck. The Fleming Mansion still stands in town today and is slowly being restored. One of Fleming's mills was located just yards away from his home. He installed a sidewalk from the house to the mill because, according to locals, he did not want his daughters to walk on the dusty path.

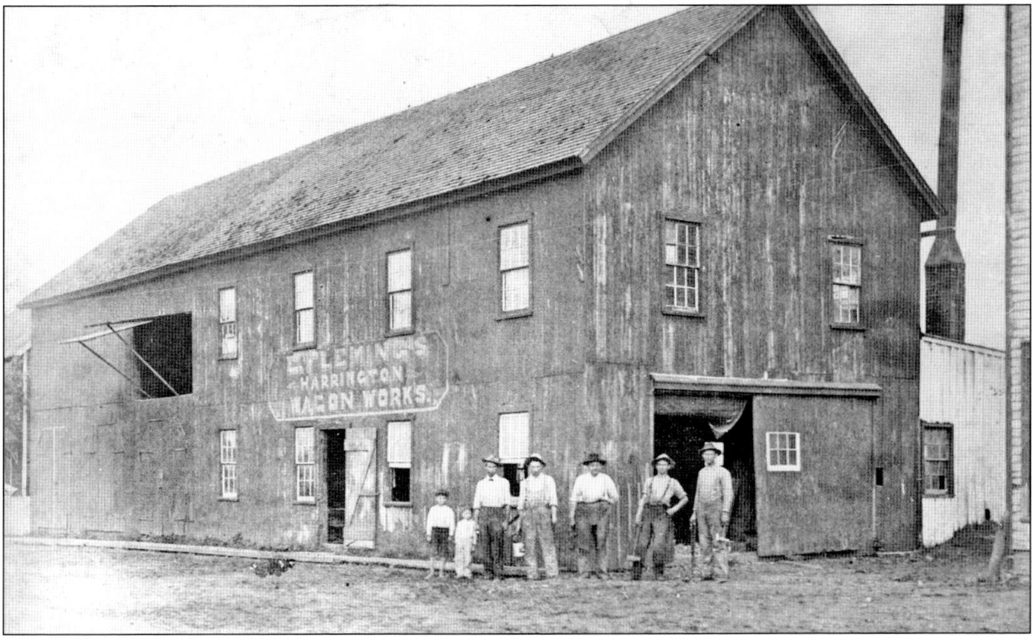

Harrington Spoke and Fellow Works was one of Ezekiel Fleming's first and largest business ventures. With farming being the primary vocation of the area and wagons, carts, and all farm implements of the day being animal powered, wooden wheels were in high demand. Since the area around Harrington was rich with quality timber, Fleming had both supply and demand at his fingertips. (Courtesy of the Delaware Public Archives.)

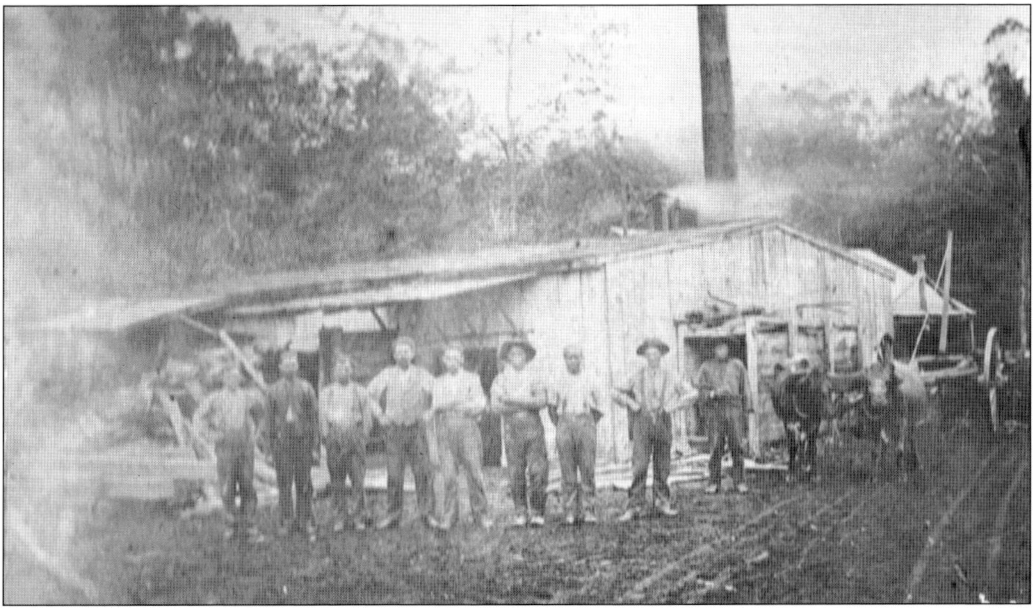

Fleming Lumber was Ezekiel Fleming's next largest mill in Harrington. Seeing that he could save money and increase his profits, he began a large lumber mill to provide his own factory with materials and to produce the lumber supplies a small town needed to grow. The lumber industry in the area was so robust that by the early 1900s, there were no less than three lumber mills and yards operating in the Harrington area.

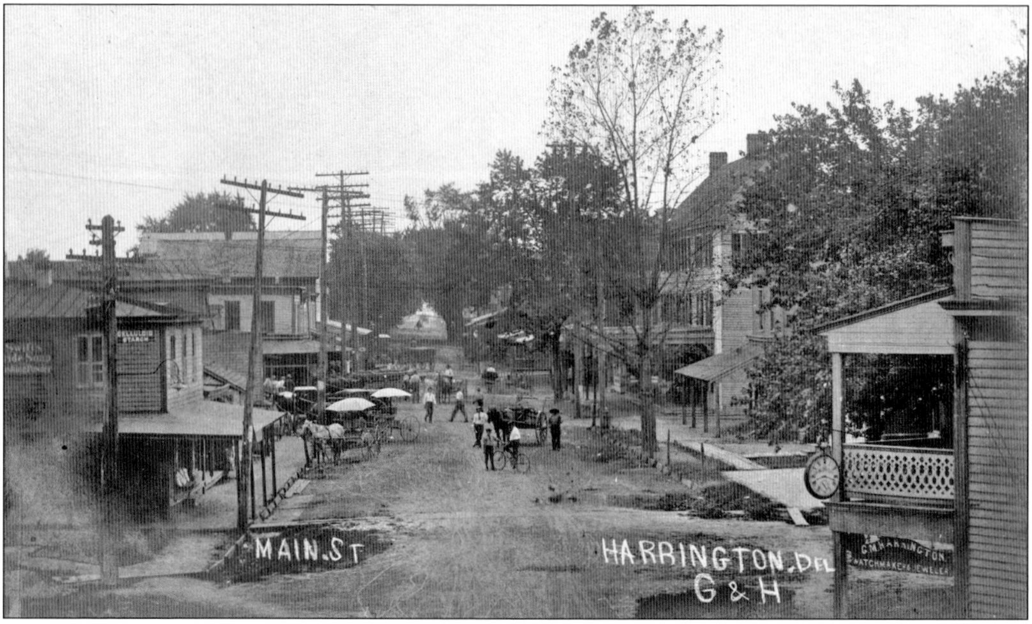

In 1906, the Phoenix Power Company, owned by William Hope, gave light to the town. The company used waterpower from nearby ponds to generate electricity for the citizens. Commerce Street grew at an even faster pace. The photograph above shows the street just after the installation of the electric lines. Hotels, restaurants, stores, and other businesses now line both sides of the street. Maps of the day show 35 businesses, three hotels, and four churches serving a population of approximately 1,500. The photograph below, taken within 10 years of the one above, shows an already changing street scene. New buildings with more refined storefronts have replaced older buildings. The trees in the distance have begun to thin as the wealthy citizens of the day build grand Victorian homes. (Below, courtesy of the Delaware Public Archives.)

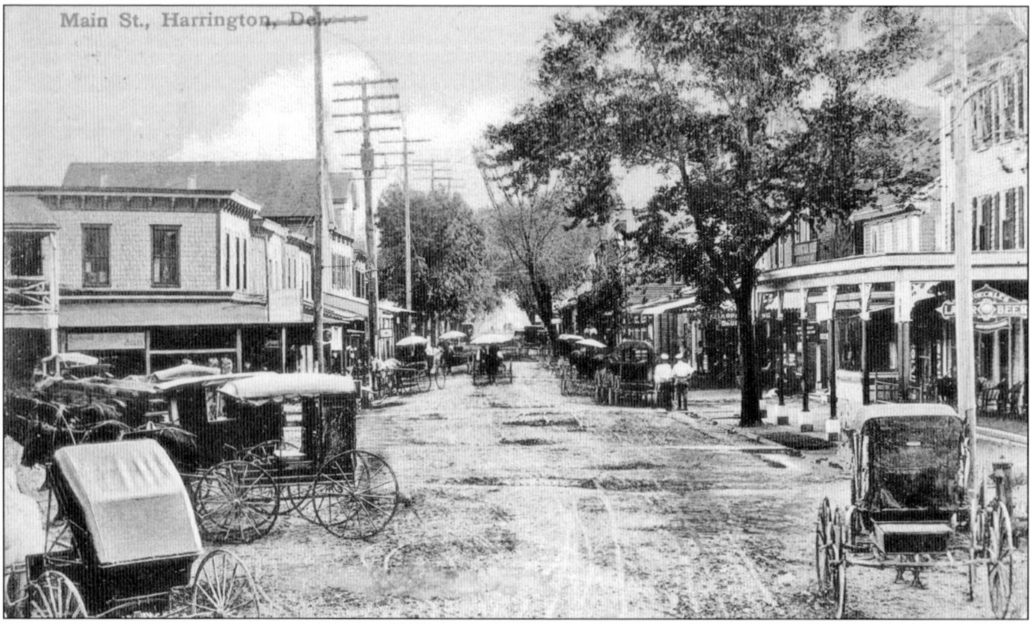

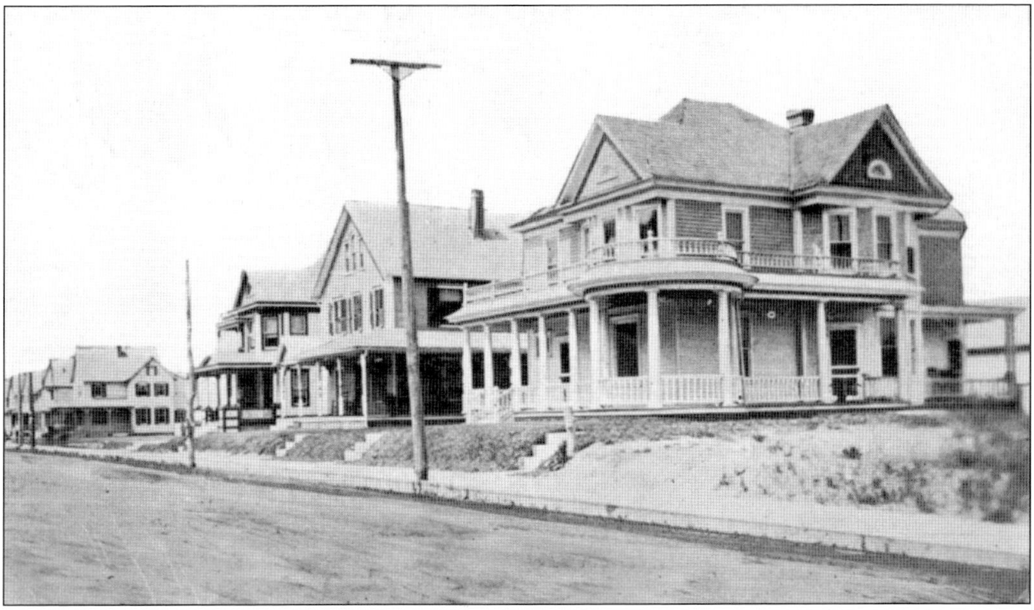

The grand Victorian homes of Commerce Street were built between 1895 and 1915 and reflected the style of the day. The home on the right in the foreground belonged to Ora Sapp, a wealthy and influential man of the town. He owned a clothier store, imported and exported goods, and was vice president of Peoples Bank and the Kent and Sussex Fair. All the homes in this photograph still exist today.

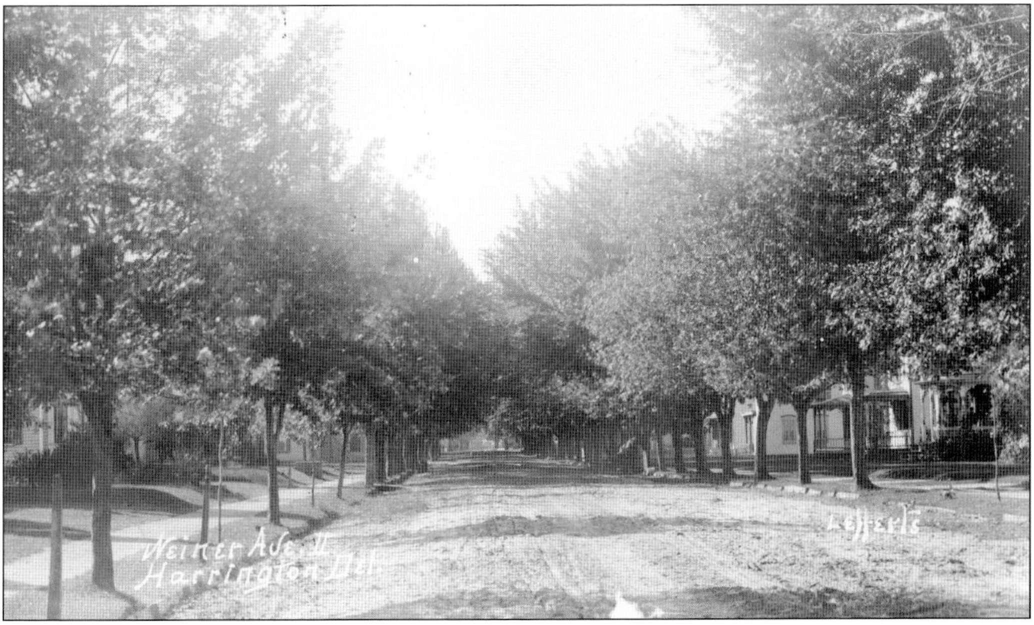

Weiner Avenue was another tree-lined street that was home to several of the town's majestic homes. Residents such as William Shaw, John Sheldrake, and several Minner families built beautiful Victorian homes along this newly created avenue. With each new home, the population in Harrington continued to grow, just as Samuel Harrington had predicted in 1856 when he believed in the area's potential.

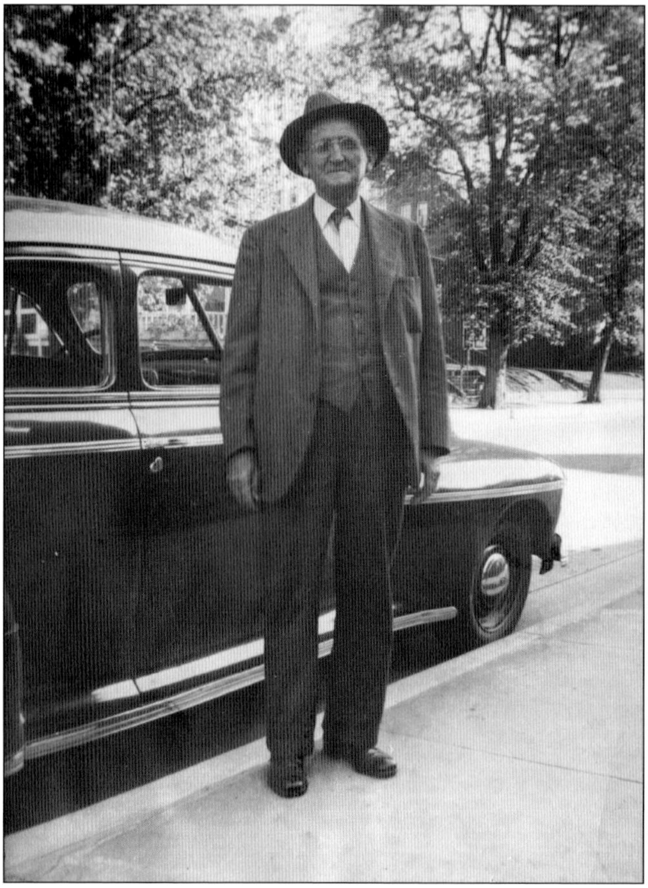

A.C. Creadick was among the many businessmen who ran factories that either supplied goods for the local farmers or processed their crops for sale. Pictured here in his 70s, he was the proprietor of several operations in the town. One of the largest was the Creadick Basket Mill. As early as the mid-1800s, farmers of the area found the soil much more conducive to produce and fruit trees than the more traditional cash crops of corn or wheat. The area—in fact, all of Delaware—became synonymous with the peach tree, which led to the peach blossom being adopted as the state flower in 1895. The Creadick Basket Mill employed 40 workers and produced baskets by the thousands. Creadick's was one of several basket companies in the area producing the goods needed to keep the fruit industry suppling sweet treats for the large cities.

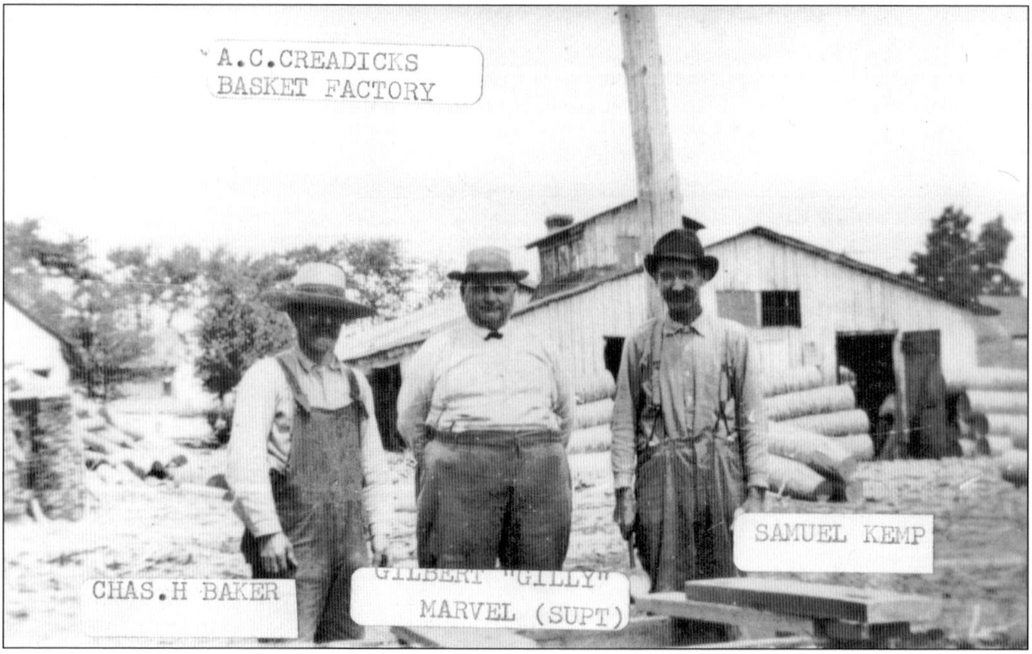

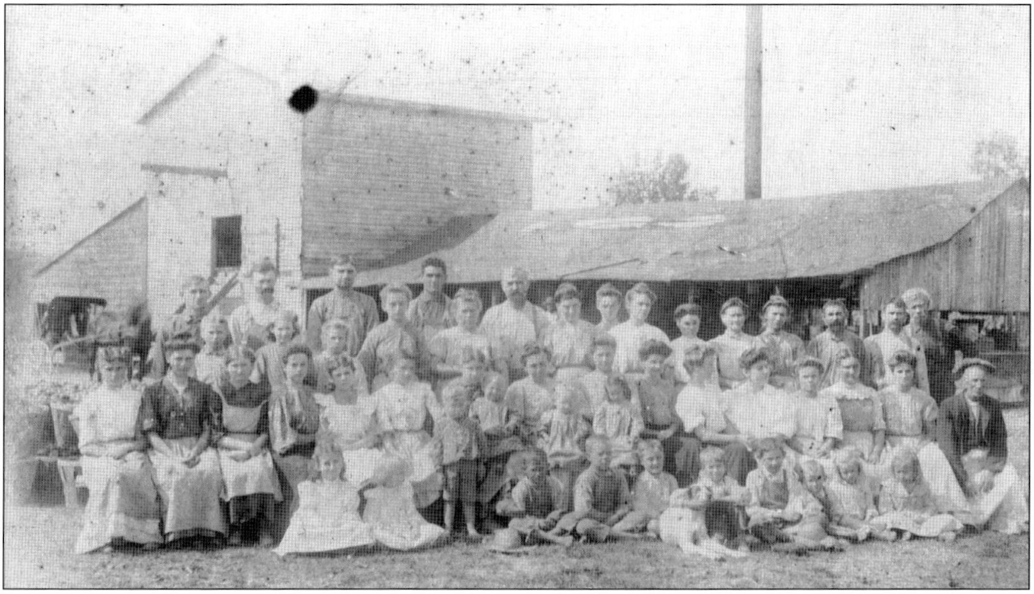

With a thriving fruit and produce industry but electric refrigeration not yet common, canning companies were in high demand. Fruit and produce would spoil before it could be sent by railcar to the larger cities. The canning process allowed these goods to stay fresh for months, providing the taste of a fresh peach well into the winter. The photograph above shows the Clint Minner Canning Company. At the peak of harvest season, Minner's cannery employed as many as 75 people working 60-hour weeks to ensure the factory could keep up with the volume of goods coming in its doors. As many as six canning factories operated in the Harrington area until the 1940s. Some smaller operations, such as the Vernon Canning Factory (below), opened even closer to the orchards and produce farms. These plants tended to serve a small group of farmers and were family owned and operated.

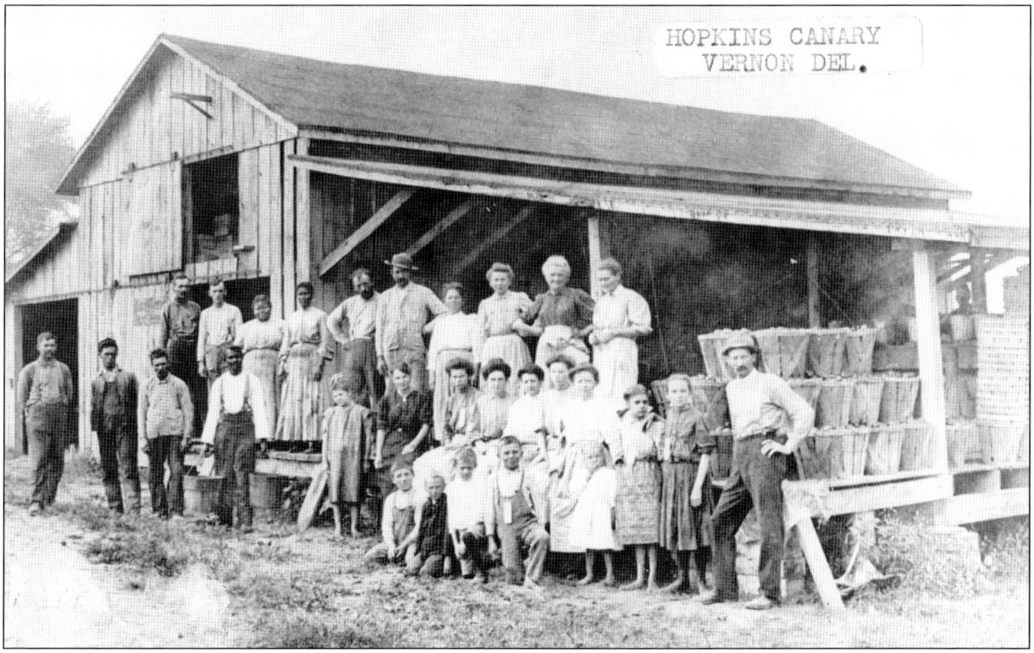

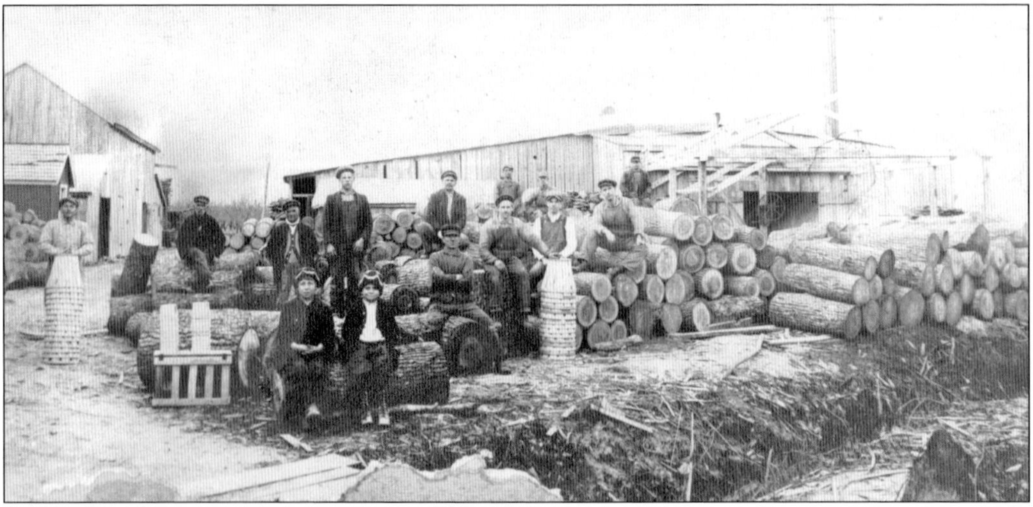

This photograph of an unknown basket mill shows the work that was performed in support of the agriculture industry. Boys as young as 12 would quit school to work on the farms and in these mills. The process of taking local trees and turning them into baskets required many hours of work. To produce the number of baskets needed for the area, a great labor force was required.

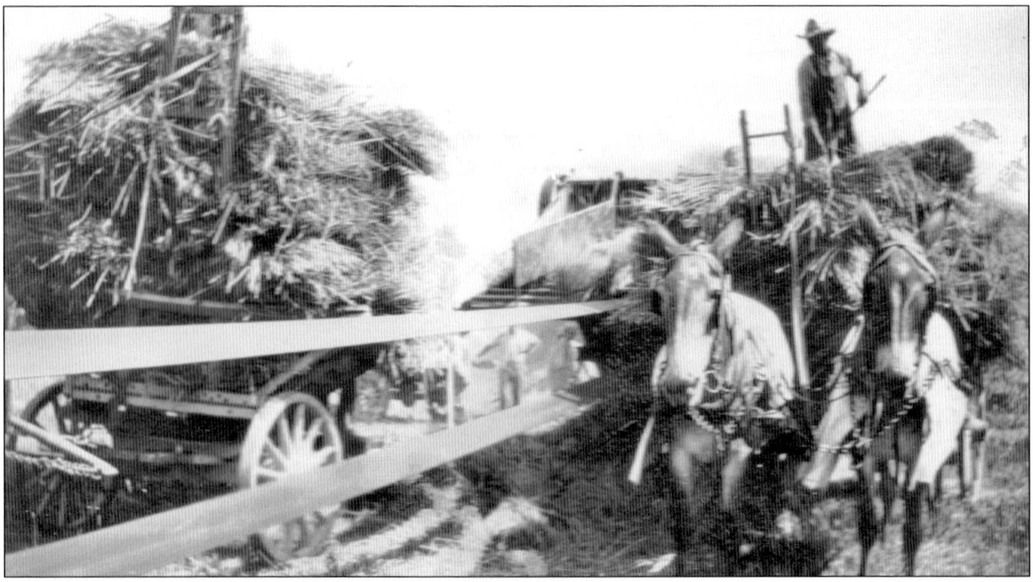

As farming techniques improved during the early 1900s, local farms began to grow cash crops such as wheat and corn. Wheat thrashing machines were first driven by horse power, but with the advent of the steam engine, what had taken days to harvest took only hours. Production in the area soared as these new implements increased productivity.

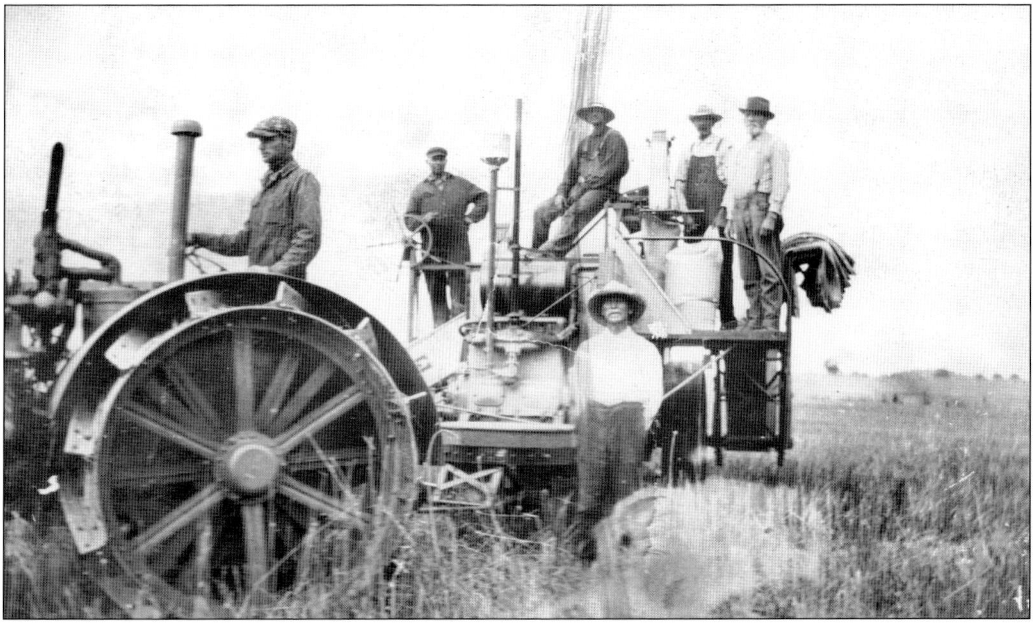

As the Industrial Revolution progressed, even smaller communities saw improvements in the methods used to perform daily tasks. Tractors replaced horses and mules on the farm, pulling ever larger and heavier equipment. Thrashing was now also done by machine and the grain bagged directly in the field. This made for quicker and easier movement to the local mills for refinement.

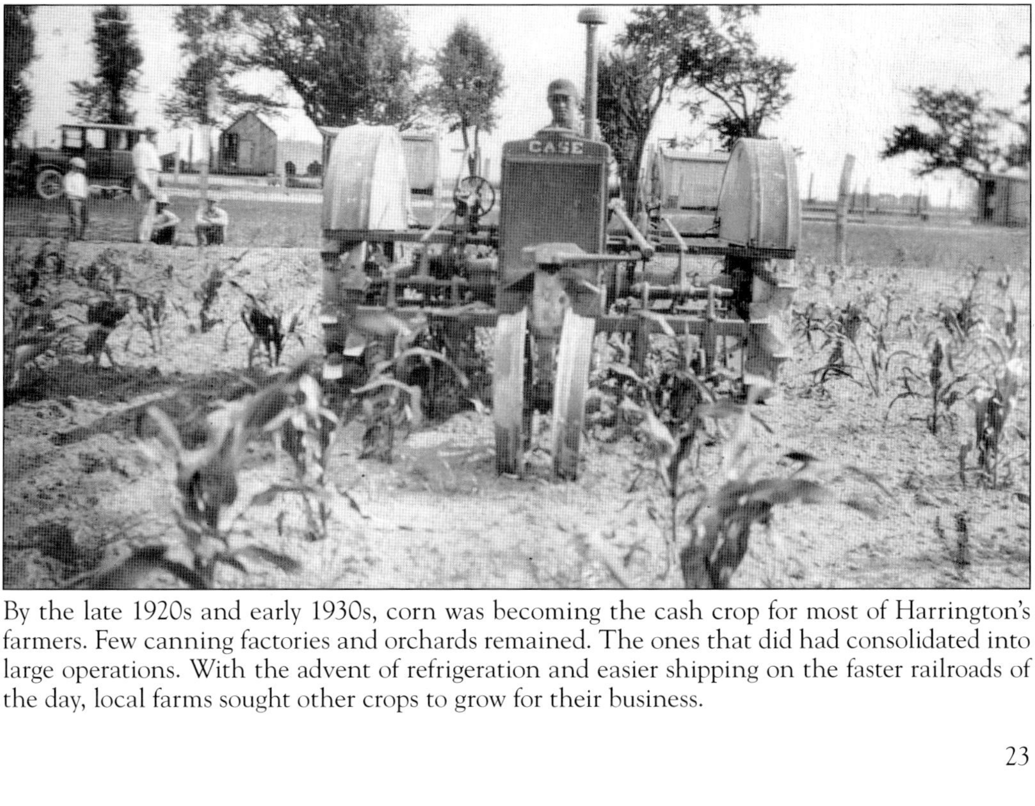

By the late 1920s and early 1930s, corn was becoming the cash crop for most of Harrington's farmers. Few canning factories and orchards remained. The ones that did had consolidated into large operations. With the advent of refrigeration and easier shipping on the faster railroads of the day, local farms sought other crops to grow for their business.

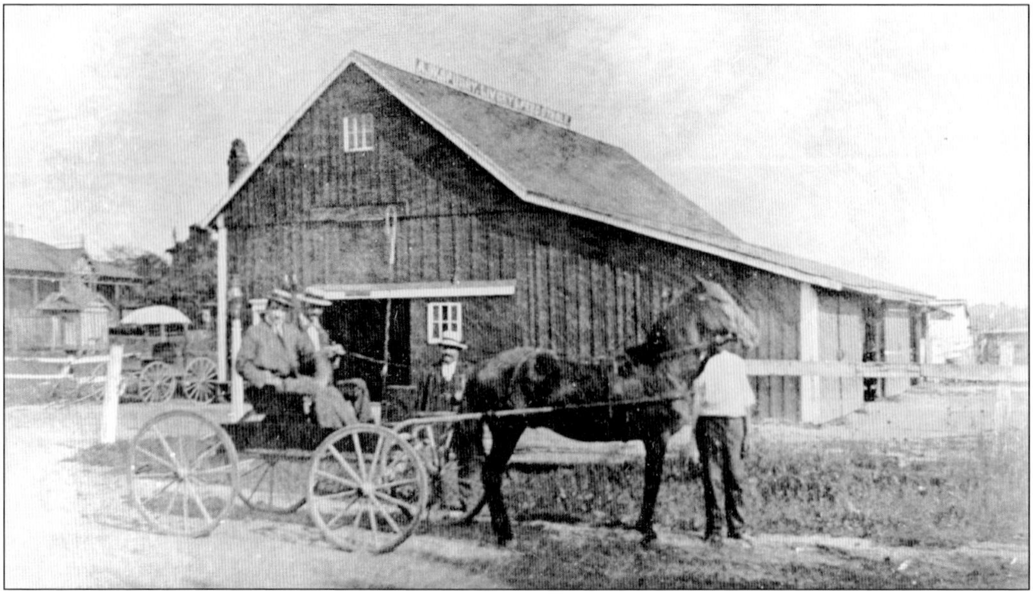

Until the advent of the gasoline-powered tractor, every town needed a blacksmith to keep trotting along. At the height of the farming, lumber, and canning industries in Harrington, no less than four blacksmith shops served the citizens' needs. One of the largest belonged to Al Spurry, pictured above wearing a hat and standing next to the horse. His shop was at the corner of Clark Street and Railroad Avenue. He had an ideal location to serve local residents and provide blacksmith and livery services to those arriving by passenger train. More common to the era was the smaller blacksmith shop shown below. Small shops like these sprang up in crossroad areas outside of town to serve the local farmers' needs.

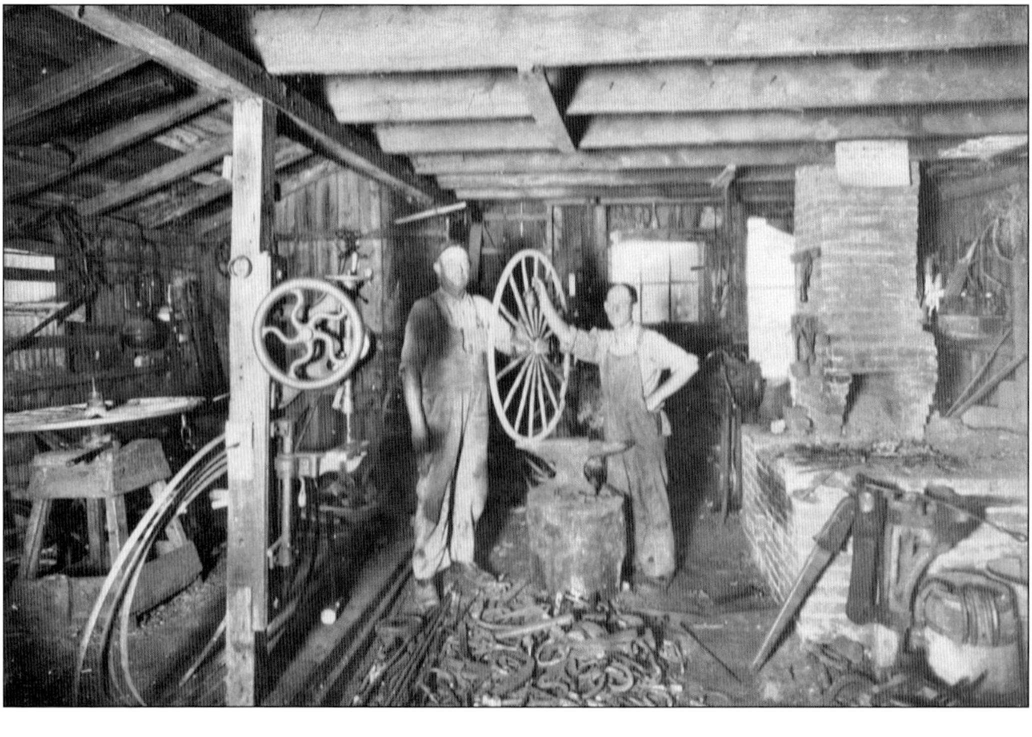

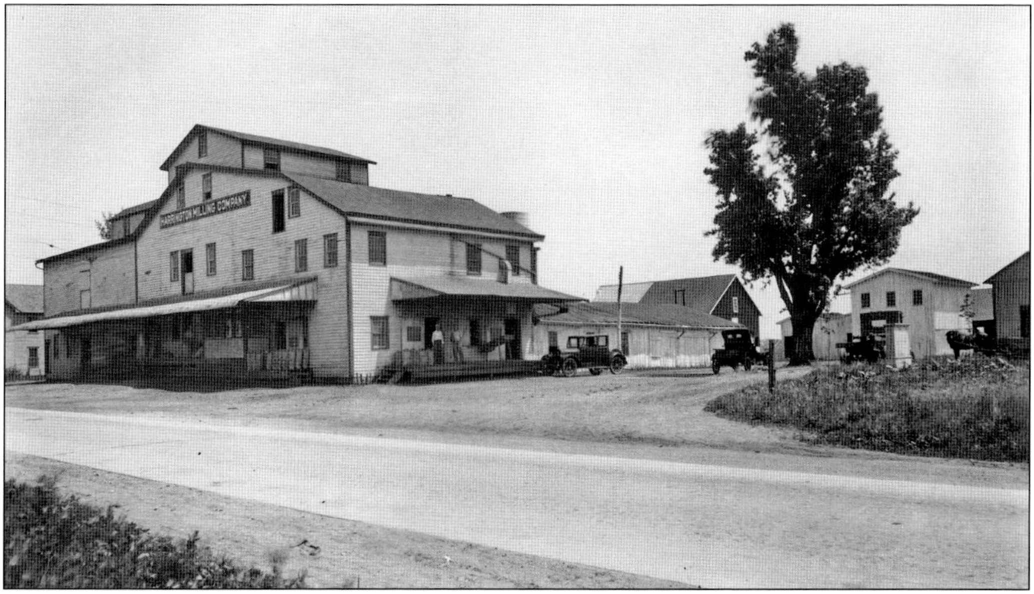

The Harrington Milling Company occupied the space first built by Ezekiel Fleming. Owned by Charles D. Murphy in the 1920s, the mill produced flour and cornmeal, which was shipped by railcar up and down the Eastern Seaboard. Even during the Great Depression, the mill still ran at full speed, and the income reached almost $1 million a year. (Courtesy of the Delaware Public Archives)

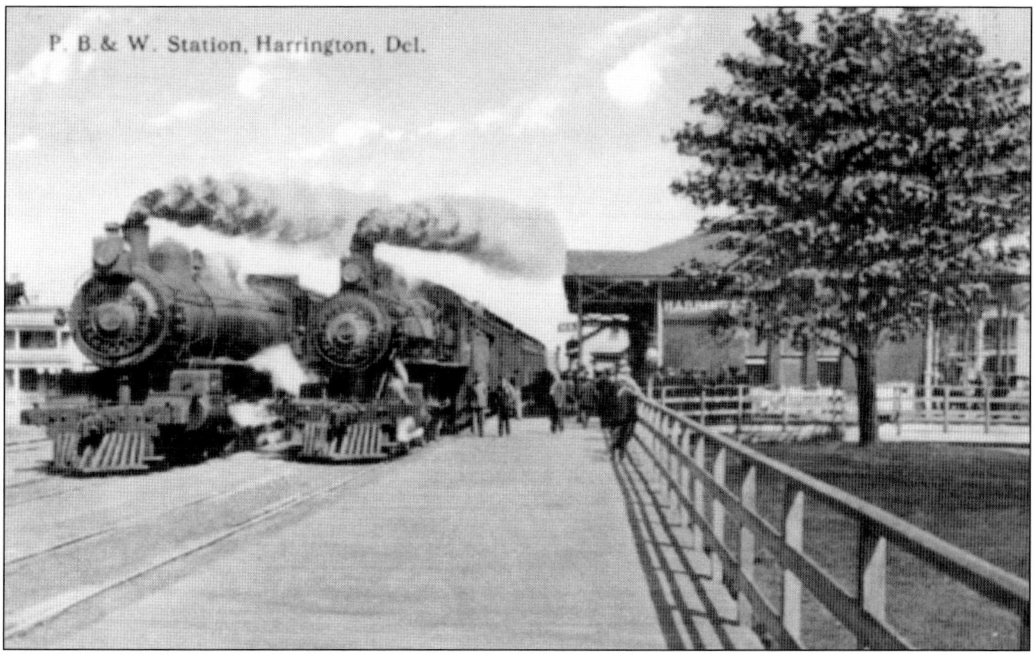

The Delaware Railroad and the Junction & Breakwater Railroad merged into the Philadelphia, Wilmington & Baltimore Railroad in the 1870s. By 1884, the line extended all the way to Cape Charles, Virginia. By 1920, the mighty Pennsylvania Railroad had taken control of the area. Small engines were replaced by massive steam-powered locomotives hauling passengers and freight from all over Delmarva. Track upgrades and yard improvements truly made Harrington "the Hub of Delaware."

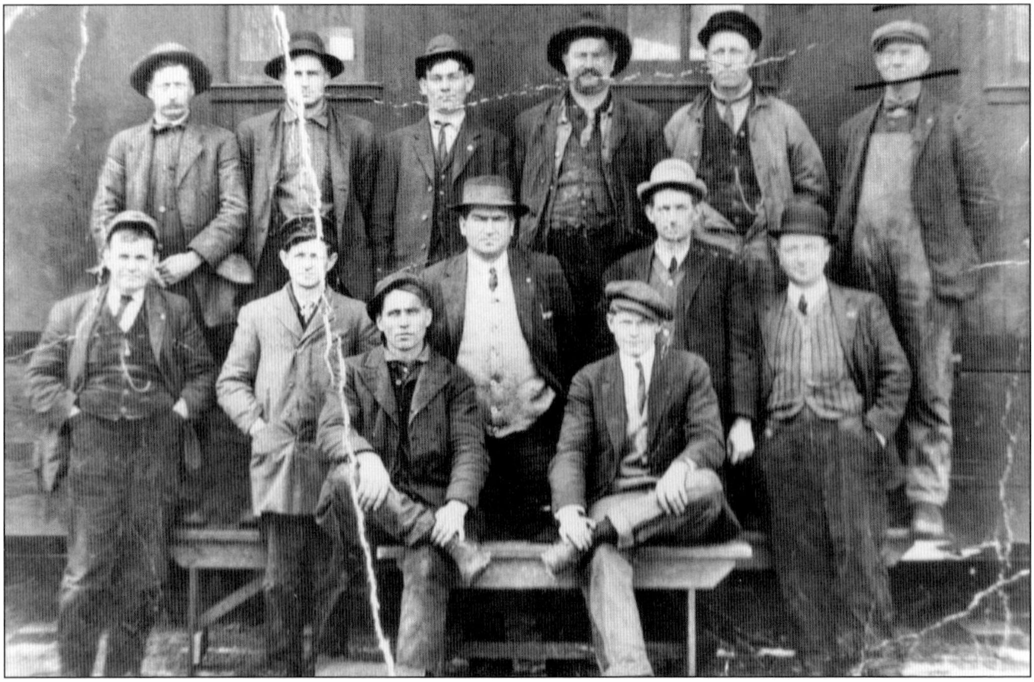

With the increasing traffic on the rail lines, maintenance was a 24-hour-a-day job. Crews were constantly on duty to repair locomotives, cars, or track as needed. With an average of over 50 freight runs a day and an additional 16 passenger trains running between Philadelphia and their destinations, workers faced ever growing maintenance tasks. With tourists using these trains to travel to the seaside communities of Lewes and Rehoboth Beach, Delaware, and as many as 120 freight trains each pulling more than 40 cars rumbling north from Harrington during harvest season, rail usage grew. All of this activity relied on the hard work and dedication of these railroad men. The work was backbreaking, in all kinds of weather, and sadly at times resulted in catastrophic injuries or death.

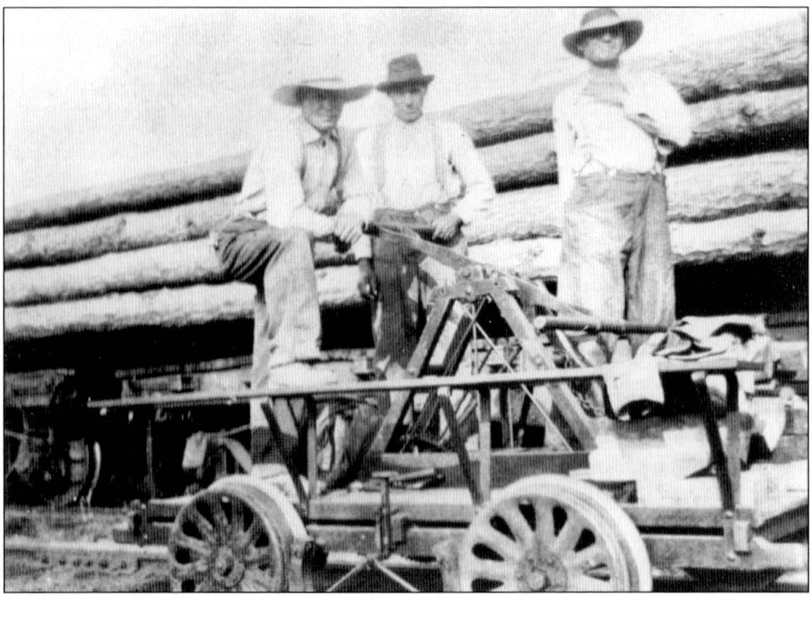

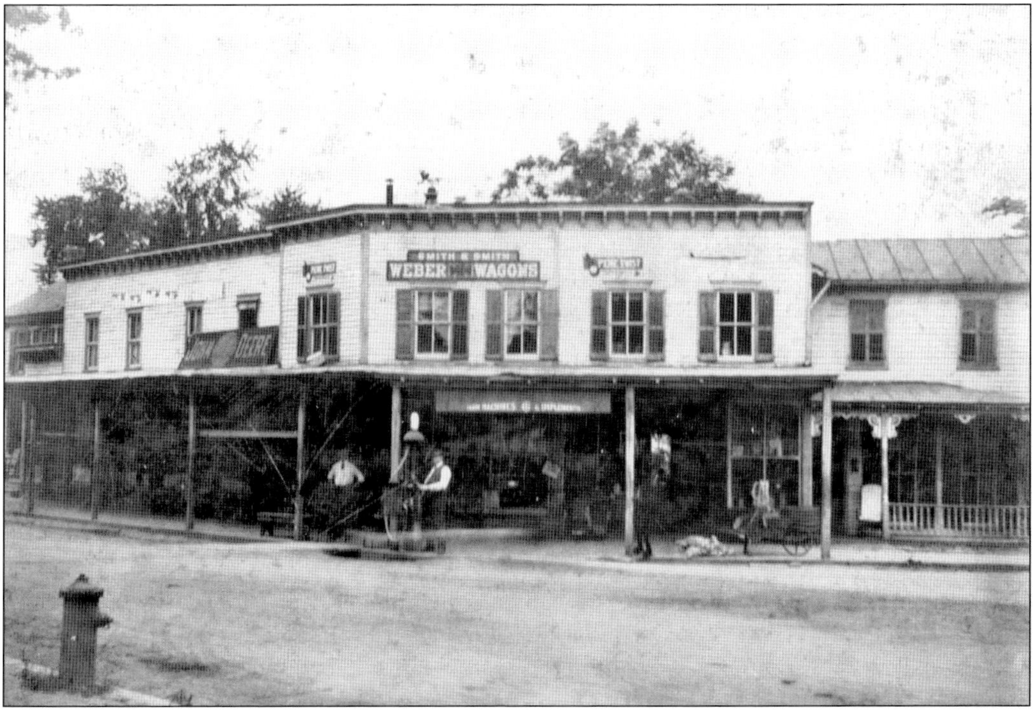

With the increased rail traffic and the employment it brought to Harrington, this small village became a center of activity. By 1920, all of the downtown area had water and sewer mains. Gas pumps, as seen in this photograph of the corner of Commerce and Clark Streets, had begun to spring up at the local general stores to supply the needed fuel for the new horseless carriages. Harrington was truly coming of age.

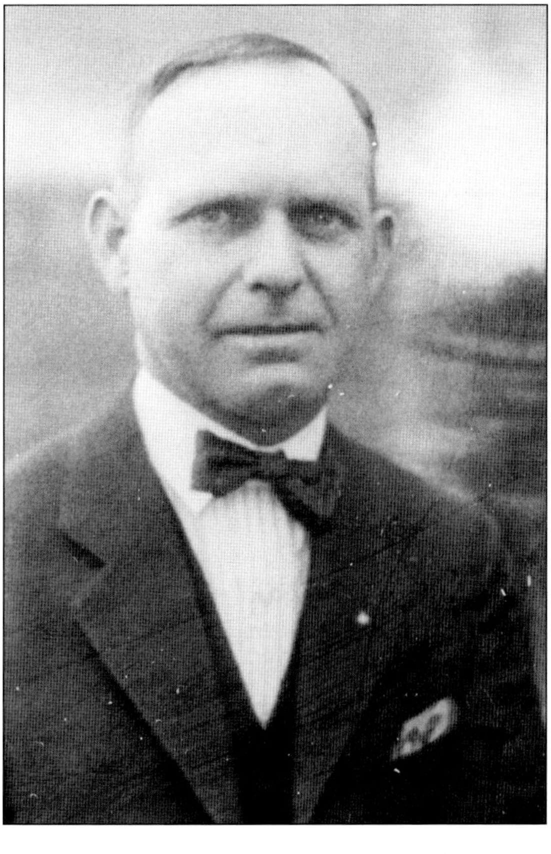

Local citizens clamored for news from the area and around the country. In May 1883, the *Harrington Enterprise* was the first local daily newspaper, but it lasted less than a year. Next, the *Harrington Bits*, a single-sheet newspaper, gave it a try, lasting for several years. Finally, in 1913, Frank Fleming began the *Harrington Journal*. This local newspaper stayed in existence until 1988, when it was sold.

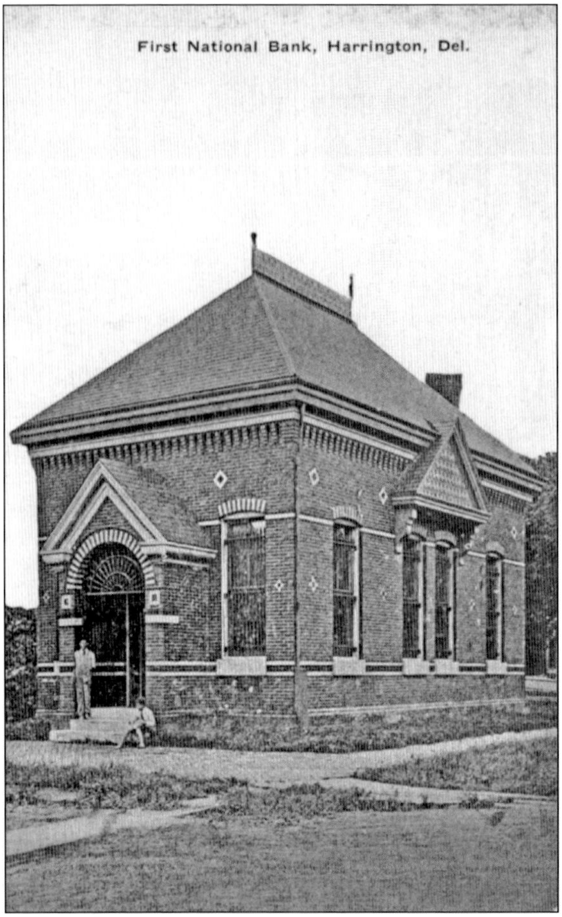

Founded in 1888, the First National Bank of Harrington was the town's first bank and is still in business today. Before then, locals who needed to do banking had to travel to Milford. The first bank was built on the site of the town's original structure, the tavern built by Benjamin Clark in the late 1700s.

By the mid-1920s, the First National Bank of Harrington had outgrown its small offices, and a new bank was built. This stately block structure still stands today. The original vault and safety deposit boxes provide the same security as they did in the 1920s. Travelers and locals alike relied on this local bank to provide much needed financial services.

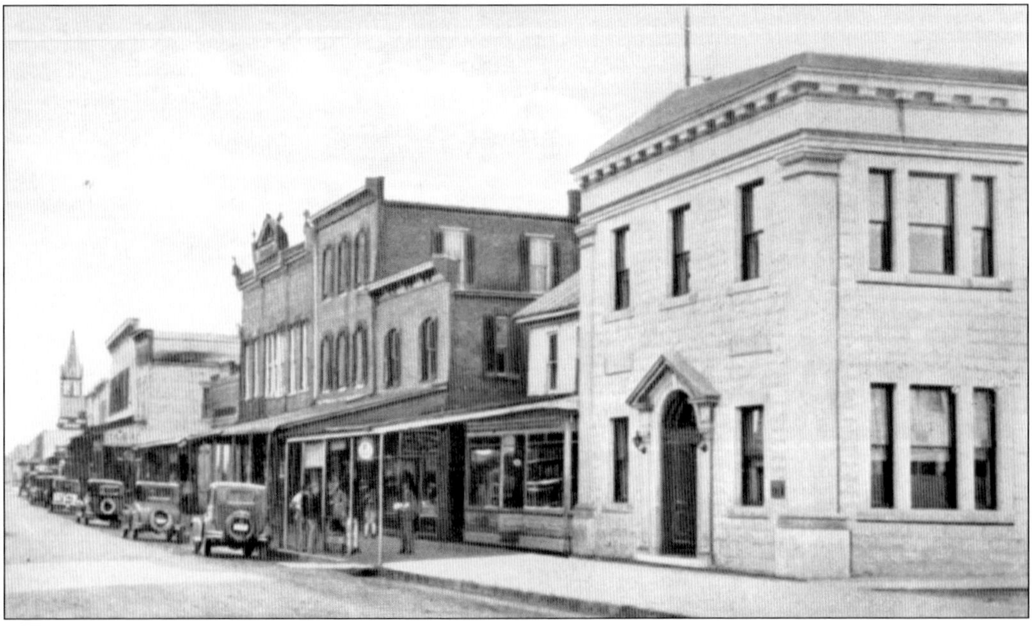

A second group of businessmen opened the Peoples Bank of Harrington in 1905. This photograph shows the first bank building, a small brick structure. Inside, it was just large enough for a single teller window. The building lasted just a few years before the decision was made to build a larger structure.

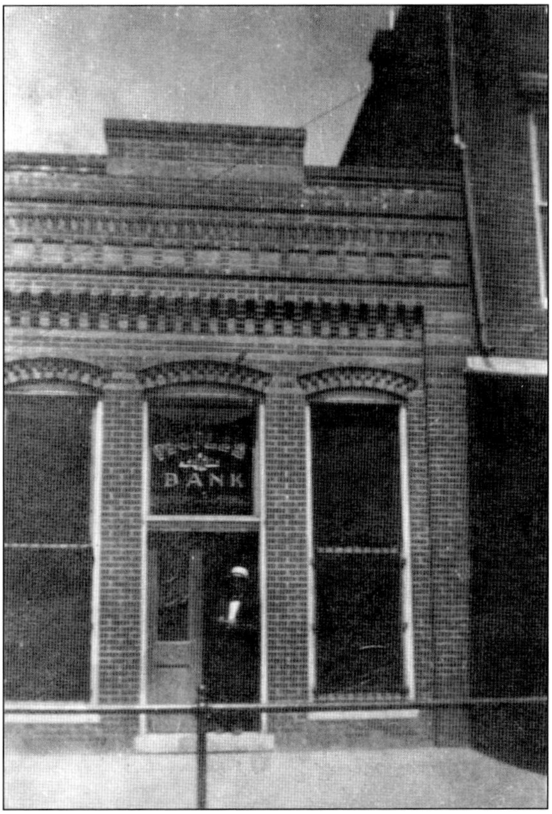

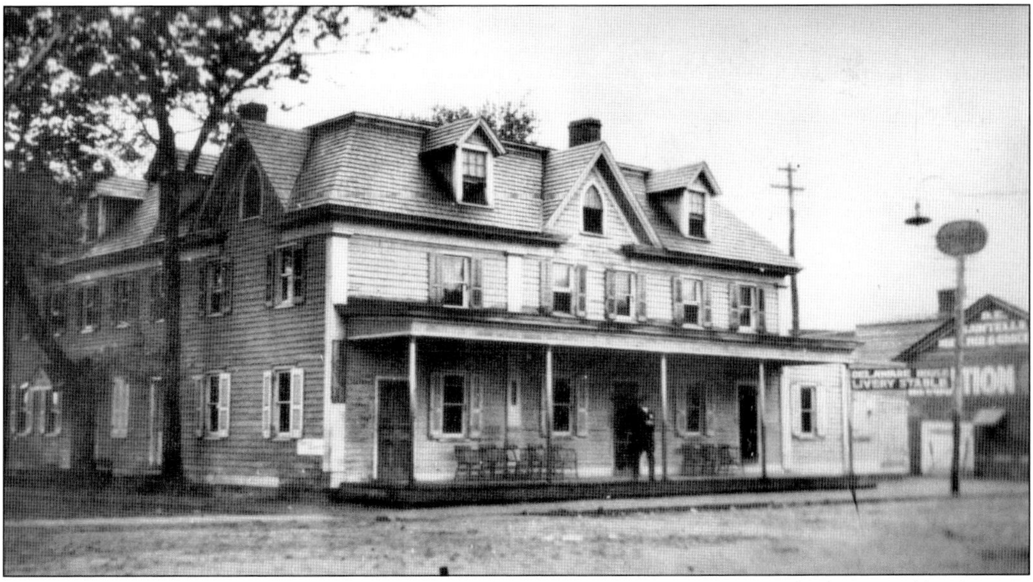

On May 16, 1914, the Newman House, formerly Delaware House, was nearly destroyed by fire. At approximately 8:00 p.m., the fire alarm rang throughout the town. The livery stable was on fire, and it was quickly spreading. The Harrington Fire Company had no motorized pumping equipment at the time, so a bucket brigade was formed. To quote local resident Albert Thistlewood, "I never saw such throwing of water!" The major buildings had damage but were spared.

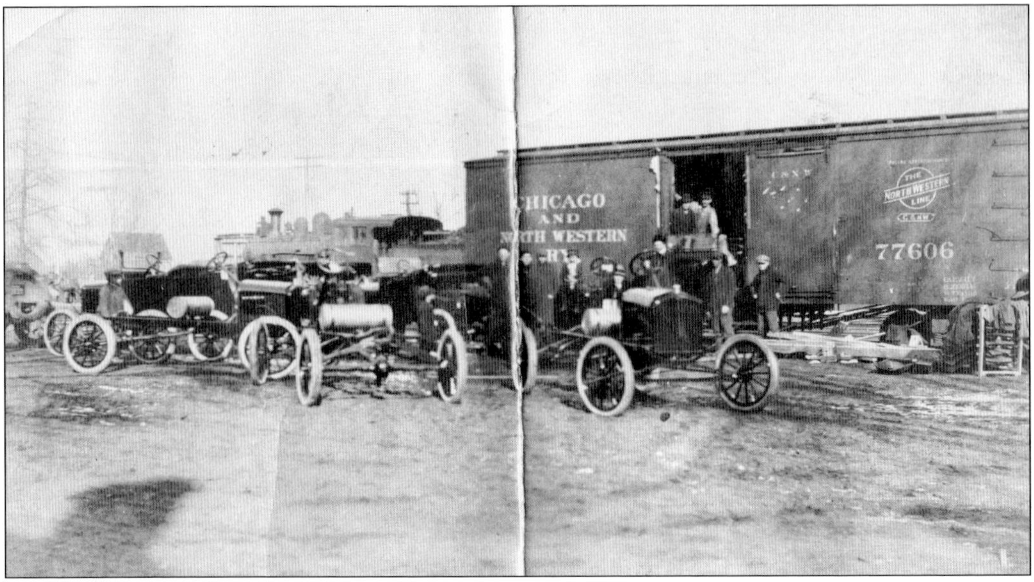

As the Ford Model A grew in popularity, citizens of the town began to want to purchase this new mode of transportation. Cars were transported by rail to the town, stacked like cordwood. Seen here at the freight yard, the cars came dissembled and were reassembled by the local dealers. Citizens quickly grabbed up these cars and were now able to travel anywhere they wanted.

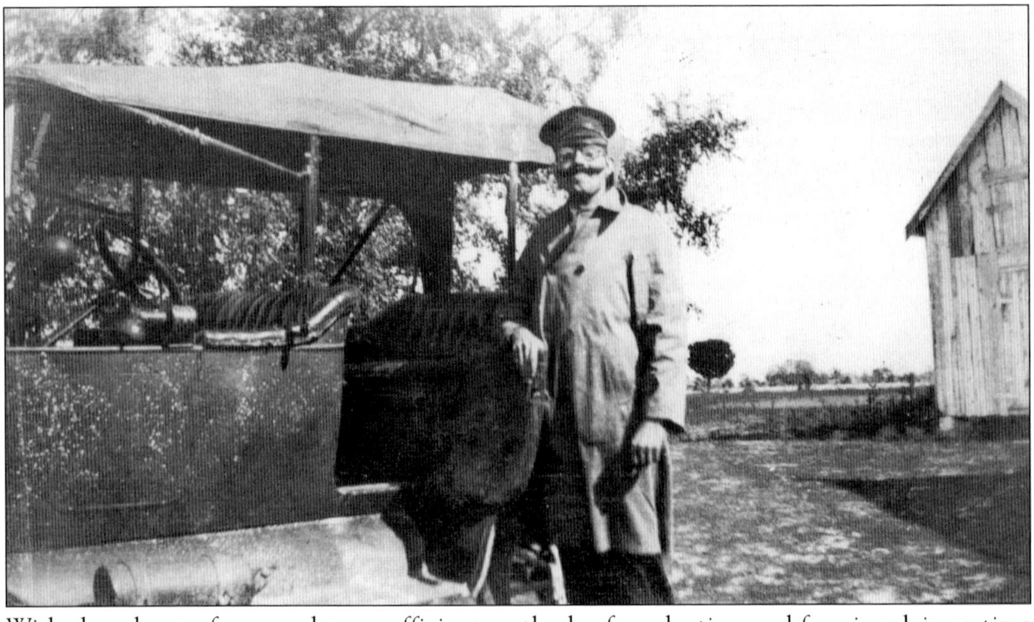

With the advent of cars and more efficient methods of production and farming, leisure time became more common. Charles Shackleford is dressed in his finest driving gear, ready for a ride in the country. Sundays became a day to visit friends and family or ride into town for a soda or ice cream treat.

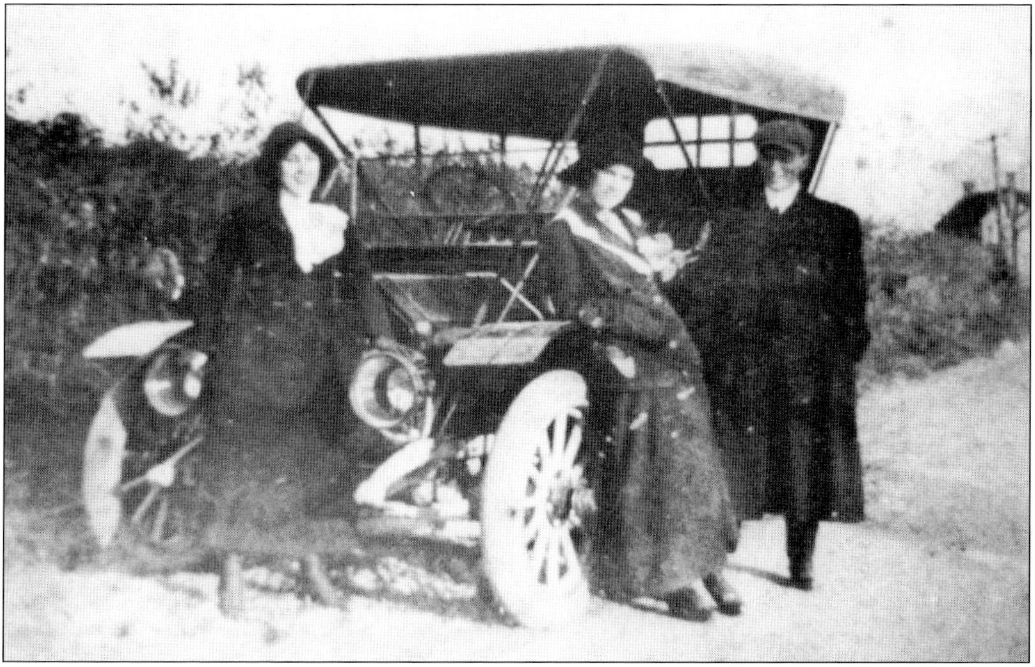

Nobody embraced this new era more than the youth of the day. The Roaring Twenties were here, and the citizens of Harrington enjoyed their new freedom. From left to right, Mary McCabe, Catharine Trice, and Olin Sapp are dressed in their finest and ready to enjoy the day's adventures.

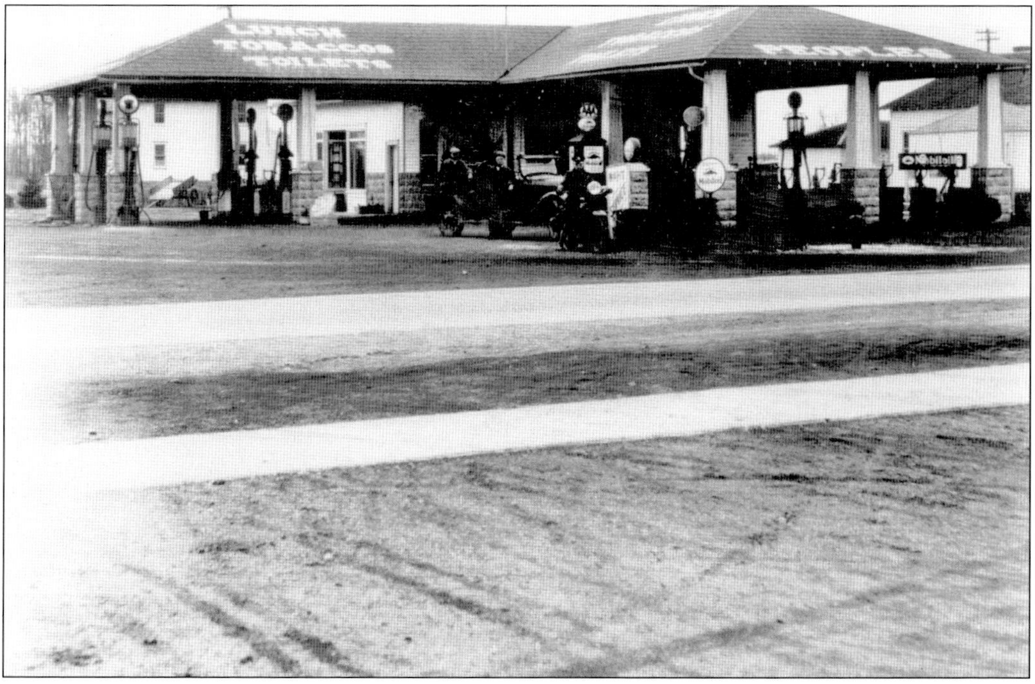

With motorized transportation, gas stations began to take center stage in the town. Peoples Service Station was built at the intersection of the newly built US Route 13 and Clark Street. Travelers and locals alike stopped here for gas, air, food, and as the building says, to use the toilet.

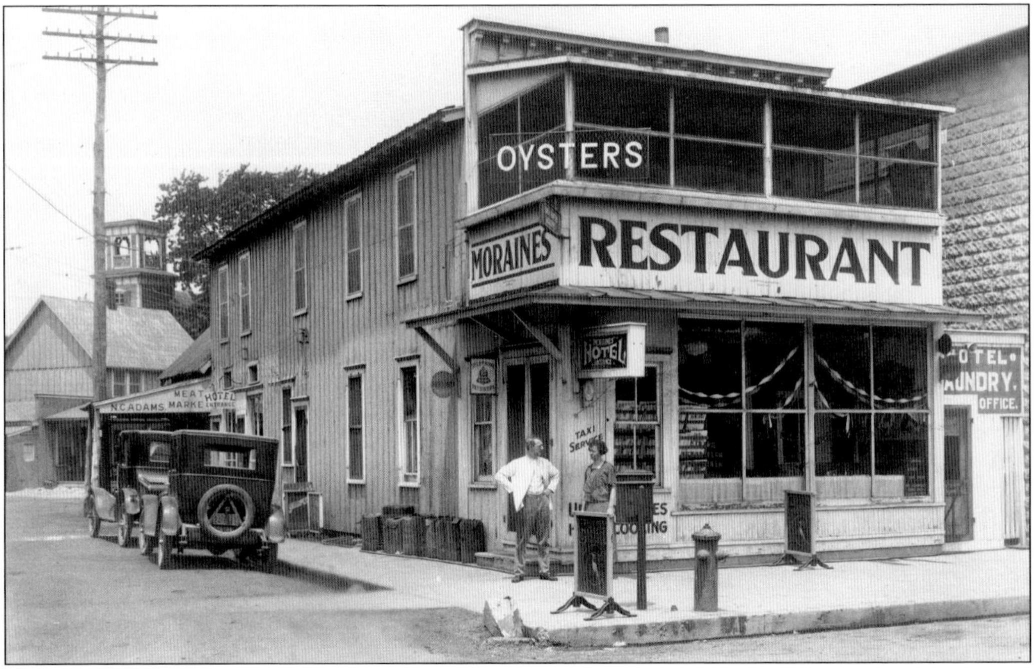

Moraines Restaurant in Harrington was a popular dining spot in the 1920s and 1930s. The restaurant took advantage of the trains traveling from the Chincoteague, Virginia, area, serving fresh oysters as one of its most popular dishes. With the advent of the oyster canning industry in the late 1800s, locals and travelers alike could enjoy this wonderful bounty of the sea year-round. (Courtesy of the Delaware Public Archives.)

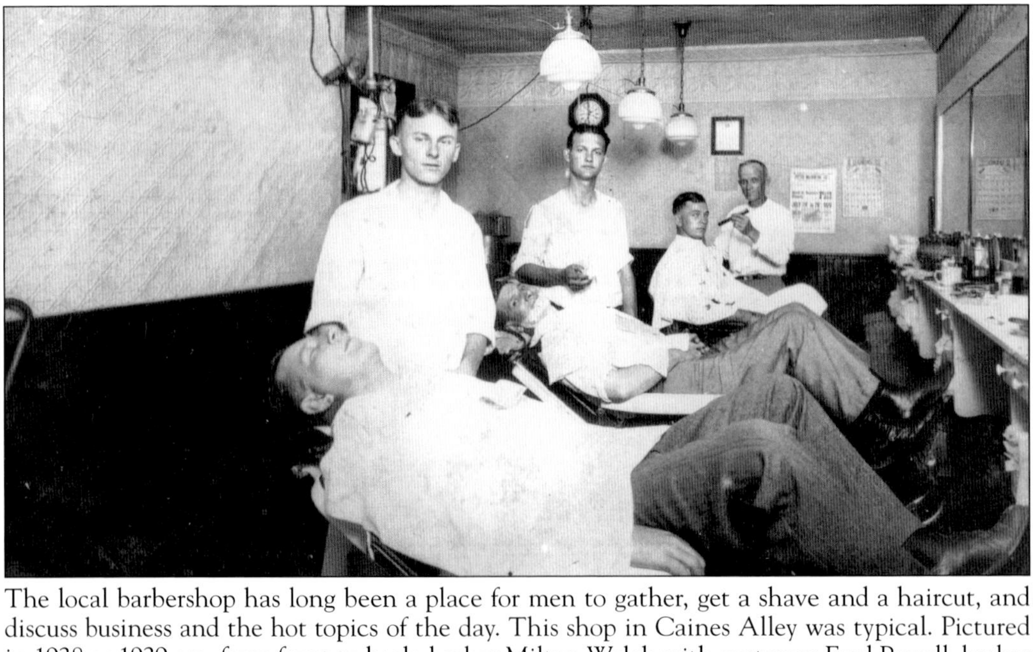

The local barbershop has long been a place for men to gather, get a shave and a haircut, and discuss business and the hot topics of the day. This shop in Caines Alley was typical. Pictured in 1928 or 1929 are, from front to back, barber Milton Welch with customer Fred Powell, barber Charles "Tony" Collins with customer Luther Johnson, and owner and barber Frank Collins with customer Lester Emory.

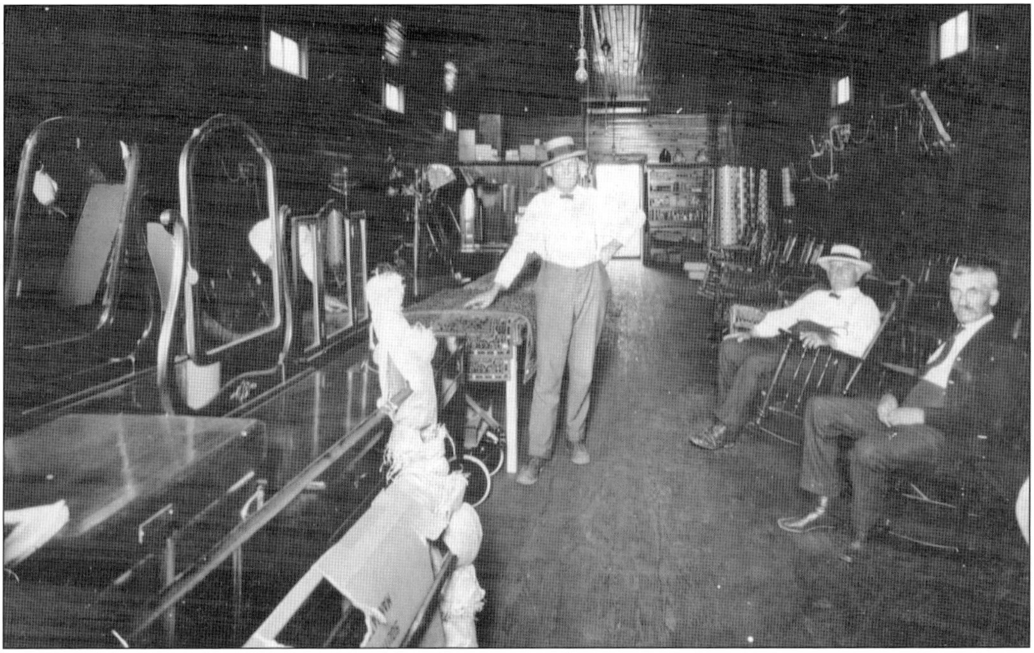

Jacobs' Store stood on Dorman Street near the intersection of Commerce Street for several years. Seated are Noah Cain (with hat) and Edward Jacobs. The store sold general mercantile goods of the day. Jacobs's son went on to serve as a state senator for over a decade and was instrumental in placing Delaware's two statues in the National Statuary Hall in the US Capitol.

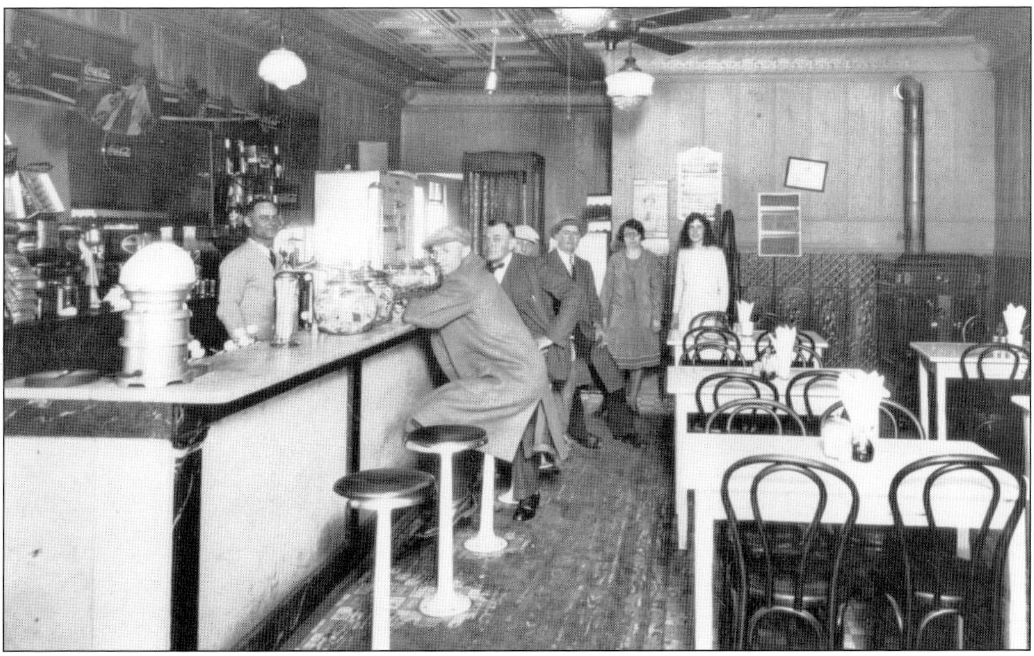

On a warm day, nothing beat a cold soda—not from a can or bottle, but from the local soda jerk. Edgar Hall's Restaurant and Soda Fountain was more than ready to help serve locals and visitors alike a refreshing drink or a good meal. Hall, standing behind the counter, was the proprietor for several years. The building, with its beautiful tin ceiling, still stands today.

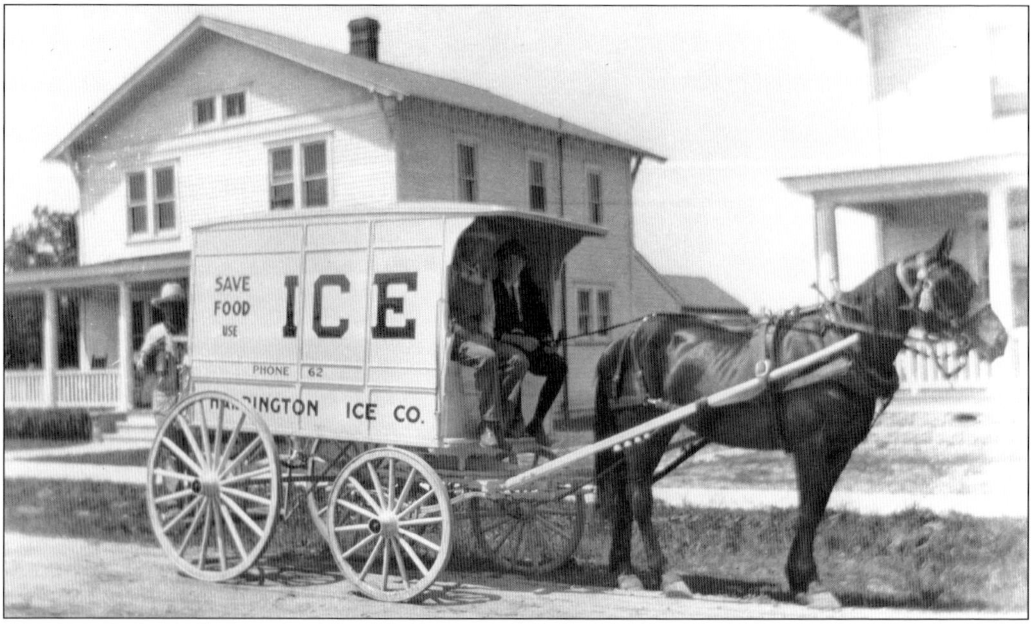

Despite electricity having come to Harrington in 1906, in 1920, an electric refrigerator averaged $250, while an icebox was $30. When the average wage was only $1,000 a year, most families chose the icebox. Ice wagons were common sights in town, and the icehouse was located near the railroad tracks, allowing it to serve locals and the railroad as well.

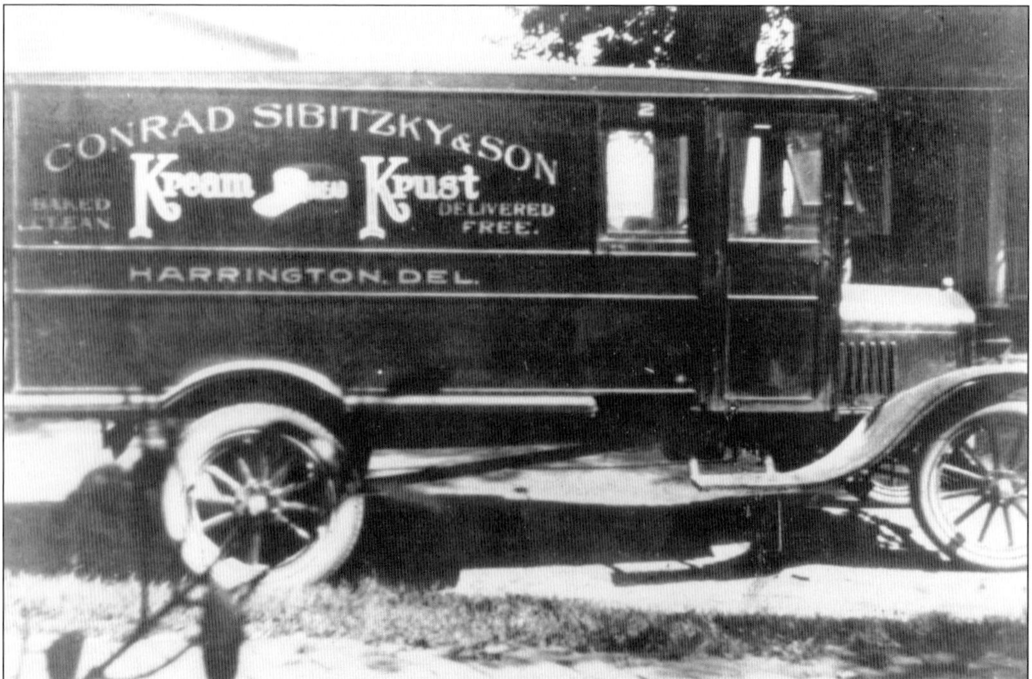

Kreme and Krust Bakery, owned by Conrad Sibitsky, provided fresh baked goods to the local stores, restaurants, and townspeople from the 1920s through the 1940s. His delivery trucks would be out early each morning dropping off wooden crates full of fresh bread.

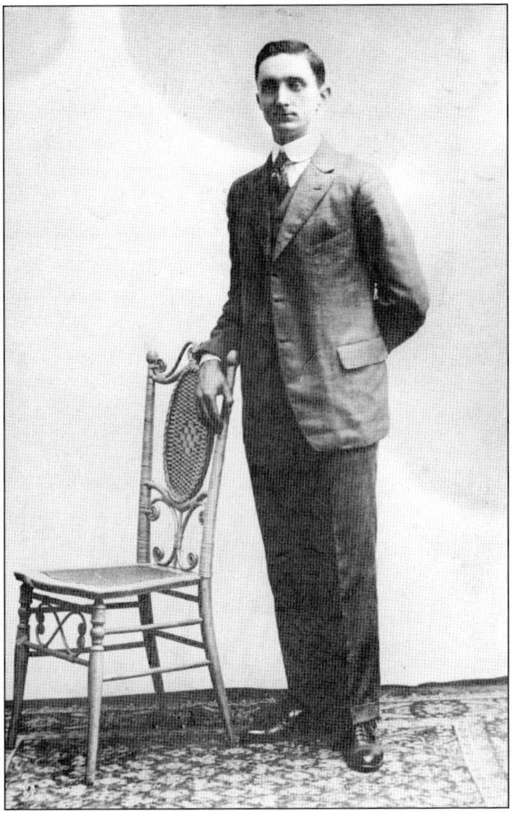

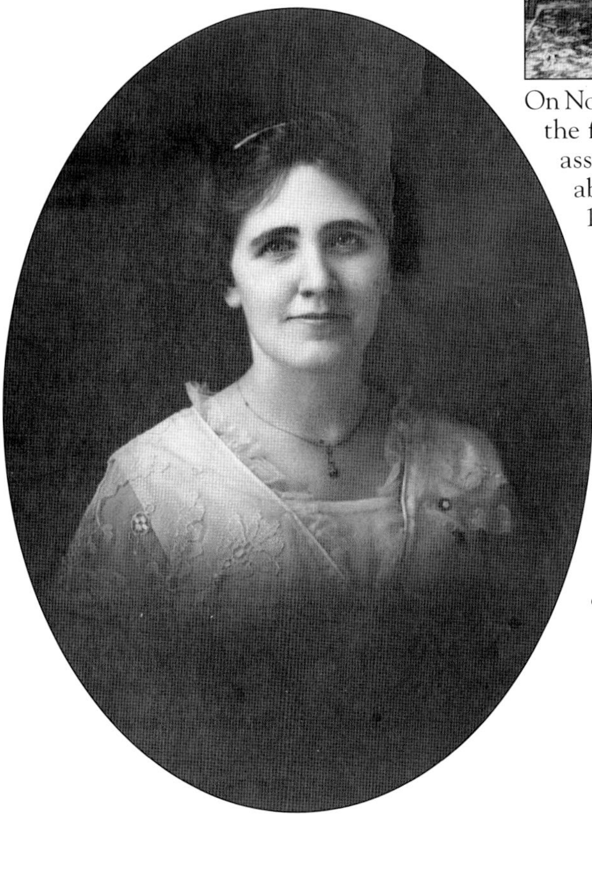

On November 4, 1887, William C. Wright opened the first funeral business in Harrington. His assistant was Mr. Major Wyatt, pictured above. Upon Wright's death in January 1920, Wyatt purchased the business from the Wright family. Wyatt married Katie Truitt, pictured at left. Sadly, less than a year later, Wyatt was deceased, and "Miss Katie," as she had become known, had to make a decision on what to do with the business. She determined to carry on her late husband's work, and through the help of associates, she was able to do just that until the spring of 1927, when she graduated from mortician's college. Katie is believed to be among the first approximately 100 women licensed in this country to perform this task.

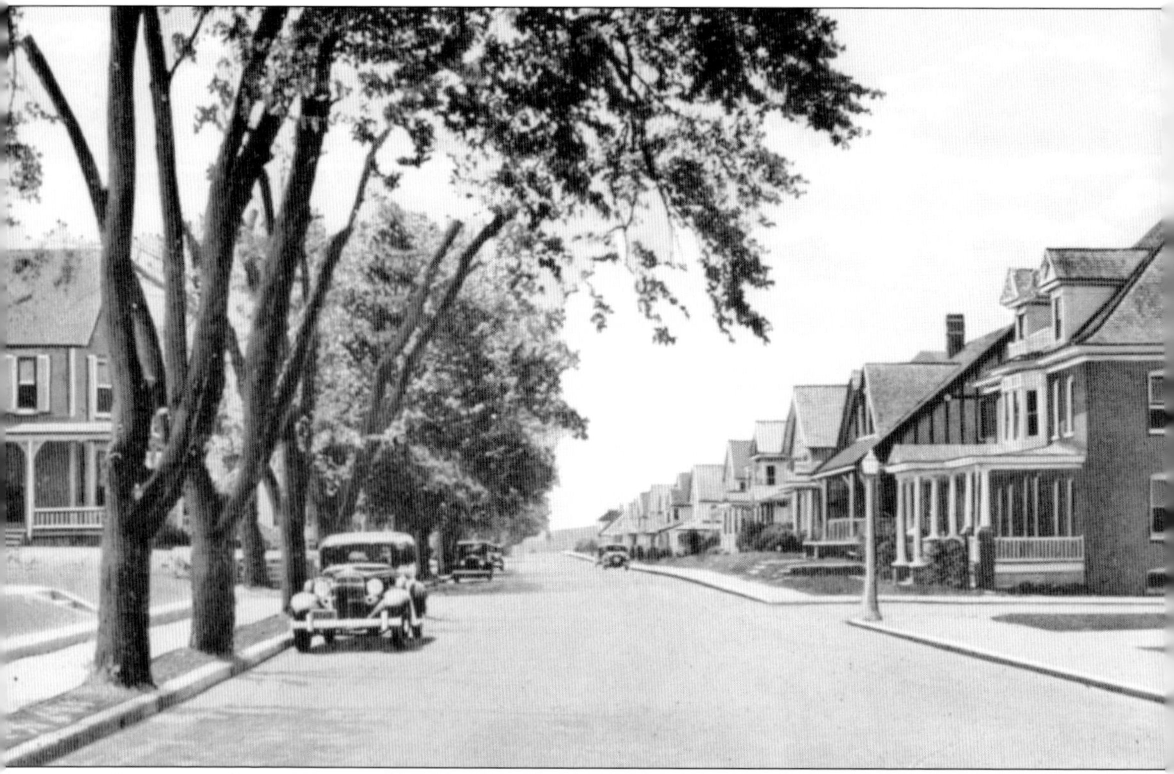

Commerce Street, pictured looking south, changed quite a bit in the short 80 years of the town. Harrington had seen its population grow from less than 500 in the mid-1800s to over 2,000 by the 1940s. The city boasted a vibrant downtown area with no less than 40 stores, restaurants, and other businesses serving local citizens and visitors. A passenger train ride to Philadelphia now took less than three hours and was done in luxury aboard air-conditioned, streamlined passenger cars. Streets, once dirty and dusty, were now paved and had tree-lined sidewalks illuminated by streetlamps each night. By all measures, Harrington had come of age. No longer just a stagecoach stop or a dot on the map, the city was now a center of commerce that still retained its small-town charm. Everyone knew everyone else, and neighbors were friends. It was as if a Norman Rockwell scene had come to life.

Three

The Many Faiths of a Small Town

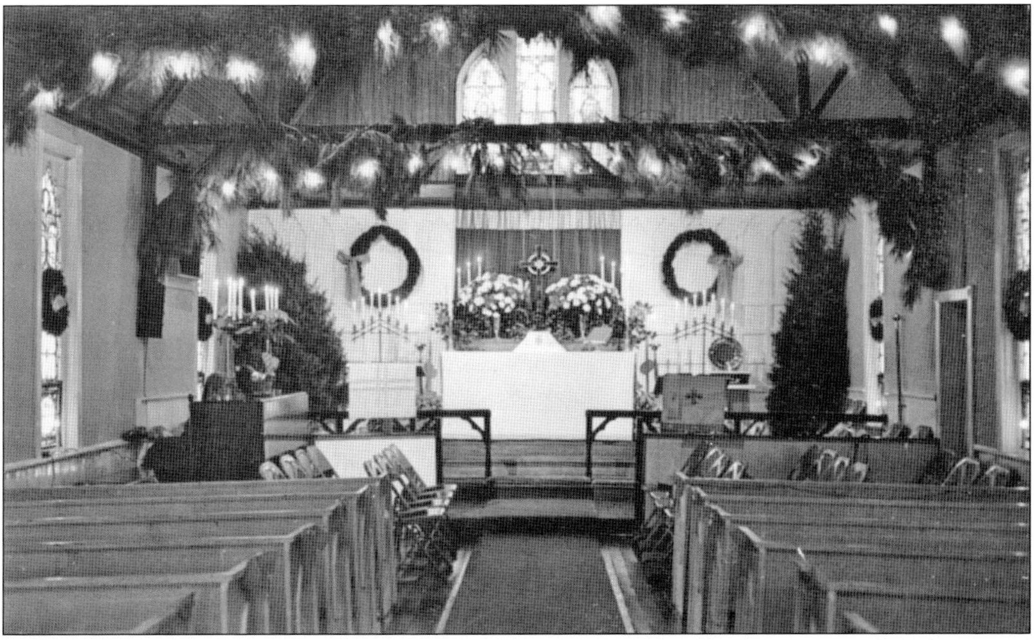

Churches in a small town such as Harrington not only provided spiritual guidance but also served as community meeting places. Churches stood as beacons, their spires dotting the landscapes and calling the faithful to worship. Harrington is steeped in many faiths, each with its own unique house of worship. St. Stephen's Episcopal Church on Fleming Street is pictured in the mid-1950s, decorated for the Christmas season.

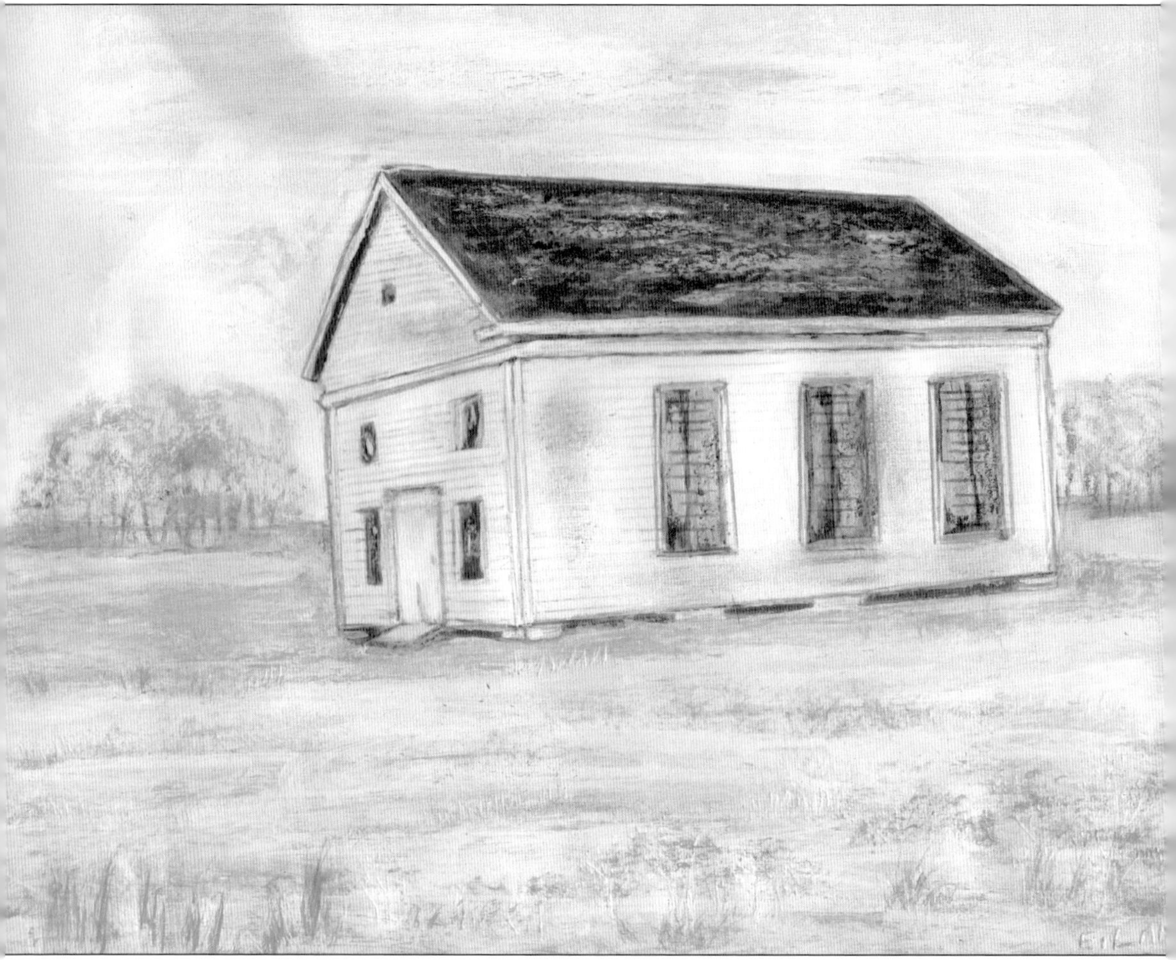

White's Chapel, just outside Harrington, played a role not only in local history but also in the founding of Methodism in the United States. The small chapel in this drawing was actually the second White's Chapel constructed in the area. It was named after Thomas White, the judge of the common pleas court in Kent County, Delaware. Judge White supported Methodism but did not support the Revolutionary War. On March 28, 1778, the Continental Congress ordered Judge White arrested and charged with the crime of being a Methodist; he was arrested on April 2, 1778. After five weeks of imprisonment and a trial, White was found innocent and returned to his home. Just prior to his arrest, White had received a house guest, Francis Asbury, who would remain for the next two years; both men would remain in seclusion for the rest of the war.

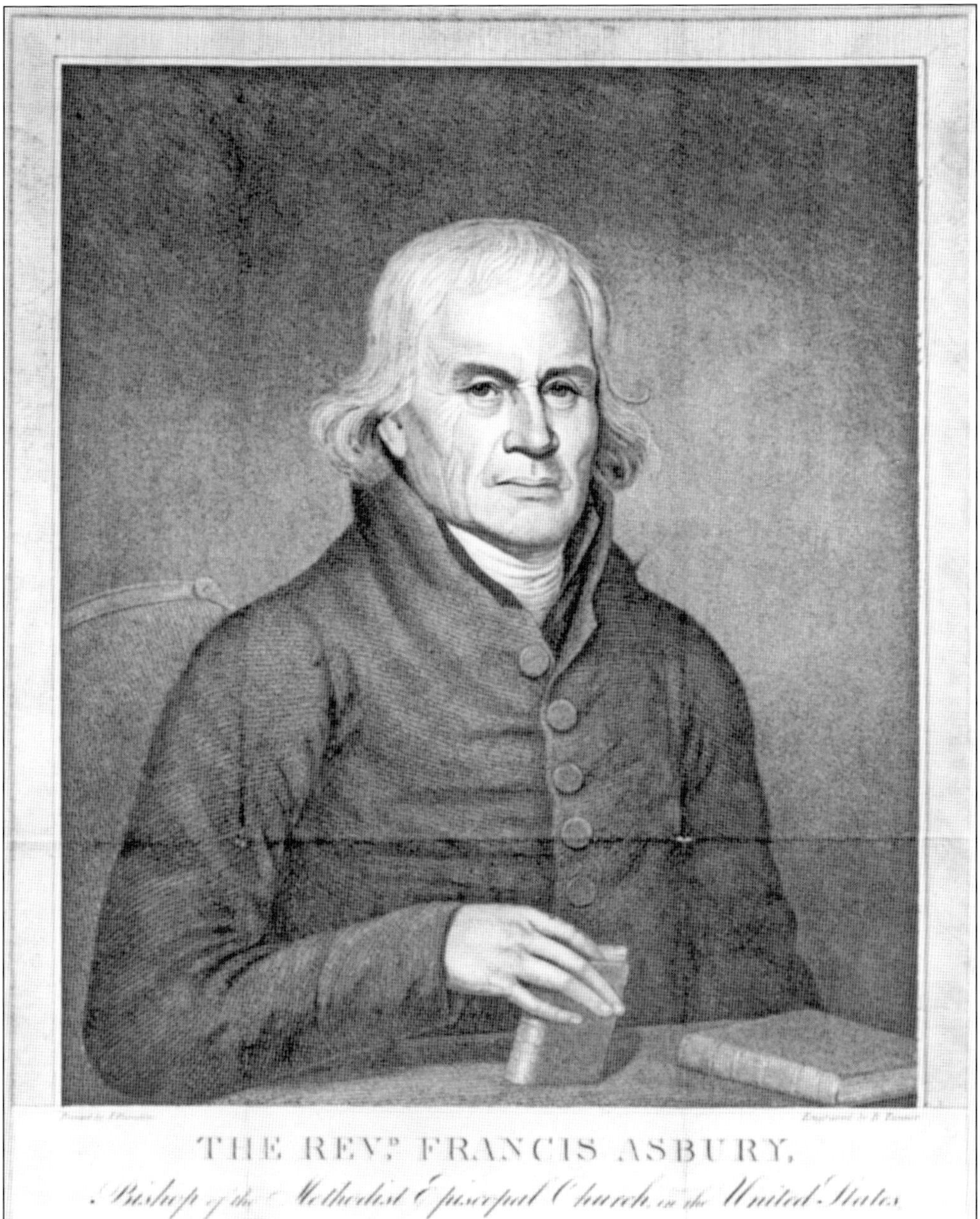

Francis Asbury was one of the two remaining Methodist lay preachers who had come to America before the beginning of the Revolutionary War. When the war broke out, Asbury tried to remain in Maryland, but ardent Patriots began to harass him at every turn. He was fined multiple times for preaching in public. Since he refused to sign the Maryland Oath of Allegiance, he had little choice but to flee to safety. The home of a nearby Methodist supporter seemed ideal. Judge White lived in a deep forest thicket off the heavily traveled roads of the day. With other Methodists nearby, Asbury could continue his missionary work. After Judge White's arrest, however, both men feared for their safety. They were desperate to continue their religious practices, and though they knew the dangers, neither one would be deterred.

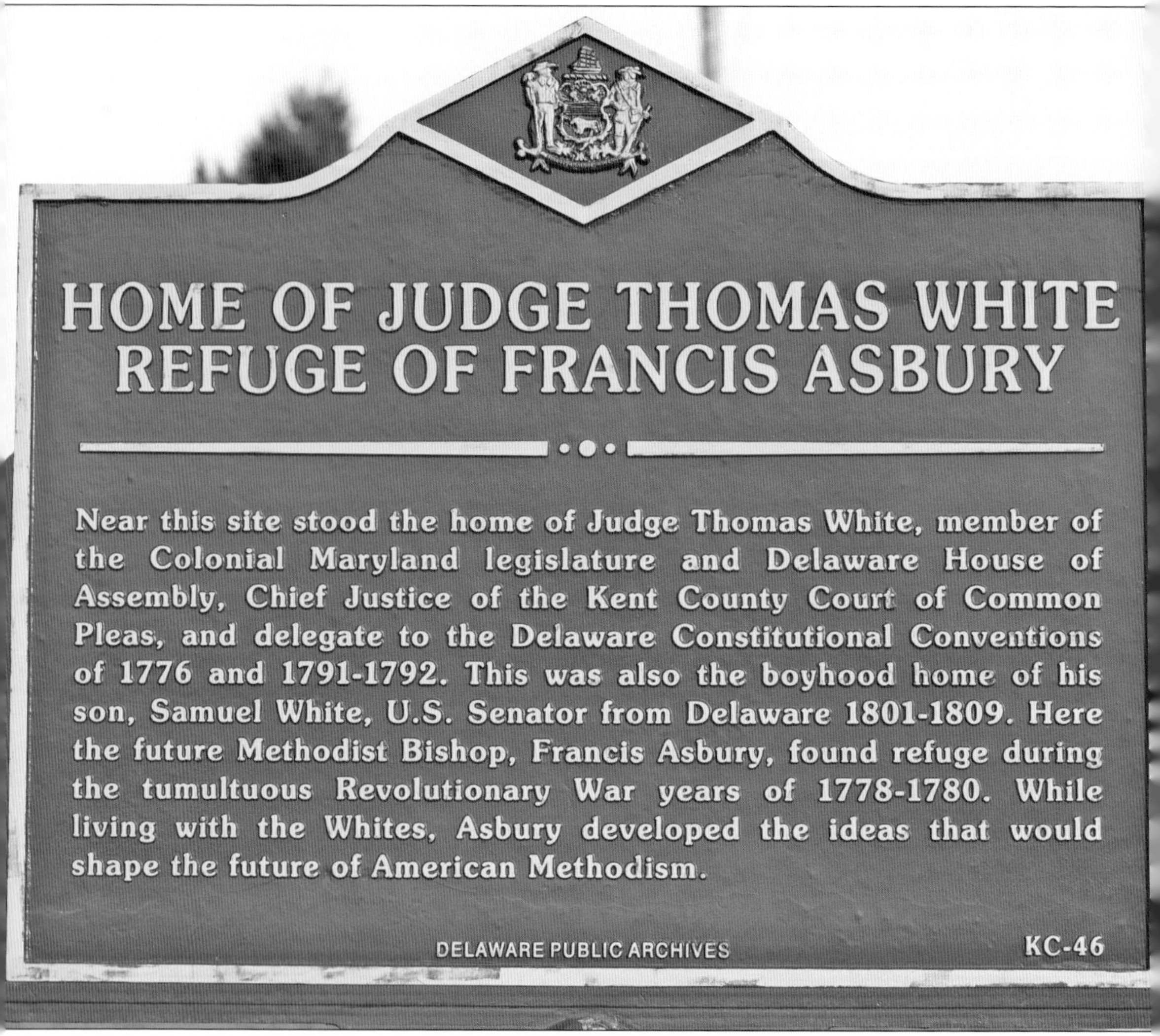

One easy way to remain free was to simply change states. Judge White's farm was a mere mile from the Maryland-Delaware state line. A historical marker has been placed denoting the location of his farm. If one state was coming to arrest the men, they could simply slip into the other. A small chapel was built in 1780 where services could be held and, if necessary, the men could claim sanctuary—most military and civilian authorities would think twice before arresting a man in a church. Francis Asbury called the building "a miserable place," but it served its purpose. For two years, the men continued to live in safety. The first two Methodist conventions in America were held on Judge White's property, the second on April 16, 1781. After the war, Francis Asbury was once again able to spread the word both he and Judge White had nearly given up their freedom to defend.

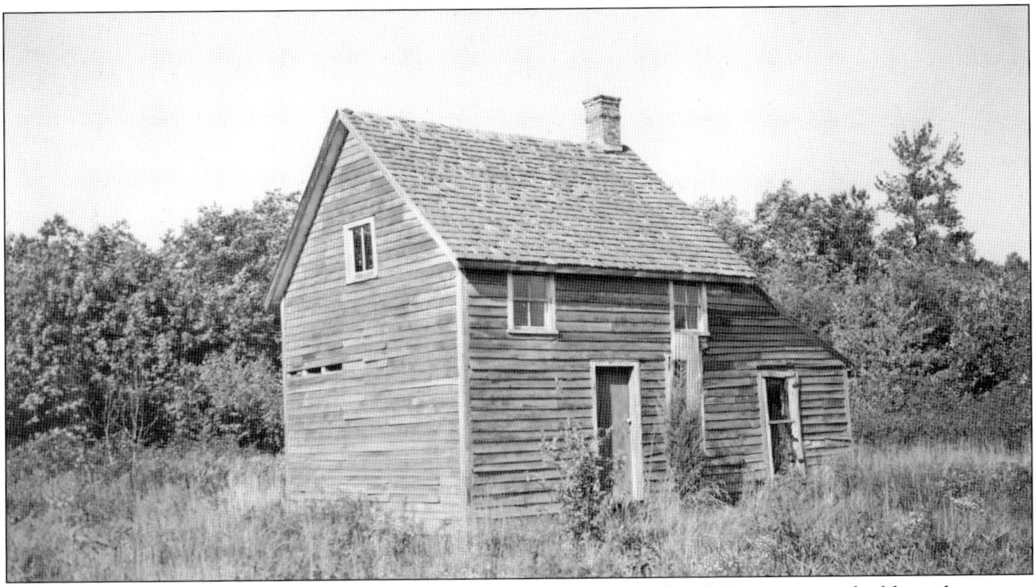

The first church to bear the name Asbury was built just north of Harrington, halfway between Harrington and Masten's Corner. Built in the mid-1810s, it is pictured in the 1940s. The church was last known to have been used sometime in 1888. Fallen into disrepair, the church was torn down not long after this picture was taken. (Courtesy of the Delaware Public Archives.)

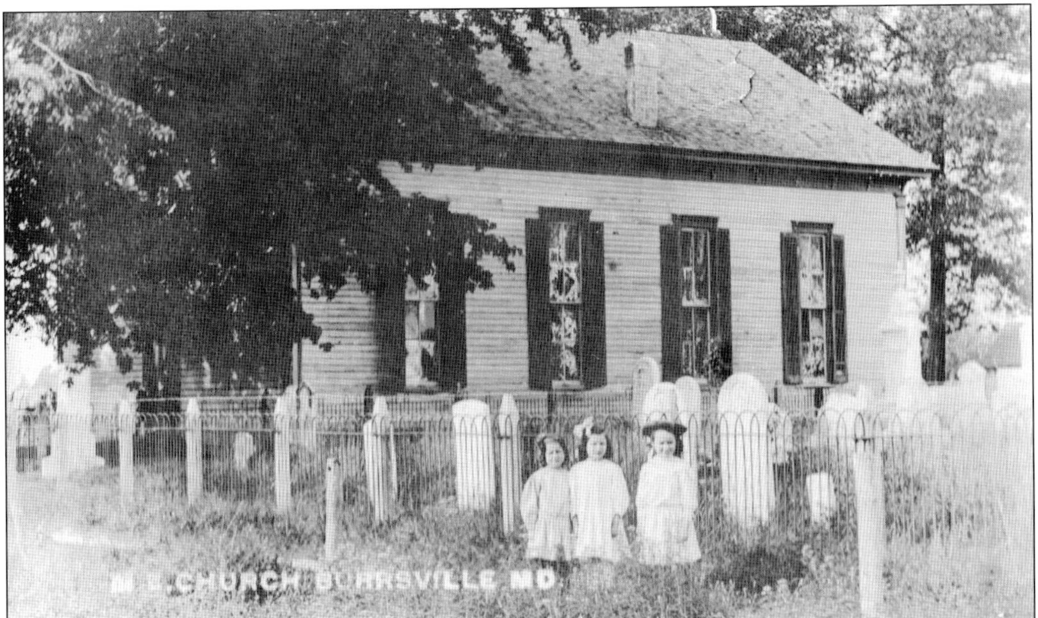

Wesley Methodist Church in Burrsville was constructed in 1834. The church served citizens from Delaware and Maryland, since it stood just feet away from the state line. The church seen here is the second, constructed in 1872. On February 18, 1934, just after morning services had ended, the church was suddenly destroyed by fire. A new church was built inside of a year and was ready for Christmas service on December 16, 1934.

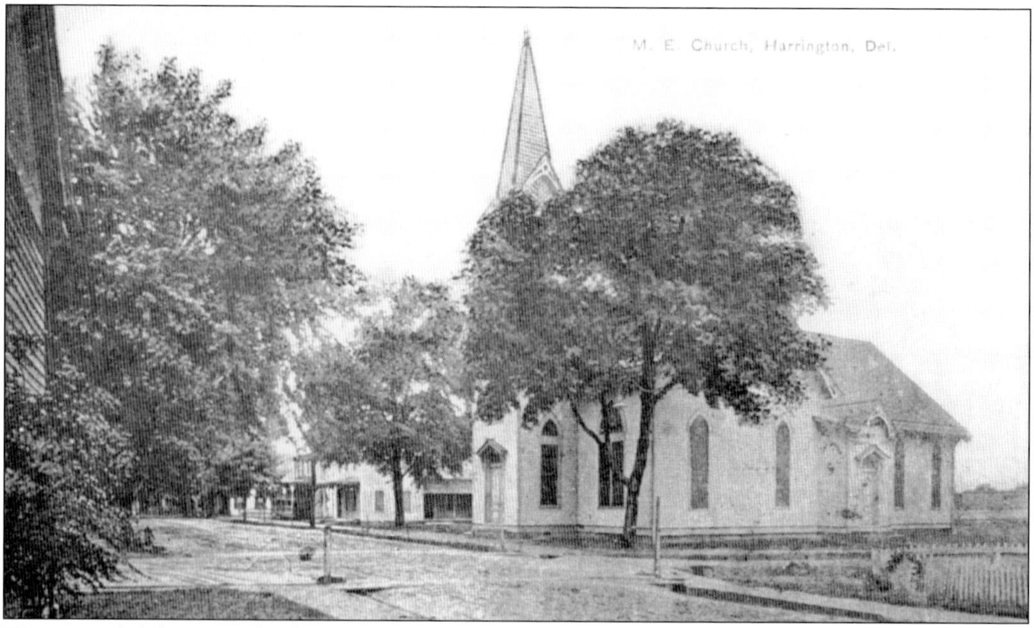

The second Asbury Methodist Church in the area began as the first Sunday school in Harrington on March 30, 1853. However, the first church building was not constructed until 1870. It was rebuilt as seen in this picture in 1890. In 1915, the church had a beautiful pipe organ installed with the financial help of Andrew Carnegie.

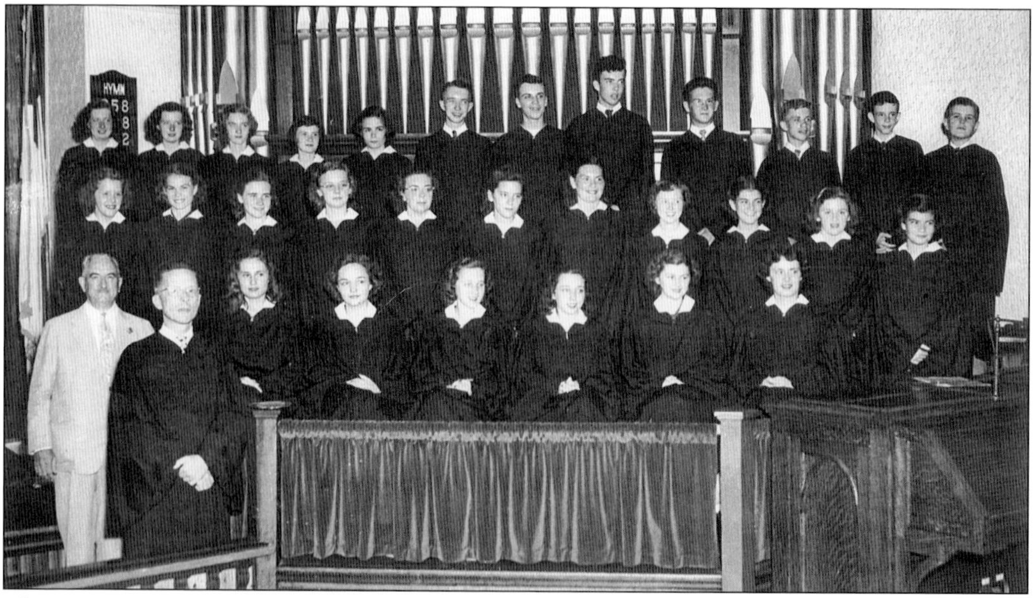

The pipe organ was restored in 1944. The Asbury choir stands in front of the organ in 1950. From left to right are (first row) Rev. J. Harry Wright, choir director Melvin Brobst, June Griffith, Phyllis Warren, Elma Stauffer, Thelma Stauffer, Betty Ann Short, and Mary Ann Hickman; (second row) Eleanor Rice, Elizabeth Greenley, Elaine Downing, Imogene Welch, Phyllis Hopkins, Roberta Rice, Ann Toppin, Mary Ellen Thomas, Connie Lord, Martha Jean Sneath, and Frances Black; (third row) Leora Biddle, Leona Biddle, Janet Kimmey, Shirley Harrington, Carol Ward, Donald McKnatt, Billy Wix, Jay Bullock, Louis Brown, Dick Pitlick, Robert Ward, and George Graham.

The Harrington Presbyterian Church was founded in 1871, and the first services were held in the local schoolhouse. The church shown here was constructed in 1873 on Dorman Street, next to the private graveyard of George Dorman. The church ceased functioning in the 1910s and was destroyed by fire in 1924. The deceased buried in the cemetery were relocated to Hollywood Cemetery outside Harrington and the land sold to the New Century Club.

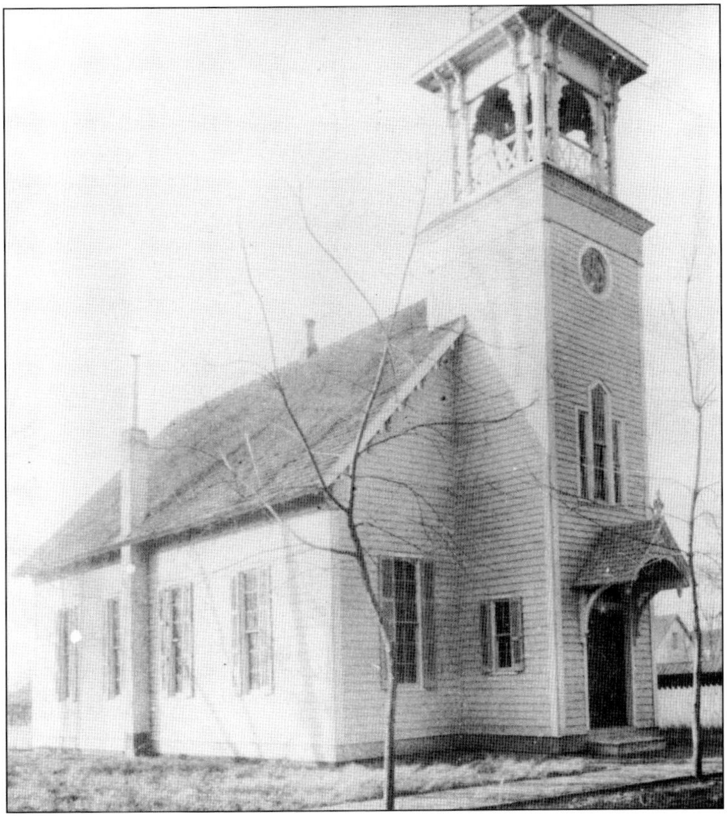

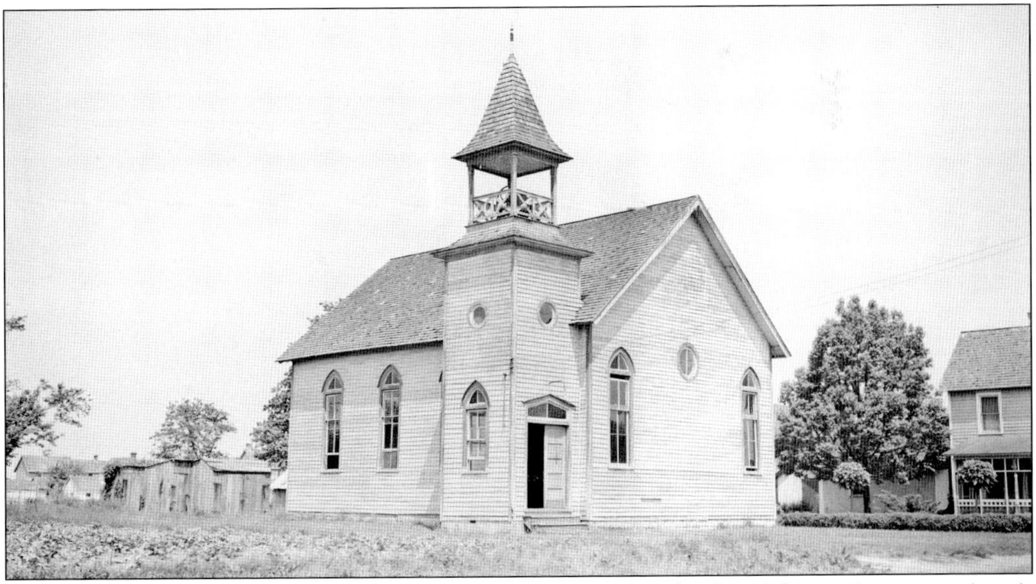

Metropolitan Methodist Episcopal Church in Harrington was the first African American church founded in the area. Organized in early 1873 by a group of trustees headed by James Friends, it purchased land to build the church, which was dedicated on October 8, 1893. The church was extensively remodeled in the 1920s, and it remains virtually unchanged to this day. (Courtesy of the Delaware Public Archives.)

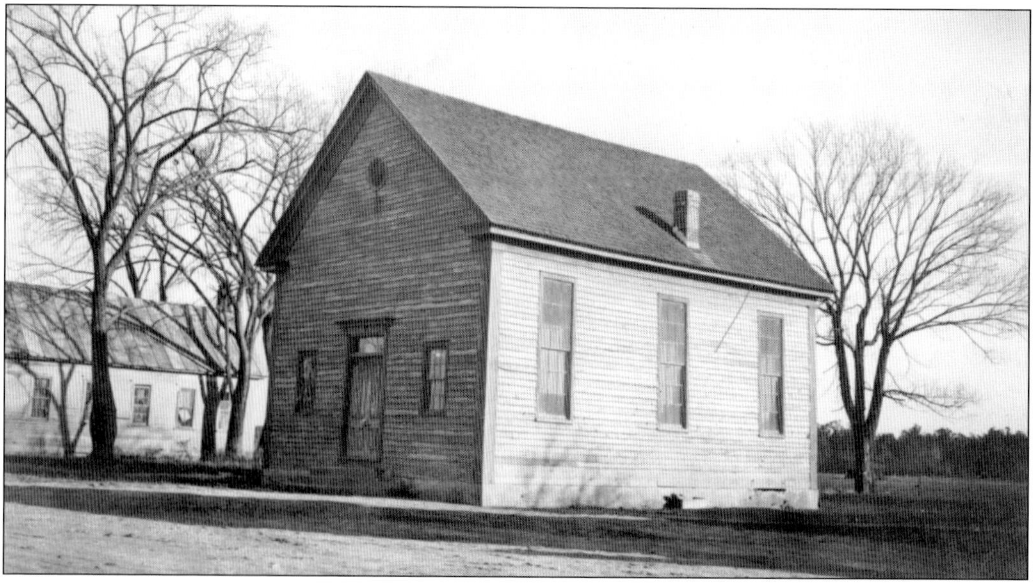

Masten's Methodist Church was located at Masten's Corner and was constructed in 1873 on land purchased from Joseph A. Masten. In 1886, the church was entirely refurnished, and in 1896, the building was completely renovated. The church remained in use for several decades, serving the citizens of the area despite many moving into the city of Harrington as it boomed. The church was last used in the late 1940s or early 1950s. It was demolished in the 1960s. (Both, courtesy of the Delaware Public Archives.)

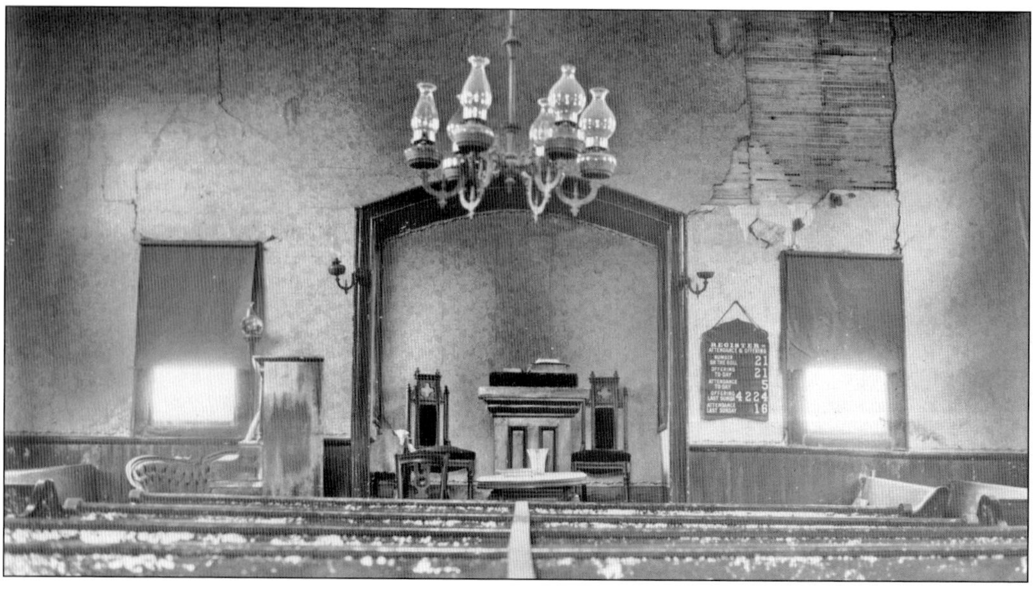

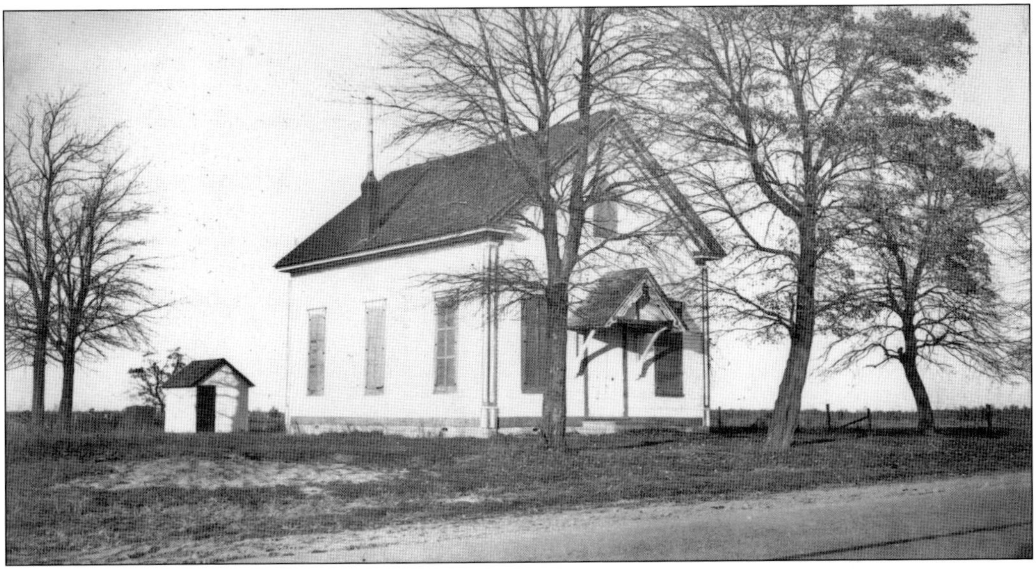

Prospect Methodist Church is just east of Vernon, a small country crossroads about four miles west of Harrington. On April 23, 1835, Jacob Graham, Clement Anderson, Isaac Graham, Charles Wroten, and William Wix bought 60 perches (three eighths of an acre) for 50¢ per perch and donated the land to John Rawley, Nathan Todd, Peter Callaway, Joshua Cranor, William Wilkerson, and their successors, trustees of Prospect Chapel. The original church cost $500 but was soon outgrown. The present church was constructed in 1874 and dedicated by Bishop Levi Scott. Sunday school rooms were added as needed in 1961, 1967, and 1973. This small but thriving church is still in operation today. (Both, courtesy of the Delaware Public Archives.)

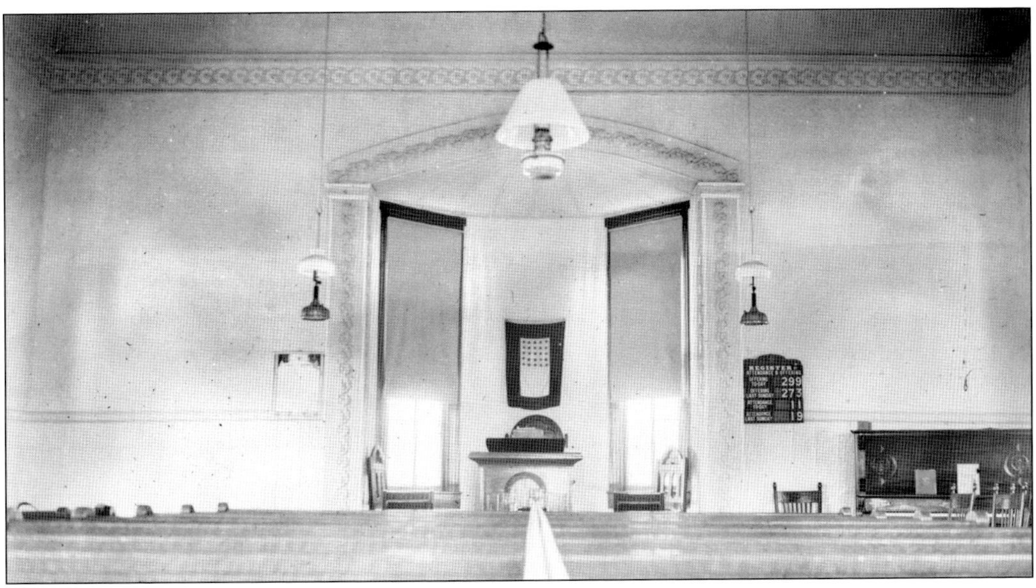

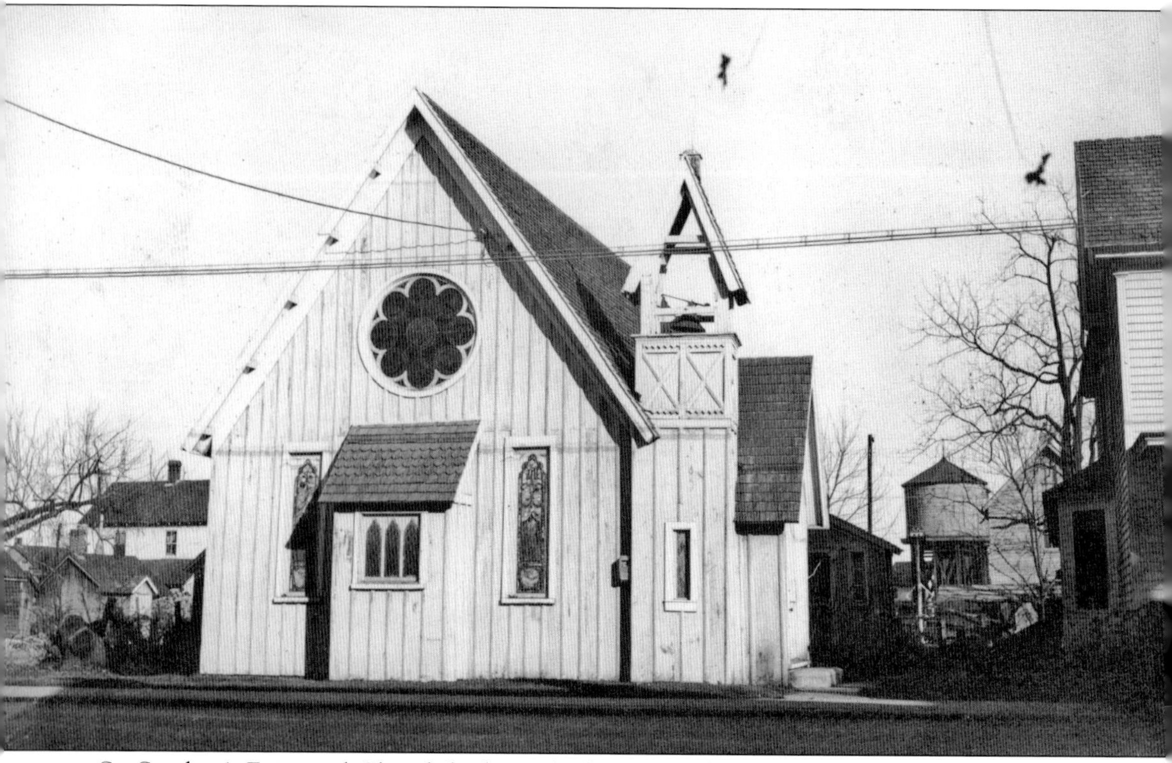

St. Stephen's Episcopal Church had a rocky beginning but today stands out among the other churches of the town. Services were first held in the local school beginning in 1868 by Rev. J. Leighton McKim. The foundation for the church was begun in 1871, but work was then halted for three years as there were issues over the deed, which had been promised as a gift. Finally "the Little Red Church," as it had come to be known, was consecrated on June 6, 1878. Included in the church was a beautiful rose window depicting the gospels of Matthew, Mark, Luke, and John. The window cost $75 in 1877. The small church remained virtually unchanged for almost 80 years. (Courtesy of the Delaware Public Archives.)

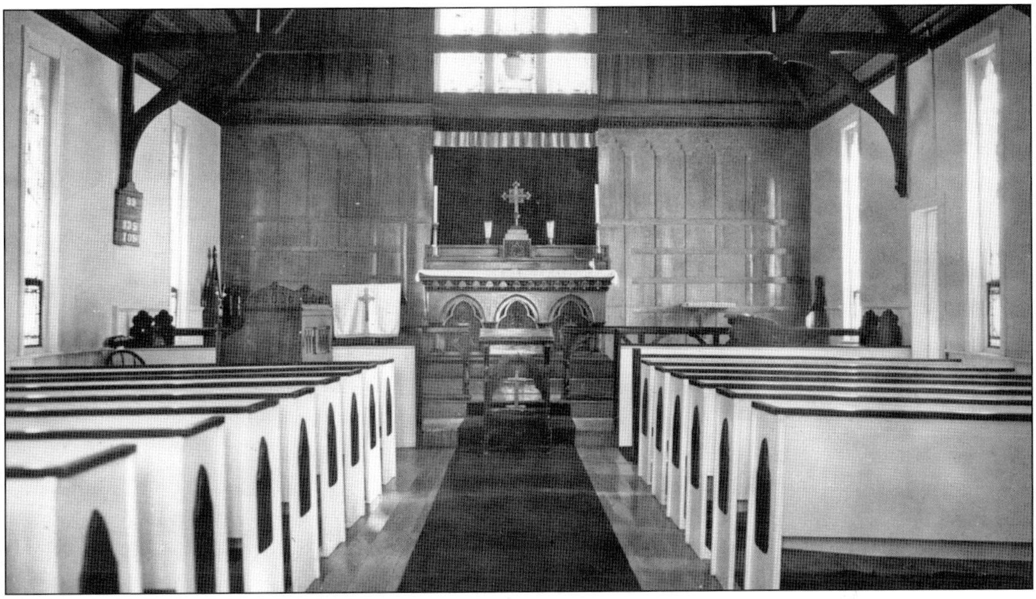

In 1959, St. Stephen's built a new church on the edge of Harrington, and the Baptist Church of Harrington purchased the old building. The church was used until 1966, at which time it sat abandoned and began to show its age. But at 100 years old, this little church was about to find new life. Donated to the Greater Harrington Historical Society, it underwent major repairs to restore it to its former glory, which included the return of the beautiful rose window. The church turned museum was dedicated on May 3, 1987. On October 8, 2014, the Little Red Church was listed in the National Register of Historic Places. It remains to this day almost exactly as it was in 1878. (Above, courtesy of the Delaware Public Archives.)

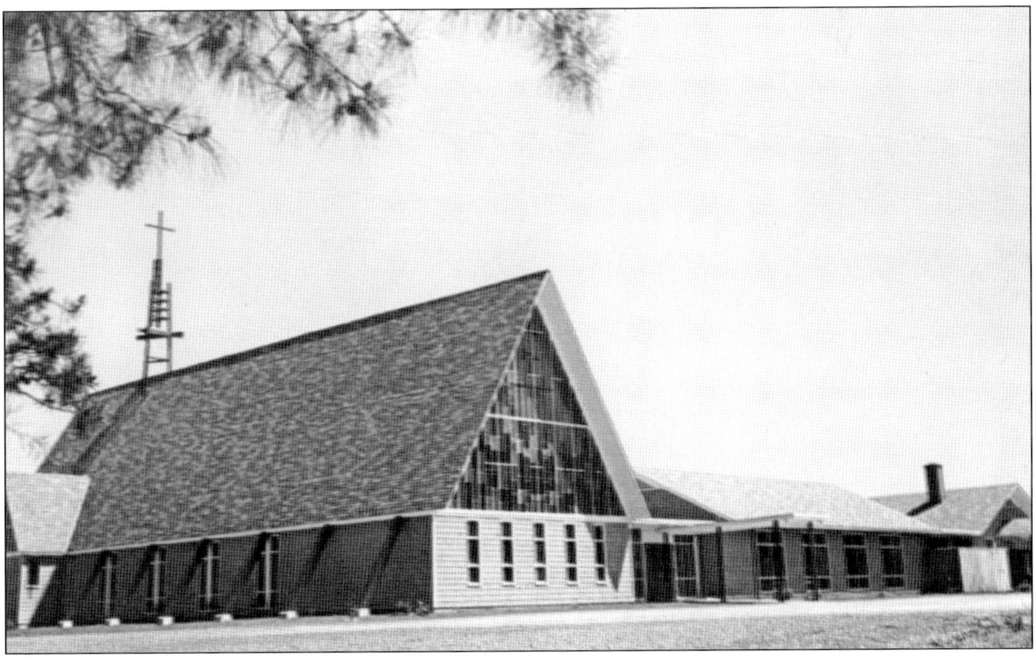

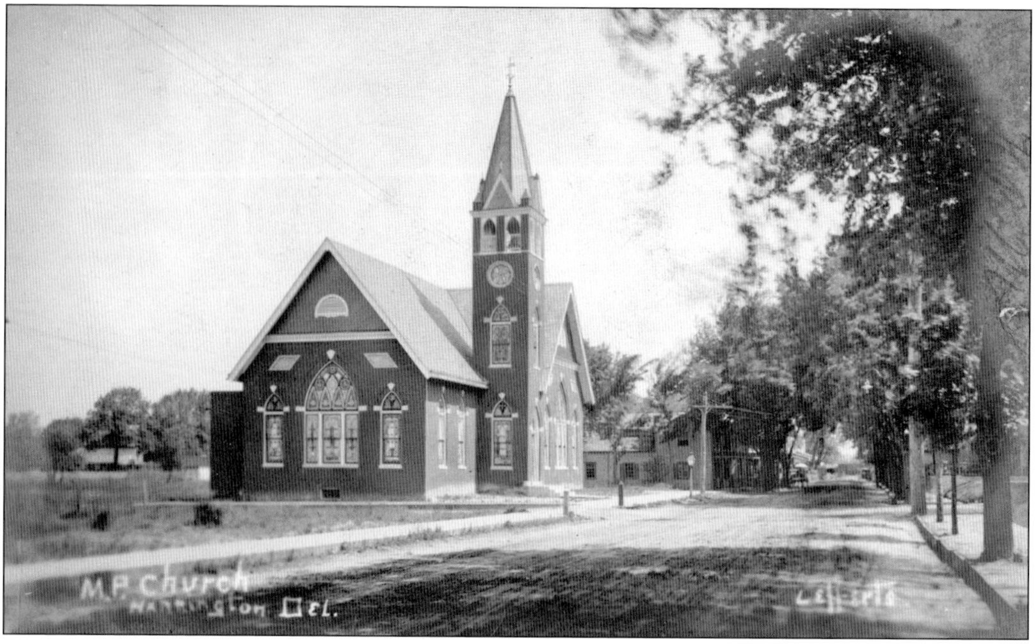

Trinity Methodist Church had the same beginnings as many other churches in Harrington. The first services were held in the local school when the church organized in 1880. The first church was built on Mechanic Street on land purchased from John Clymer and was dedicated on August 19, 1881. As the town grew, the small church was no longer large enough to hold the growing congregation. On June 6, 1904, new property was purchased, and the new church was completed later that same year. A large pipe organ was added in 1924, and the Sapp Memorial Building was added in 1926. (Below, courtesy of the Delaware Public Archives.)

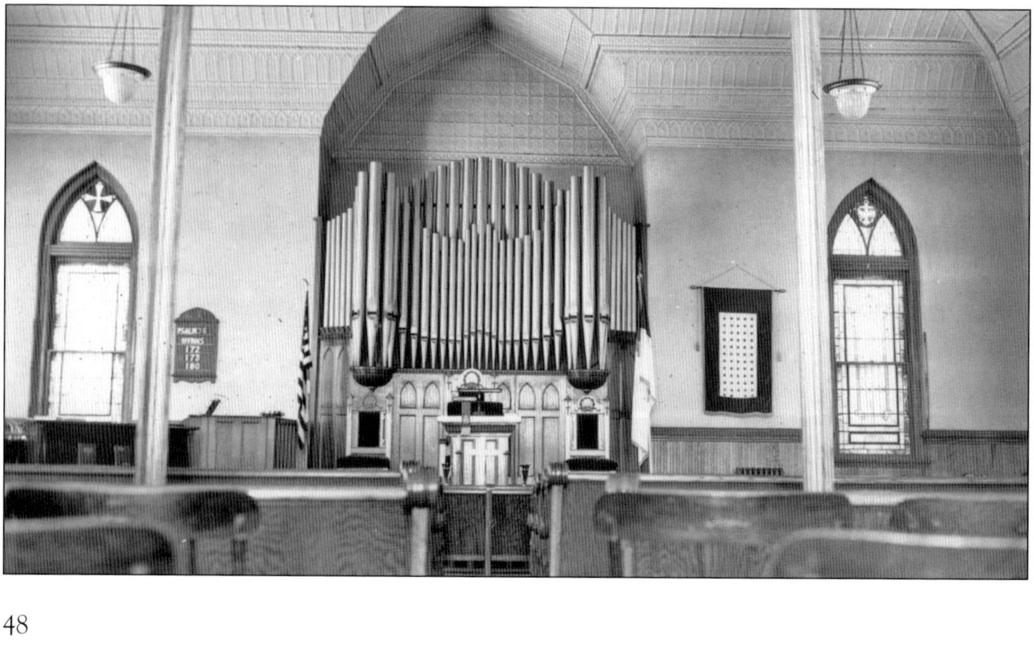

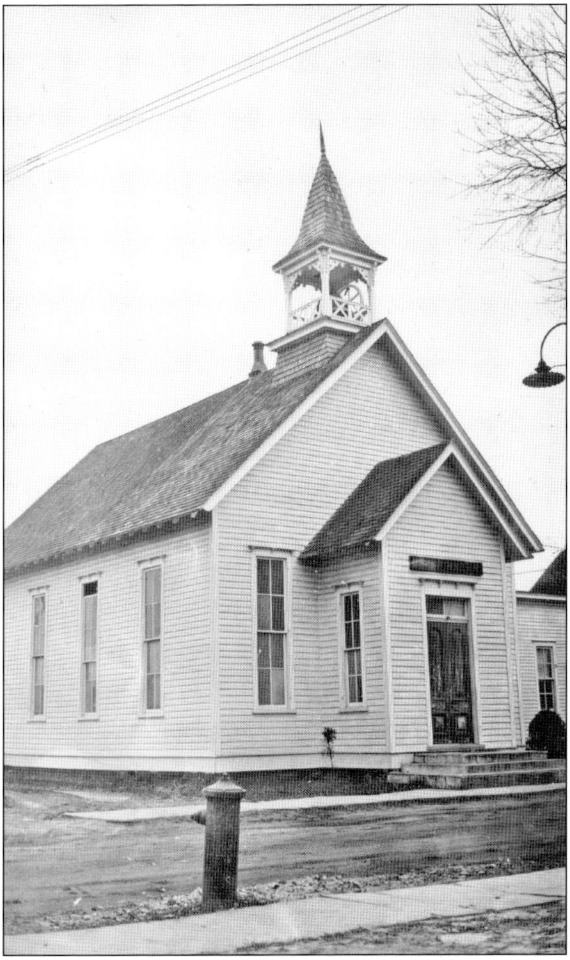

Currently home of the Mount Carmel Seventh-Day Adventist Church, this building has undergone major expansion since this photograph was taken in 1934 and served as a home to several religious bodies. The church was built in 1889 by the Delaware Baptist Union. It was then sold to Harrington Pilgrim Holiness and the Church of the Nazarene on March 25, 1903. In 1909, a split occurred between these two groups, and by a bare majority vote, the church was turned over to the Pentecostal Church of the Nazarene. It was later sold to the Seventh-Day Adventists, who call it home today.

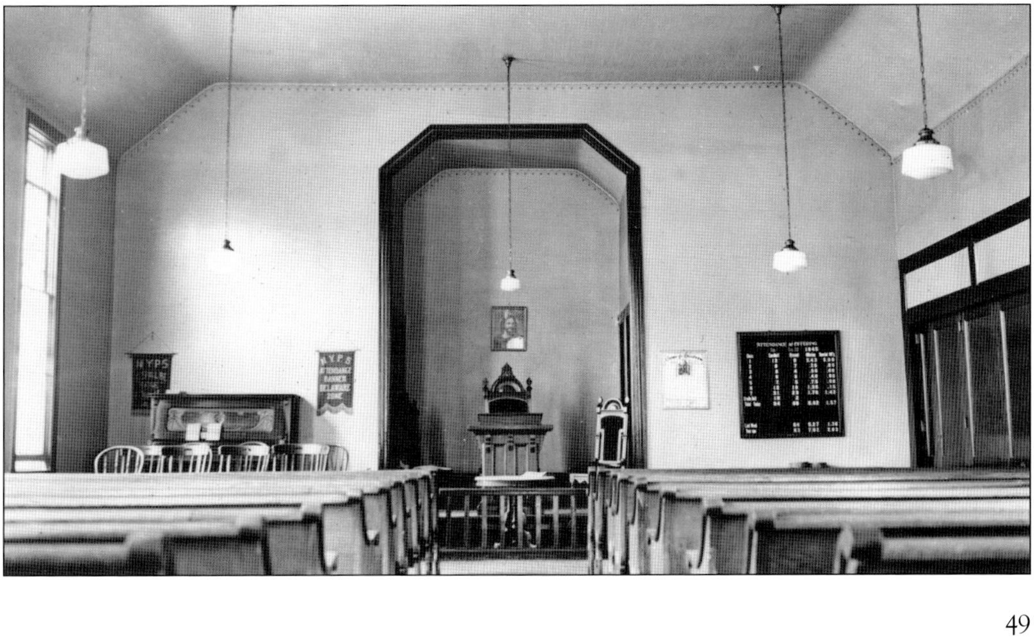

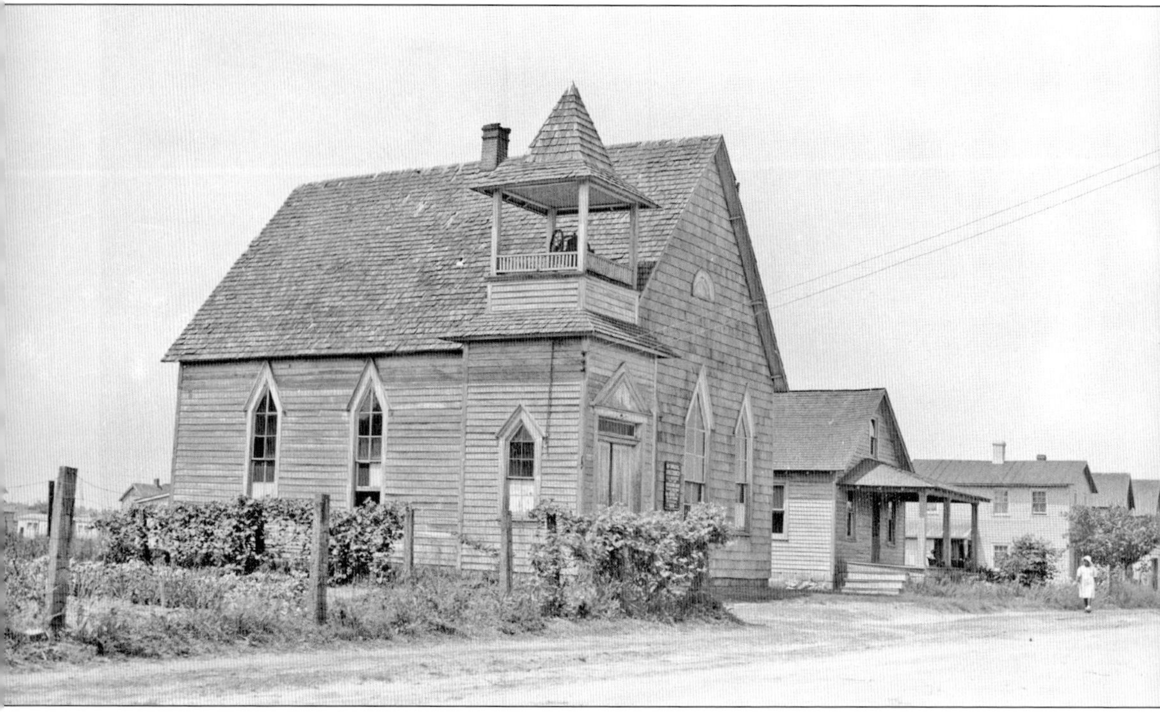

St. Paul's African Methodist Church was constructed in 1895 on land purchased from Henry C Wolcott. It was the last of the 11 AME churches built in Kent County between 1867 and 1895. Established in 1830, it is the oldest documented religious organization in Harrington and has been in practice continuously since that time. The church was organized just 17 years after the founding of the AME movement by Richard Allen, a former slave and a Delaware resident before moving to Philadelphia. Pastor Allen successfully sued in 1807 and again in 1815 for the rights of the AME Church to exist independently. The church building was nearly destroyed by fire in 1993, but it was repaired and serves to this day. (Courtesy of the Delaware Public Archives.)

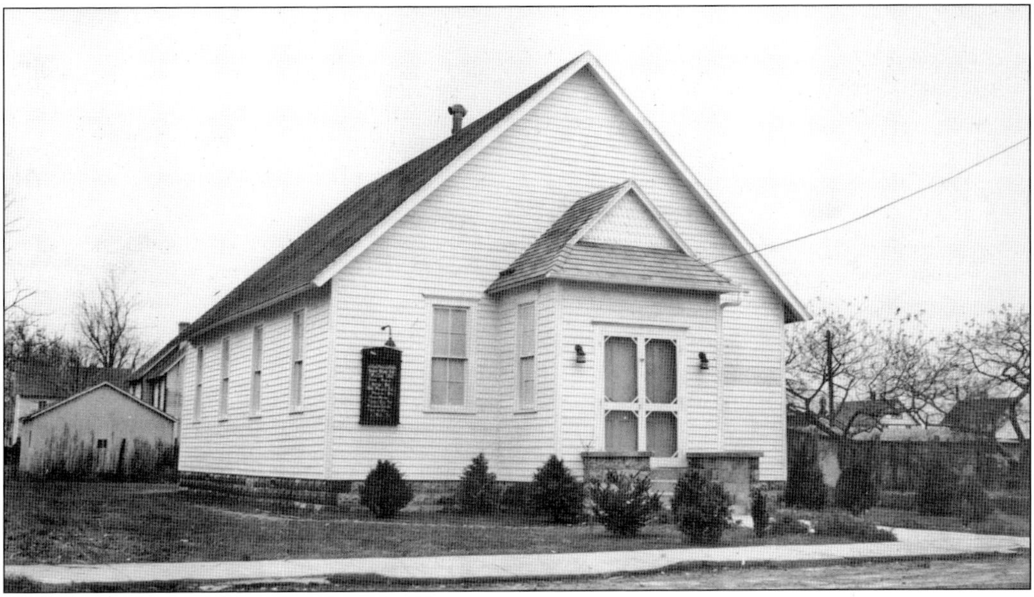

The Pilgrim Holiness Church was founded in March 1909 after a split from the Church of the Nazarene. First holding services in Masten's Hall, the church was given land on Liberty Street by Cyrus Dorman on May 26, 1909. A structure was quickly built, and on November 28, 1909, the church was dedicated. In September 1937, it was found that the church was over the property boundary and had to be moved. The organization purchased the lot next door, and the entire building was shifted the required distance. Closed in the 1970s, the church is now home to the Dover Miracle Revival Center. (Both, courtesy of the Delaware Public Archives.)

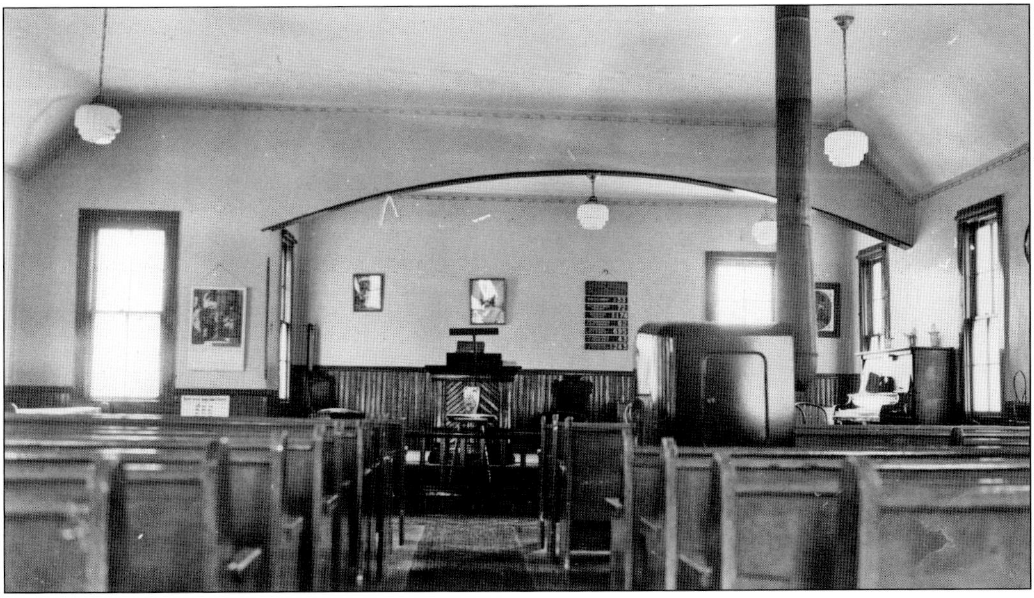

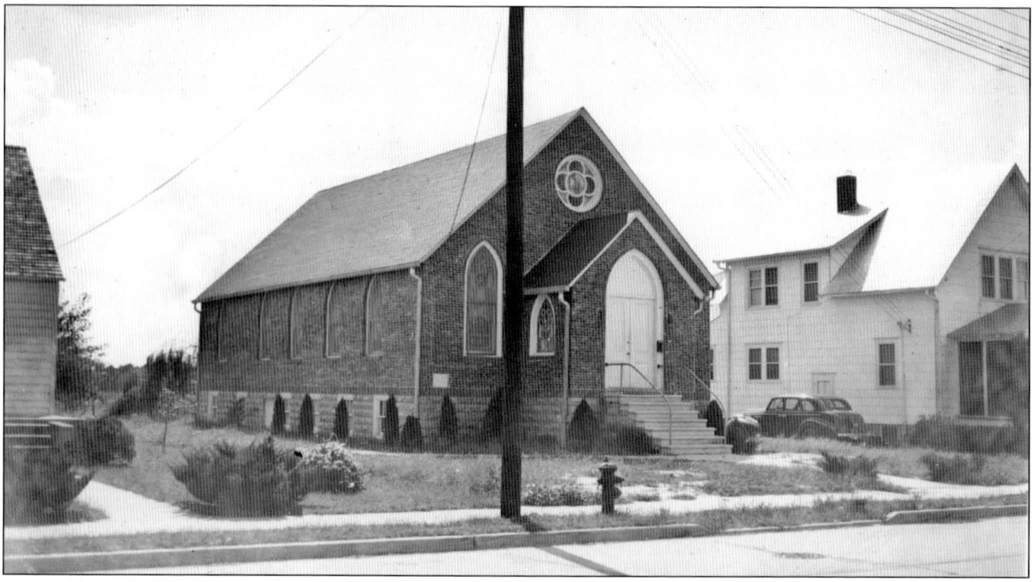

The Harrington Seventh-Day Adventist Church was founded by a group in Hollandsville, Delaware, on March 8, 1890. In December 1913, it moved to a newly constructed church in Whiteleysburg, Delaware, and was renamed the Whiteleysburg Seventh-Day Adventist Church. On September 23, 1939, a second group of Seventh-Day Adventists began to worship in Farmington, Delaware, at the home of the Tatum family. These two groups merged and formed the Harrington Seventh-Day Adventist Church on April 30, 1944. The church was approved for construction despite most new buildings being banned due to World War II. The congregation believed that divine intervention allowed its small church to be built. Materials, including the stained-glass windows, were recycled from a much older church in Pennsylvania. The church was constructed entirely by the membership and dedicated on May 6, 1944. (Both, courtesy of the Delaware Public Archives.)

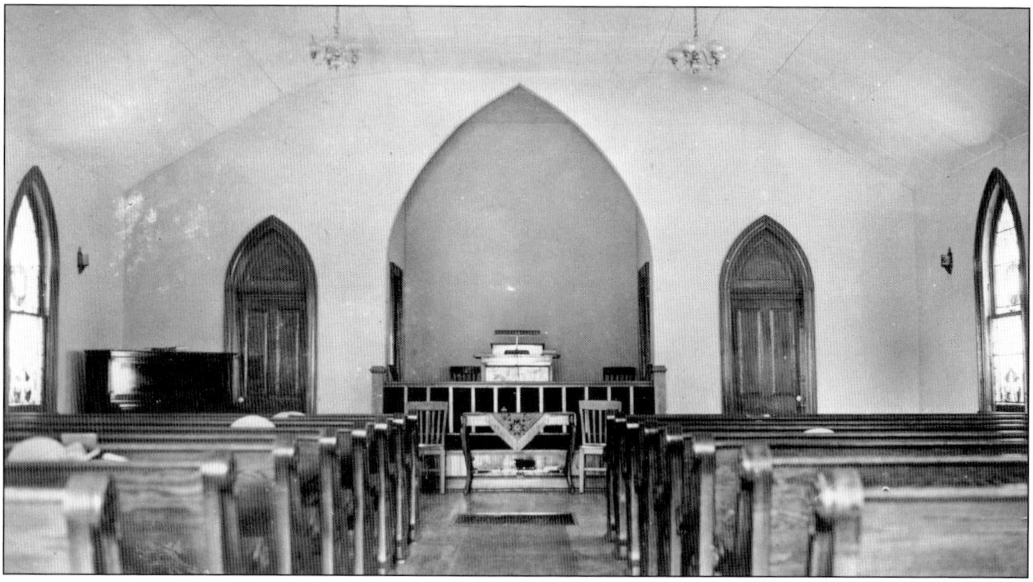

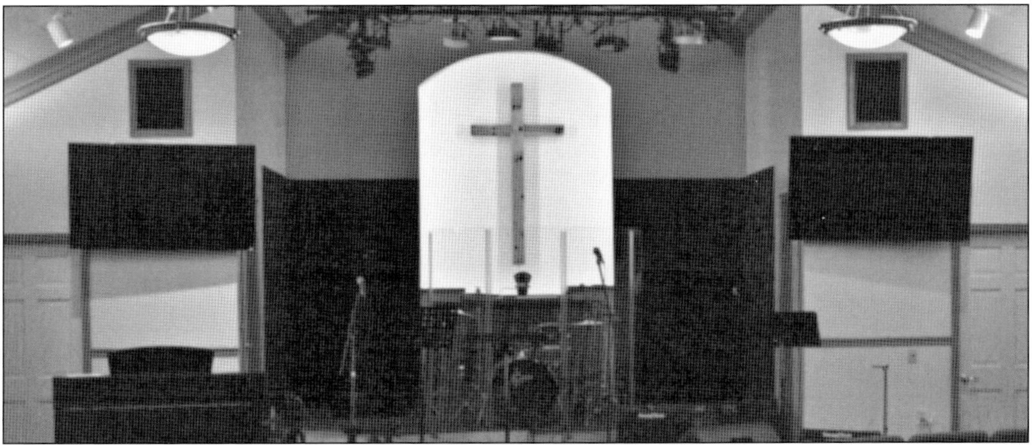

Harrington Baptist Church had its beginnings in 1889. After leaving town for several decades, a part of the congregation based in Greensboro, Maryland, chose to once again form a church in Harrington. Using several buildings beginning in 1959 to conduct services, the congregation purchased the former Episcopal church on Fleming Street on November 2, 1960, for $75,000 and utilized it for services beginning on February 19, 1961. These photographs are of the new church, which was constructed in 1966. The fellowship hall and educational wing were added in October 1978.

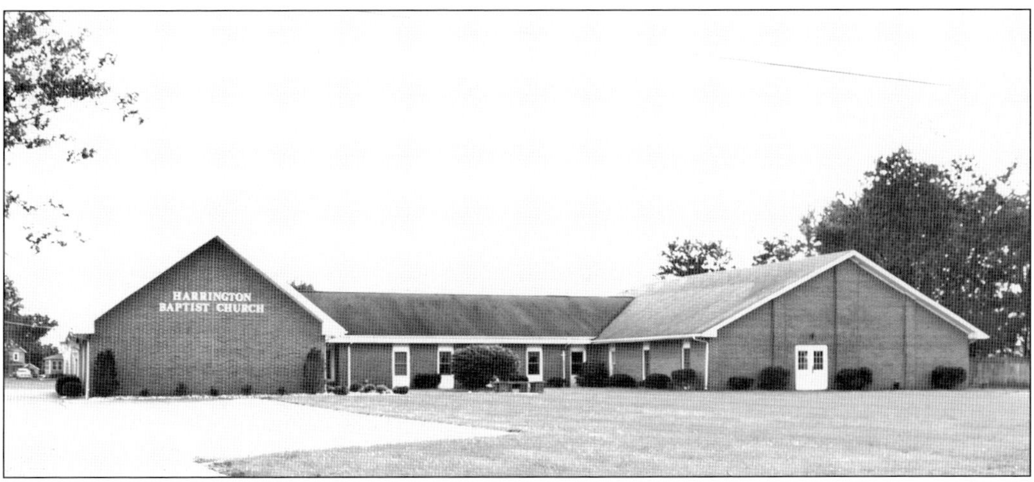

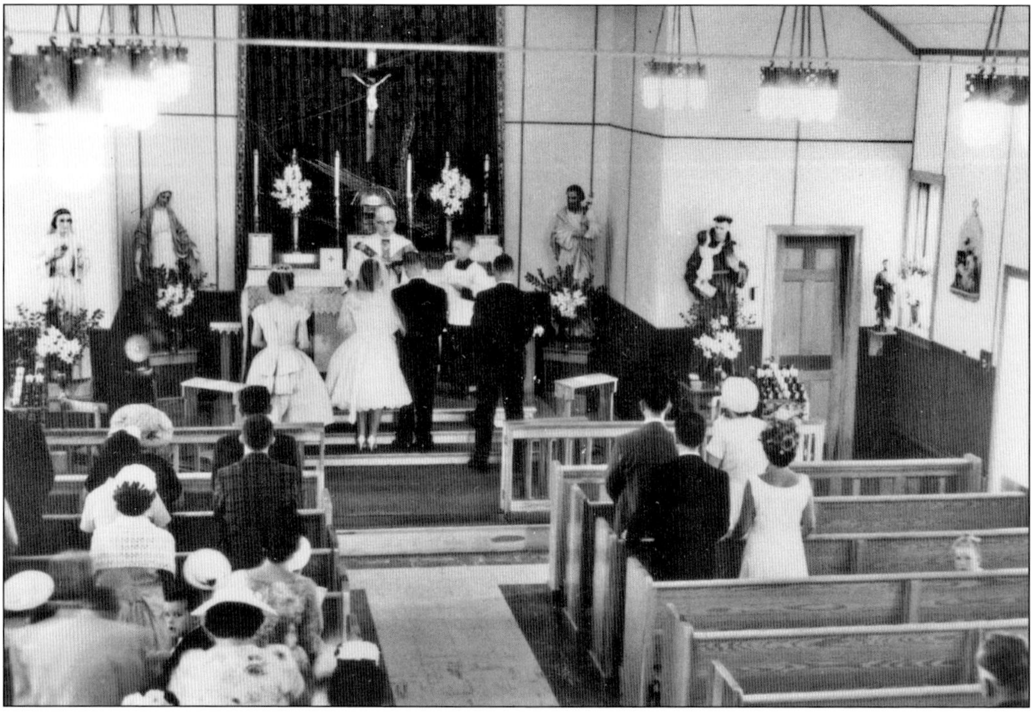

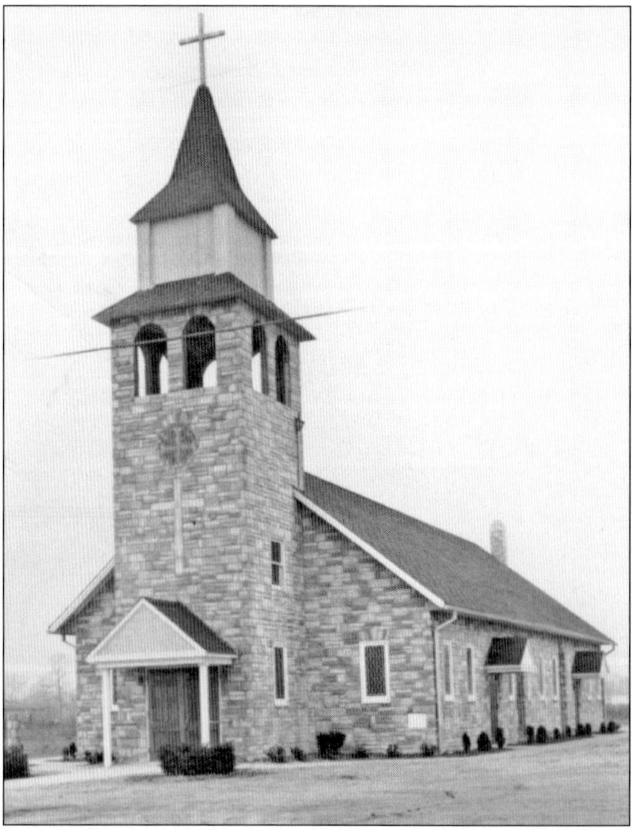

St. Bernadette Catholic Church is new to the city, but Catholic mass has been held here since the early 1900s. Mass was first held in the Newman Hotel, then in local homes. However, local Catholics still yearned for a place to call home. Due to difficulties Catholics faced in being accepted in the local community, they could not secure a building site. Local merchant Harry Greenburg offered to purchase land on behalf of the church. On September 6, 1952, Greenburg purchased 20 acres, and the next day, he sold it to the church. The families of the church agreed to supply the needed funds, and they constructed the church themselves. Beginning on November 23, 1953, crews hand-dug footers, and by Easter 1954, only the roof remained unfinished. This was the only part hired out to a contractor. The church was opened and dedicated on September 6, 1954.

Four

The School Bell Rings

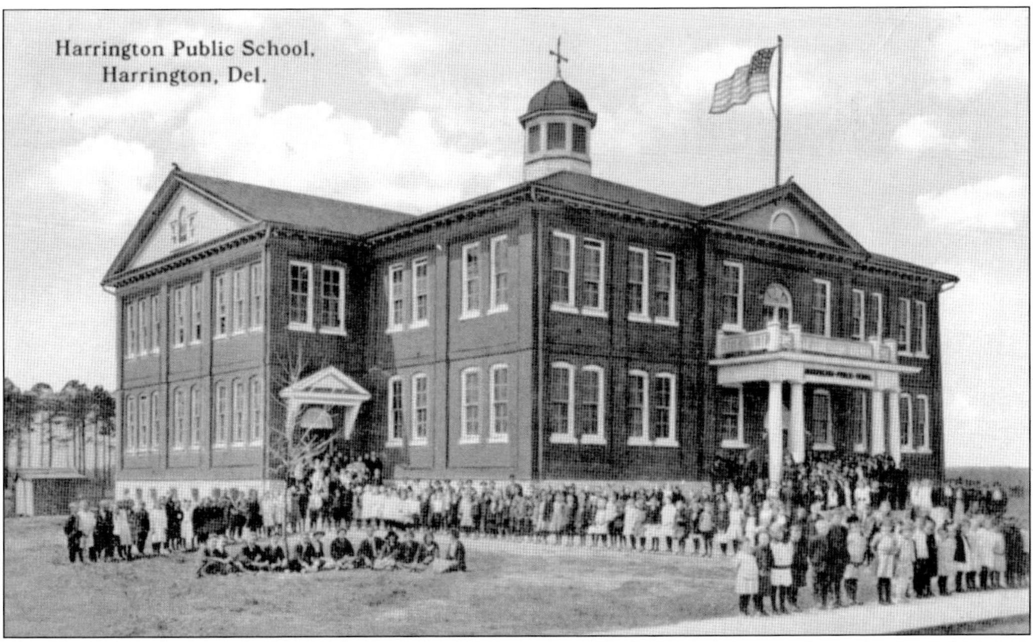

In 1910, the previous school had been outgrown, so the decision was made to borrow $25,000 to erect a new, modern school facility. The new building was a two-story structure designed to house 500 students and teachers. It included a laboratory and a nurse's office, a first for a school in Harrington.

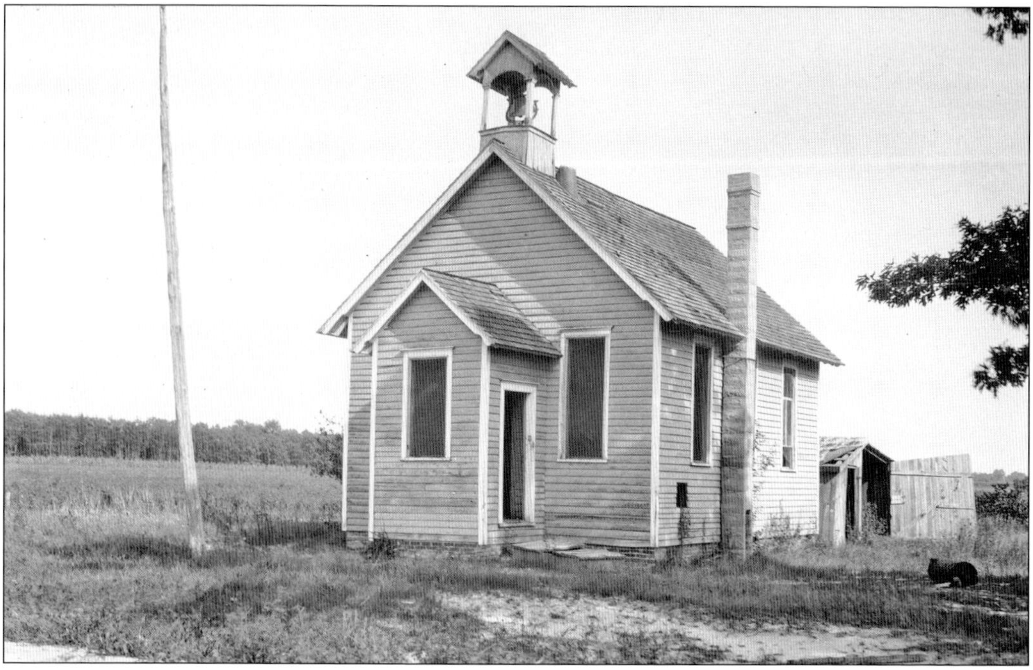

On July 1, 1919, the State of Delaware combined several one-room schoolhouses in the countryside surrounding Harrington into the Harrington School District. Until that time, Harrington School, which had been created as District 94 on March 1, 1883, had served just the town's residents. These schools were Powell's No. 48, Brown's Neck No. 38, and Old Masten's No. 35. When this occurred, it greatly increased the number of students attending Harrington. On June 28, 1928, the district was combined with other small one-room schools. Pictured above is Marvel's No. 63; below is Masten's Corner No. 58. (Both, courtesy of the Delaware Public Archives)

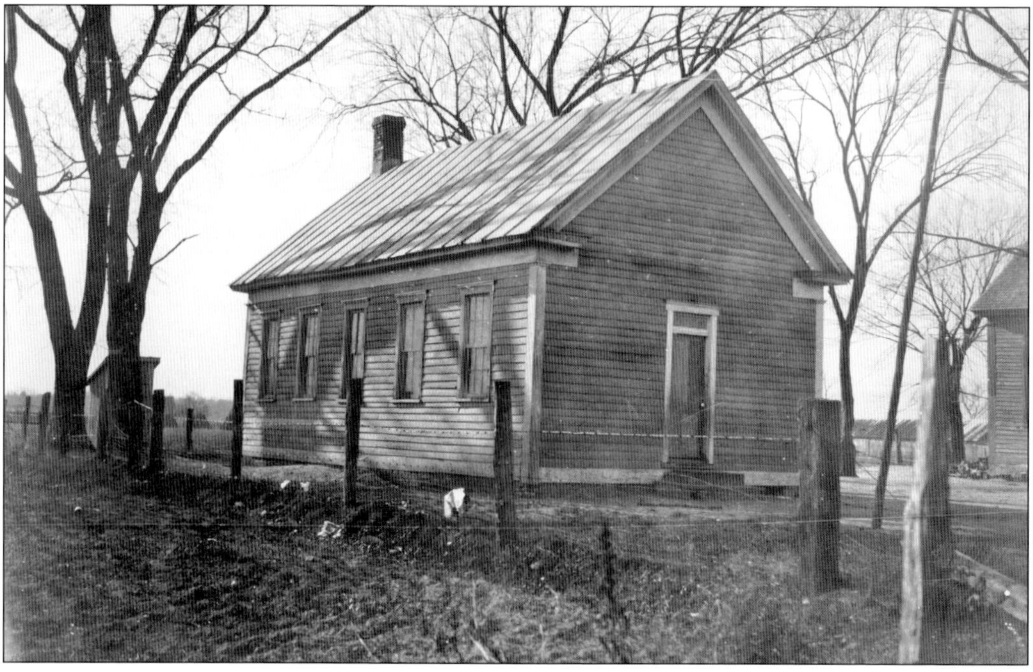

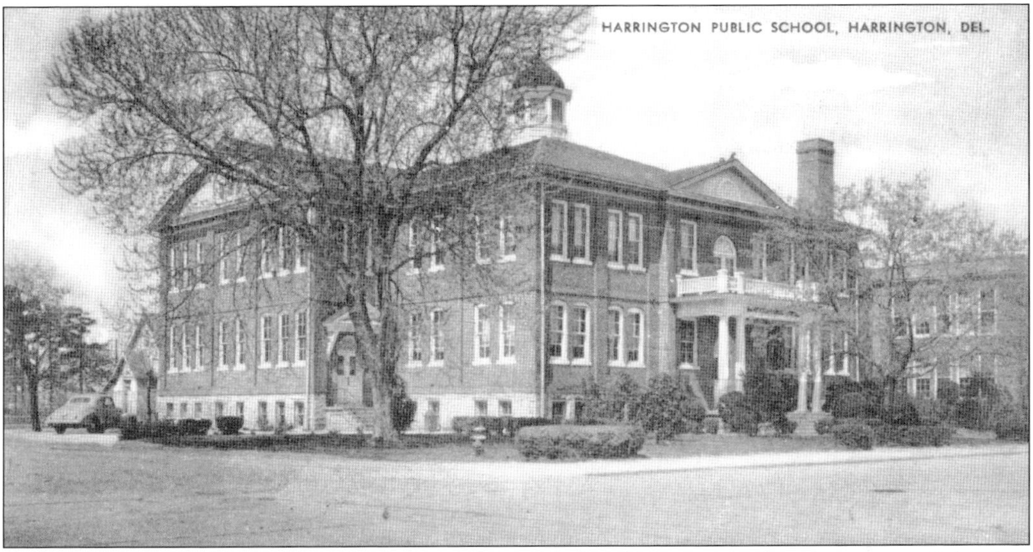

When the first consolidation occurred, Powell's School had been moved to Harrington School to provide additional space for a home economics classroom. With the addition of over 150 students, the brick structure on Dorman Street was expanded to add much needed classroom space for first through 12th grades and over 1,000 staff and students.

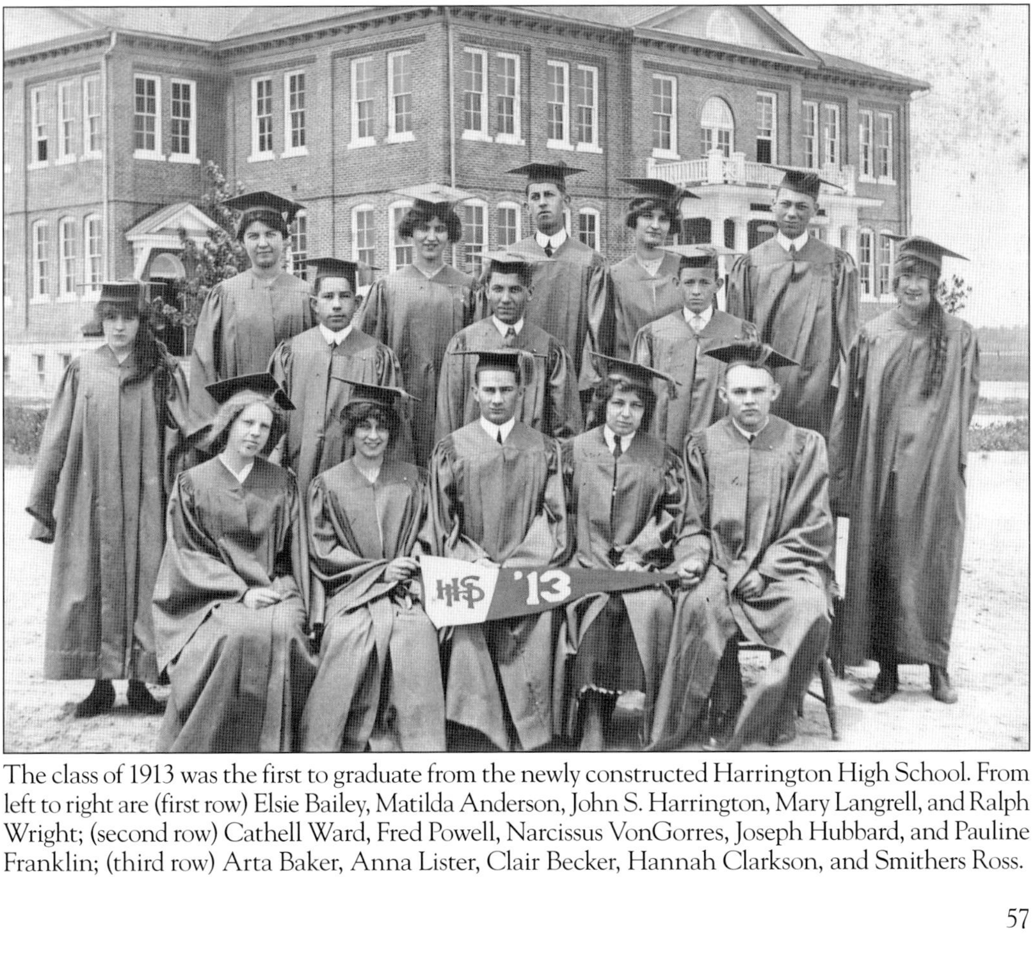

The class of 1913 was the first to graduate from the newly constructed Harrington High School. From left to right are (first row) Elsie Bailey, Matilda Anderson, John S. Harrington, Mary Langrell, and Ralph Wright; (second row) Cathell Ward, Fred Powell, Narcissus VonGorres, Joseph Hubbard, and Pauline Franklin; (third row) Arta Baker, Anna Lister, Clair Becker, Hannah Clarkson, and Smithers Ross.

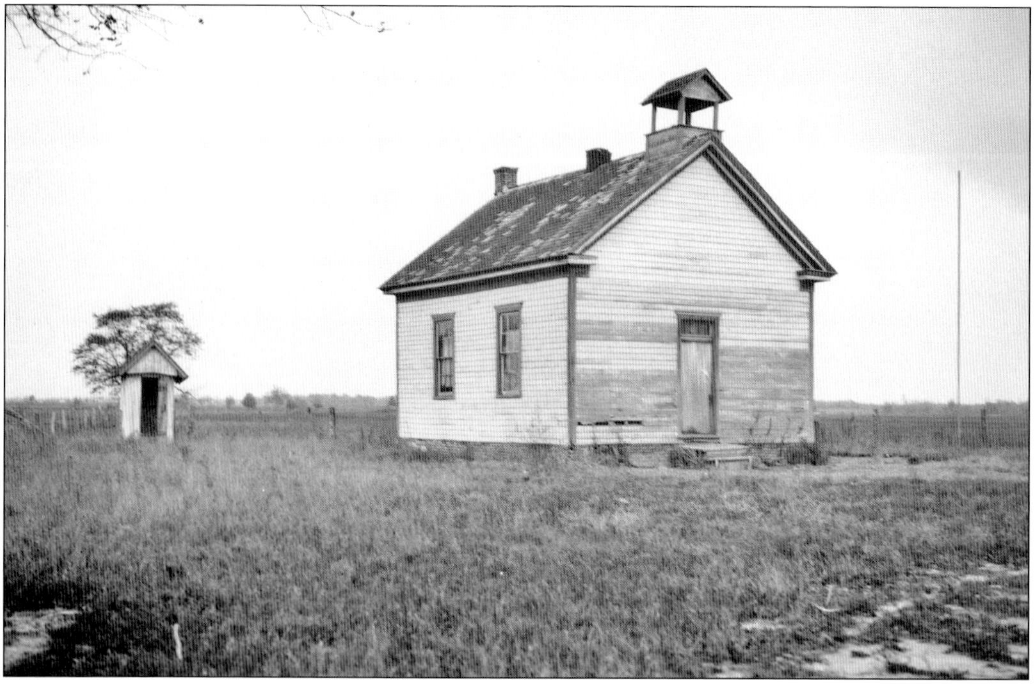

Bus transportation began in 1923, so the little one-room schools such as Prospect No. 36, seen here, were no longer viable. It too was consolidated into the Harrington District in 1928. Located near Vernon, this little school, like so many in the area, was dimly lit, cold, and sadly lacking in basic needs such as textbooks and chalkboards. (Courtesy of the Delaware Public Archives.)

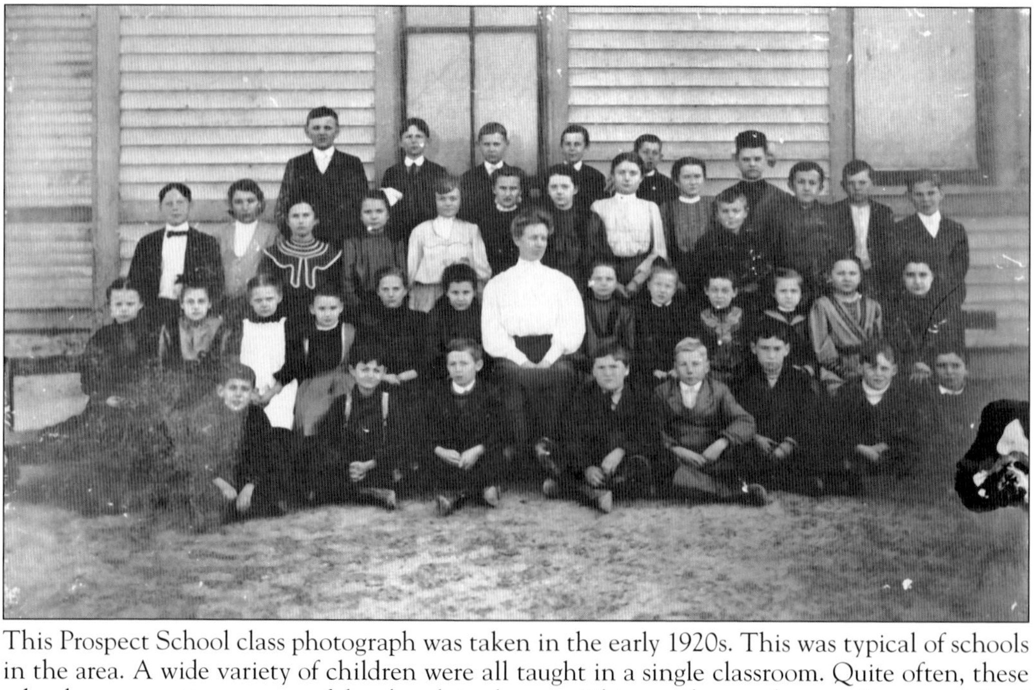

This Prospect School class photograph was taken in the early 1920s. This was typical of schools in the area. A wide variety of children were all taught in a single classroom. Quite often, these schools were next to or a part of the church in the area. This was the case here, as Prospect School was a part of Prospect Church.

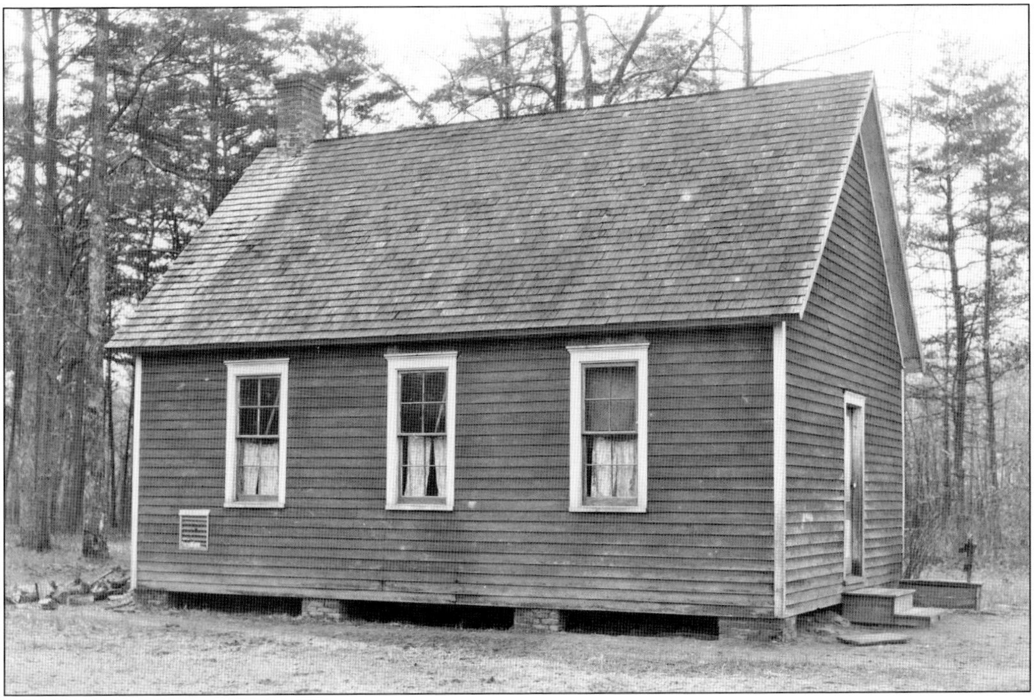

Hammondtown School No. 165 was the first "colored school," as the state called it at the time, to be brought into the Harrington School District. This occurred on July 1, 1928. Even though the school was consolidated, the black students were still segregated into a separate school building on West Street. Before the school was closed in 1928, it had been completely remodeled. The photograph above was taken in 1920, and the one below in 1923. This school, along with every colored school in the state, was remodeled by the DuPont family of Wilmington. (Both, courtesy of the Delaware Public Archives.)

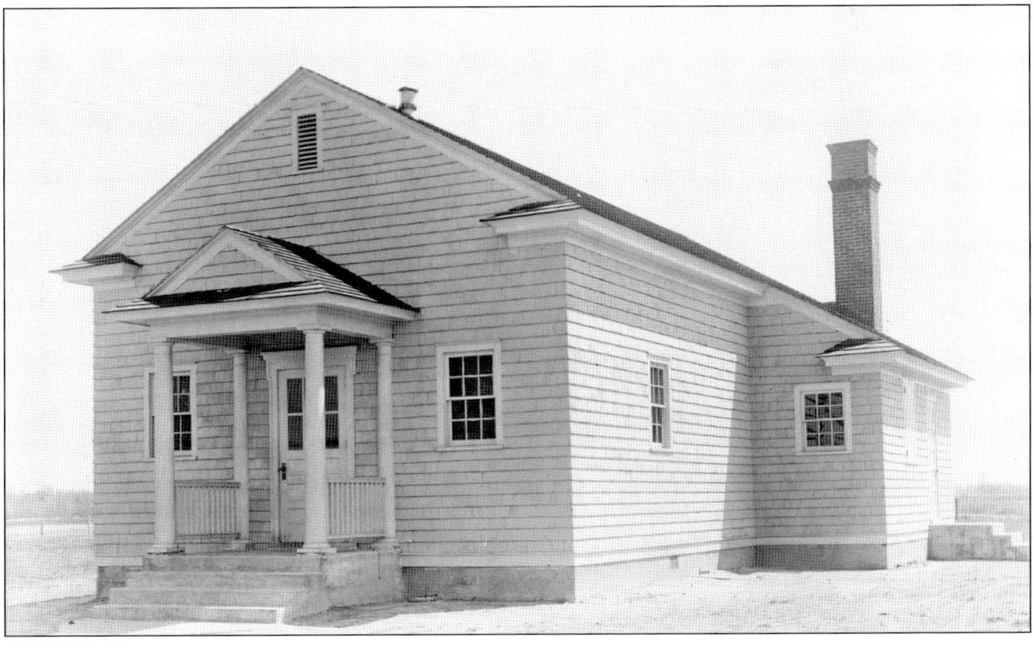

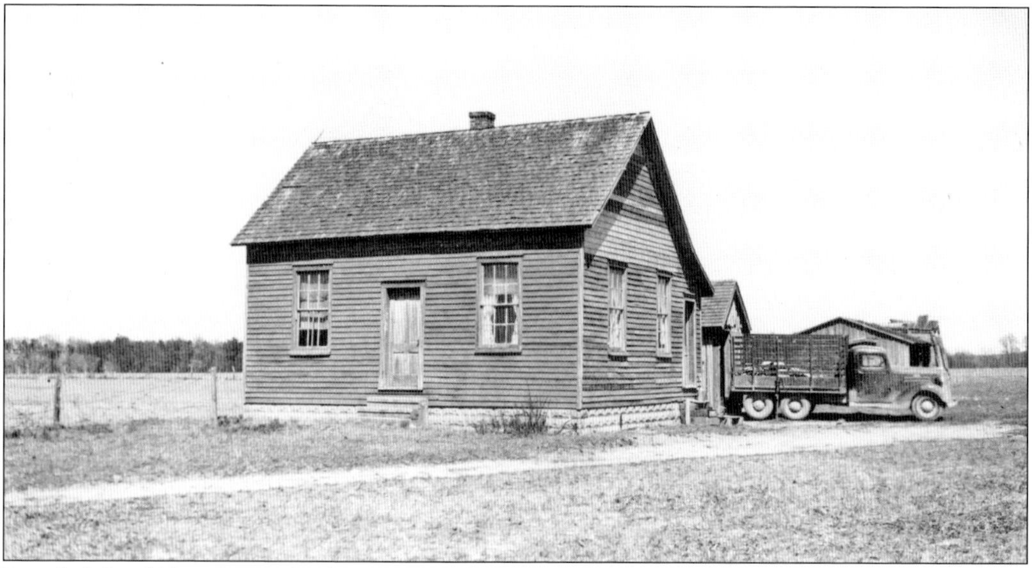

Potash School No. 100 was built in 1867 on land donated by John Porter. School districts created during this time, when one-room schoolhouses were serving the rural area, comprised on average a radius of two miles. This small school was located less than half a mile outside the Masten's Corner District. It was consolidated with Harrington School District on May 15, 1931. The building was sold and turned into a home. (Courtesy of the Hagley Museum & Library.)

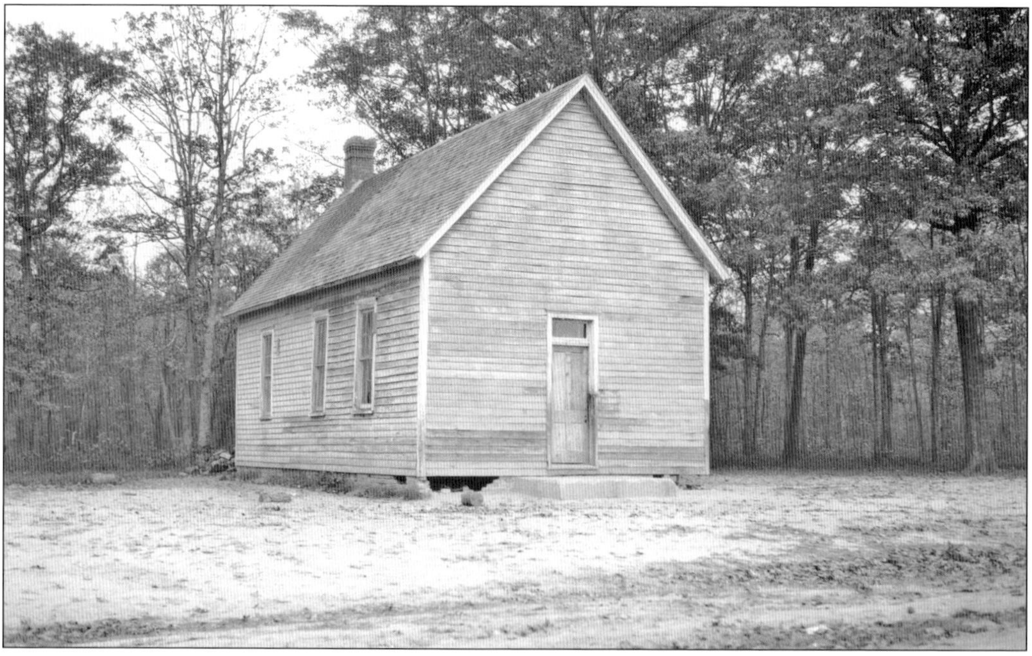

Anderson School No. 55 was situated near the crossroads of Brownsville northwest of Harrington. The location had originally been named Grape Tree Crossroads but was renamed after Outten Anderson, who donated the land for the school in 1835. The school was funded by residents of the area through subscription. In less than 10 years, this small school was serving over 50 pupils. This district was brought into the Harrington District on September 24, 1937. (Courtesy of the Delaware Public Archives.)

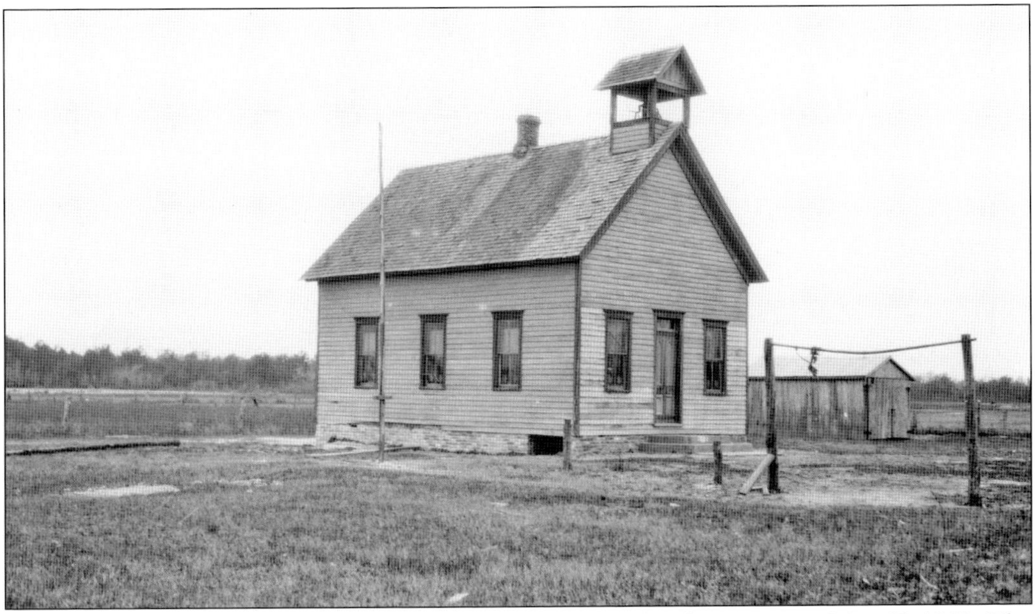

Maple Grove School was brought into the Harrington School District on May 17, 1940. The first schoolhouse was constructed in 1844, and a second building, the one pictured here, was built in 1888. Located just east of the Delaware-Maryland state line, this was one of the last one-room schoolhouses to close due to its distance from the city. Since bus transportation was very unreliable for these students, leaving them in their local school was a better choice. (Courtesy of the Delaware Public Archives.)

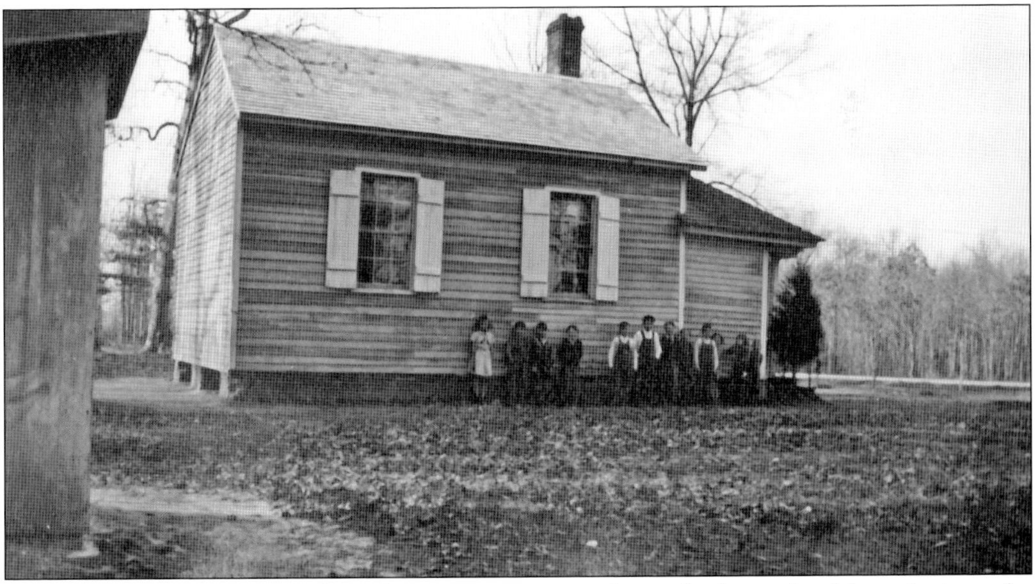

Thomas School was the farthest from Harrington and was the last school brought into the district, on May 21, 1943. Again, transportation of the students was the cause for the delay in consolidating this school. The spring report from the Kent County School Commission dated May 24, 1918, describes the roads in this area as the worst the commission encountered during its entire inspection tour of the schools in the county. Until the roads were improved, it was impossible to provide school bus service. (Courtesy of the Delaware Public Archives.)

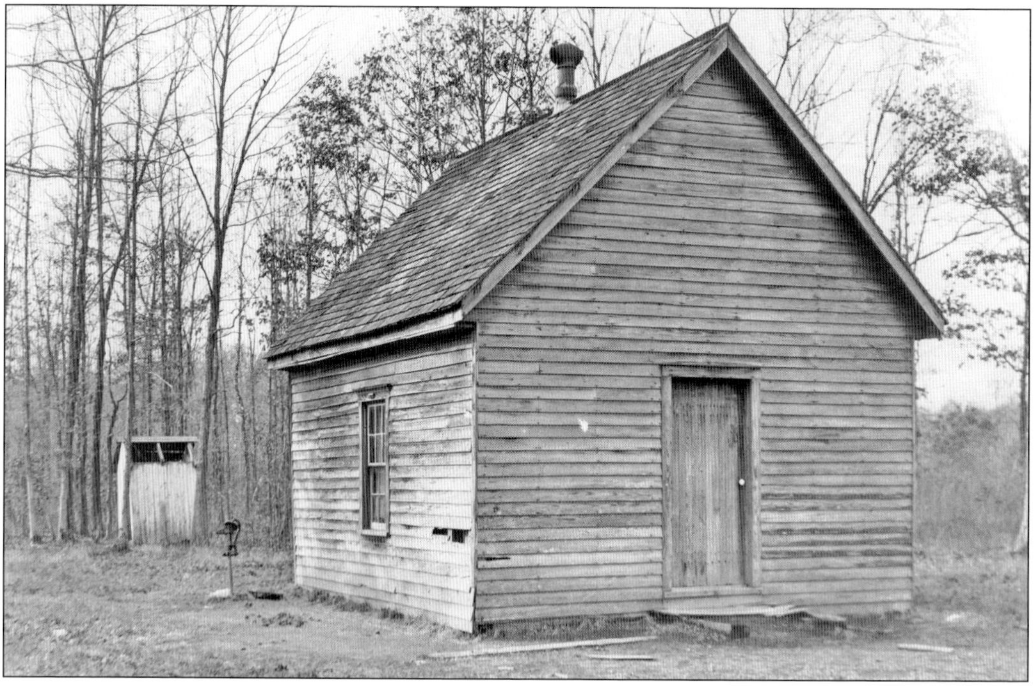

Brownsville Colored School was approximately six miles from the town of Harrington. Records of this school's beginnings are lost, but it is believed to have been built by local farmers wanting to educate the black families living and working on their farms. The school was closed in 1928, and the students were transported to the newly built school. The students only attended up to sixth grade, as that was all that was offered to black children at the time. (Courtesy of the Hagley Museum & Library.)

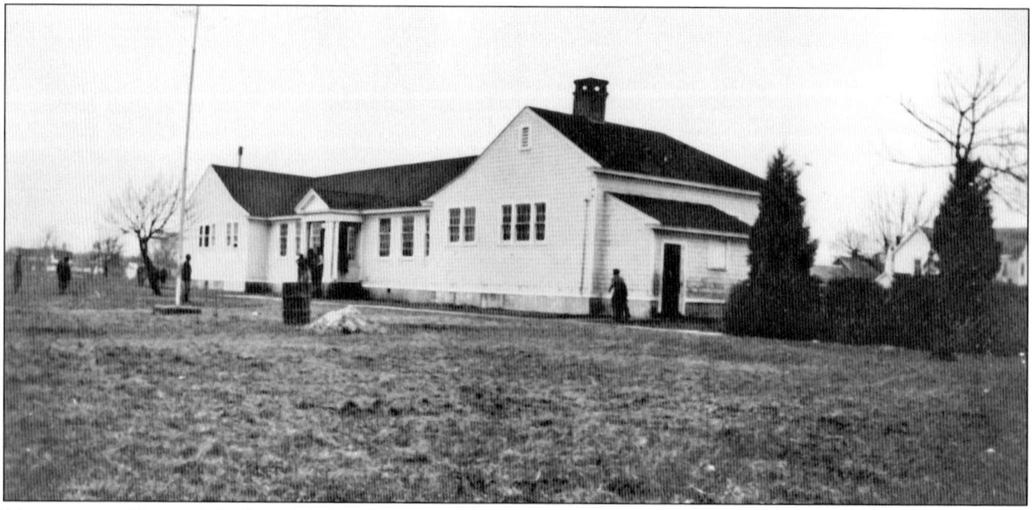

Harrington Special Colored School opened in 1929 and by Delaware law educated black children through the ninth grade. That same law created a single high school for all black students in the county, but no transportation was provided, so most students completed the ninth grade and had no other opportunities to further their education. Beginning in 1966, African American students began attending Harrington High School. The first to attend was Vivian Tribbett, who graduated in 1967. (Courtesy of the Delaware Public Archives.)

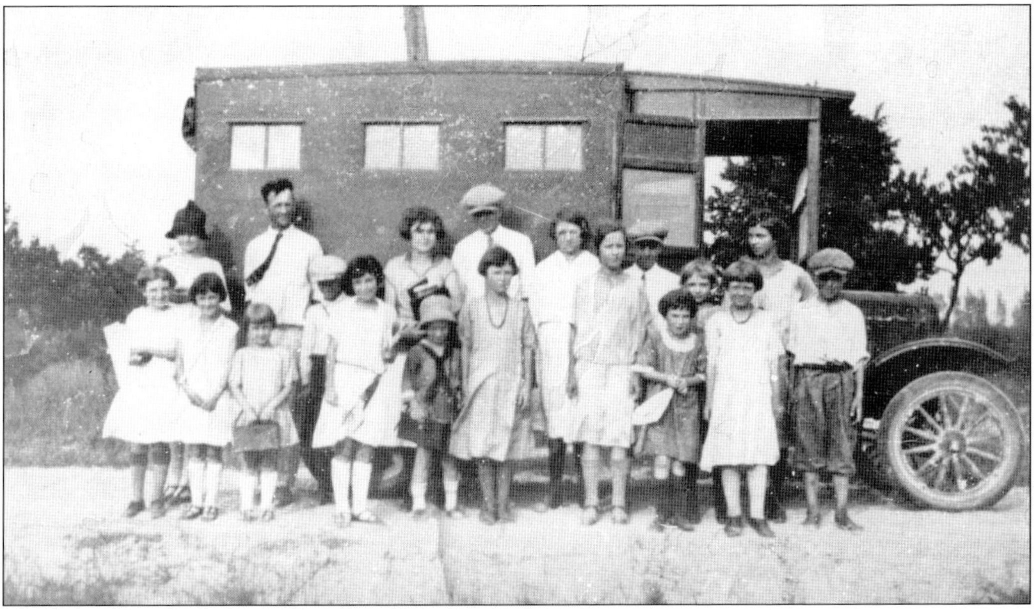

Early on, school buses were homemade by locals for districts that wanted to provide students with a ride to and from school. Harrington had buses made by Al Spurry, Orville Wright, and Stanley Wyatt. The bus shown here was made in 1923 by Spurry. From left to right are (first row) Ida Bland, Sarah Martin, Marie Martin, Walter Taylor, Virginia Martin, three unidentified, Lorena Moore, Clara Goldinger, Florence Sherwood, and Joseph Taylor; (second row) Helen Keyes, bus driver Orville Wright, Margaret Bland, George Tatman, Evelyn Sherwood, Russ Salmons, and Elizabeth Goldinger.

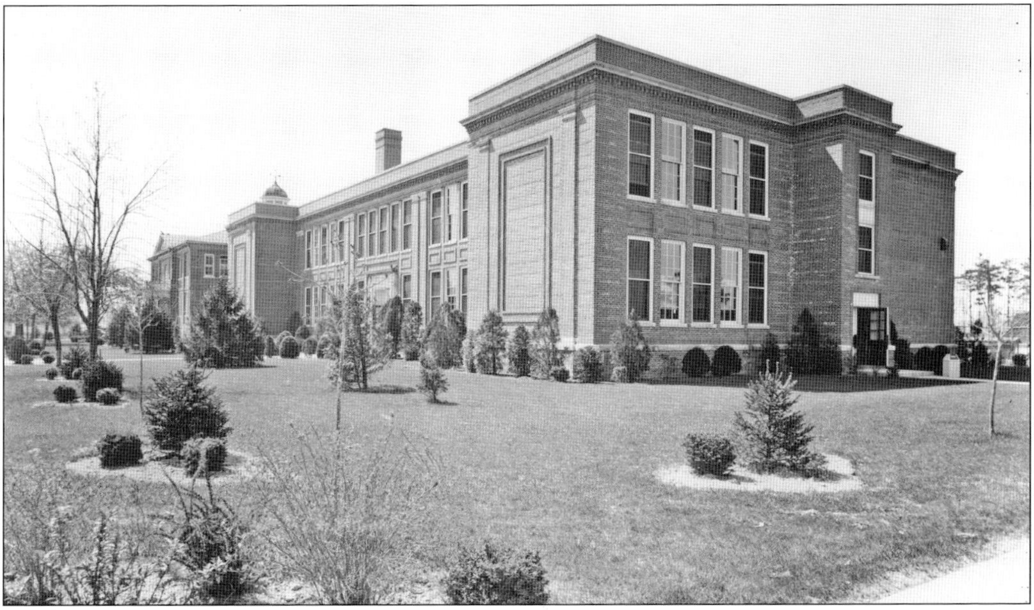

Harrington High School, pictured around 1955, was expanded once again to house an increasing population. An elementary school had been added, so the entire Harrington Special School District was now housed in one building. Playground equipment had been added, new sports such as football were offered, and the marching band filled the streets when it played. (Courtesy of the Delaware Public Archives.)

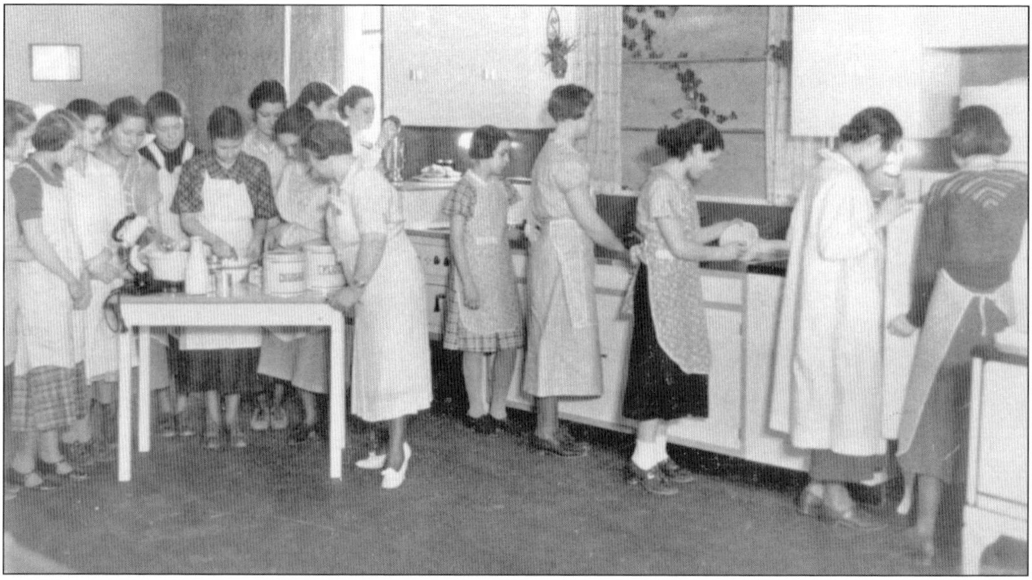

Home economics was required for all female students in the 1950s. It was first made a requirement at the school just after the 1900s, and the newly expanded school housed a complete kitchen so students could learn to cook, sew, and manage a household. Meanwhile, the boys were required to take shop class. It would be several years before all students had to take both classes.

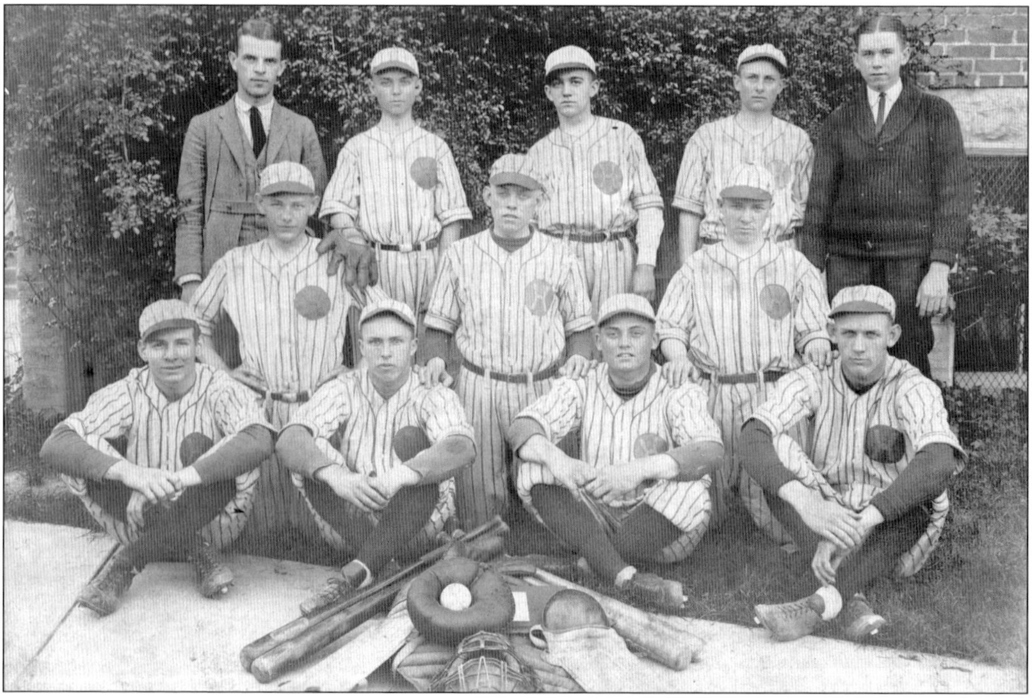

Baseball was the first organized sport played at Harrington High School. The school won multiple state championships over the decades. From left to right are (first row) William Cahall, Townsend Masten, George Short, and Herman Ryan; (second row) Darwin Schaub, William Wood, and Carrington Burgess; (third row) coach Lake Vane, Maurice Hall, Wilbur Richards, Harvey LeGates, and manager Edward Cannon.

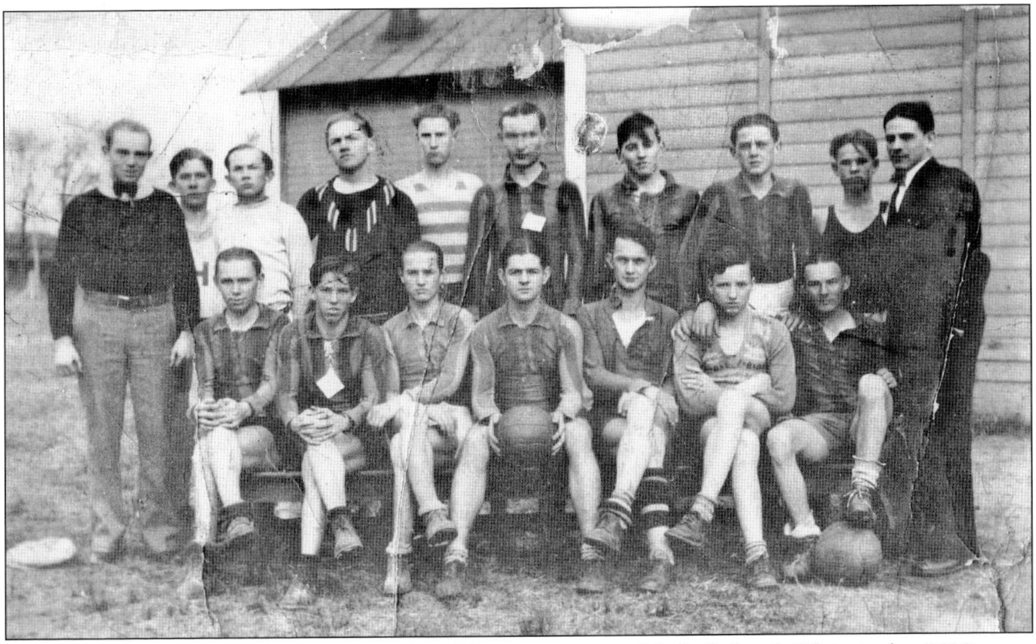

Soccer was the second sport to be played by Harrington High School. This is the 1929 state championship team. The school could not afford uniforms, so the students had to make do with whatever clothing they had. A few athletes chose to buy matching shirts to give them a sense of team pride.

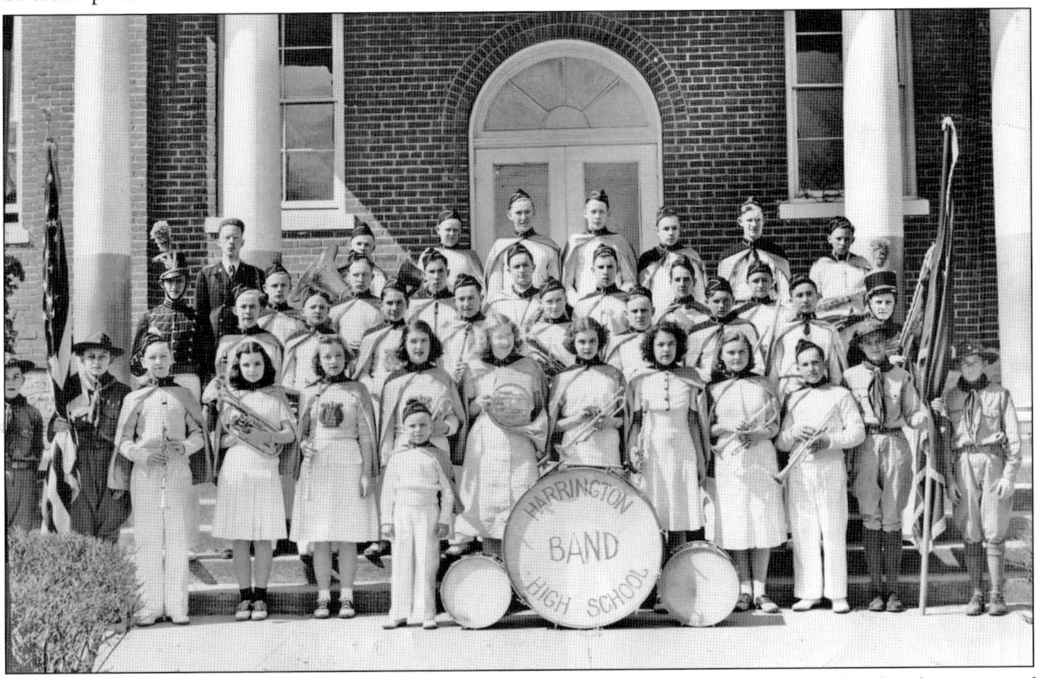

The Harrington High School marching band was the pride of the school. Under the direction of Melvin C. Brobst, who came to the school in 1939, the band participated in parades all over the area, bringing home trophy after trophy. The band exemplified the small town that it came from. The director worked with students and parents alike to ensure they were the best around.

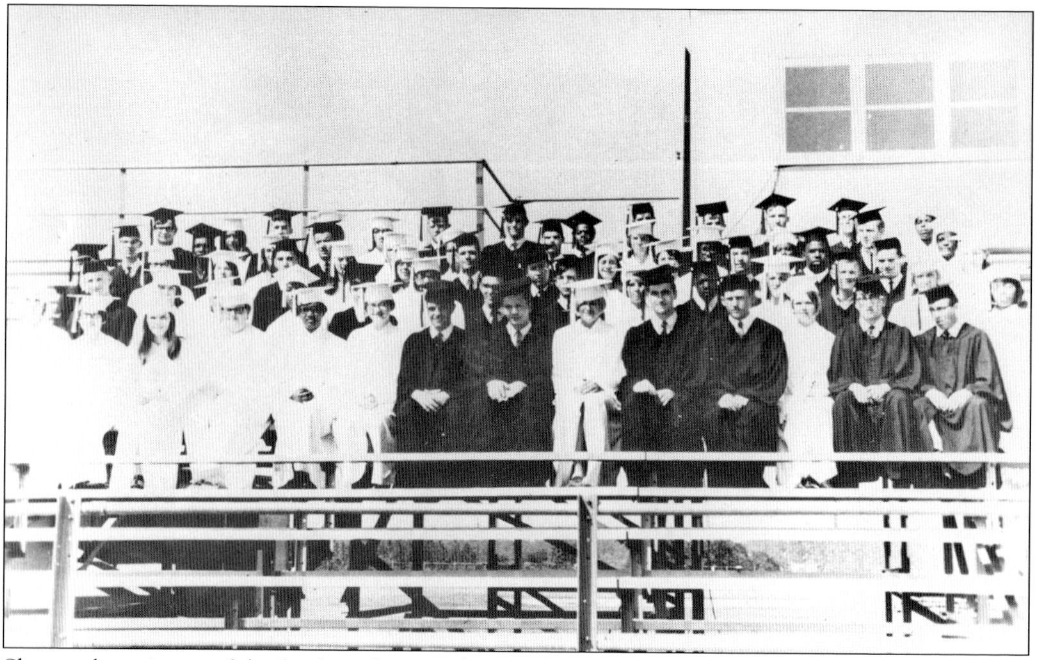

Shown above is one of the final graduating classes of Harrington High School. In 1969, Harrington High School closed. In order to reduce education costs, the State of Delaware decided to again consolidate school districts. Felton and Harrington High Schools combined as Lake Forest High School. The school facilities continued to serve the community as an elementary school and the W.T. Chipman Junior High School within the Lake Forest School District. But sadly to the citizens and alumni of the town, the Harrington High School lion would roar no more.

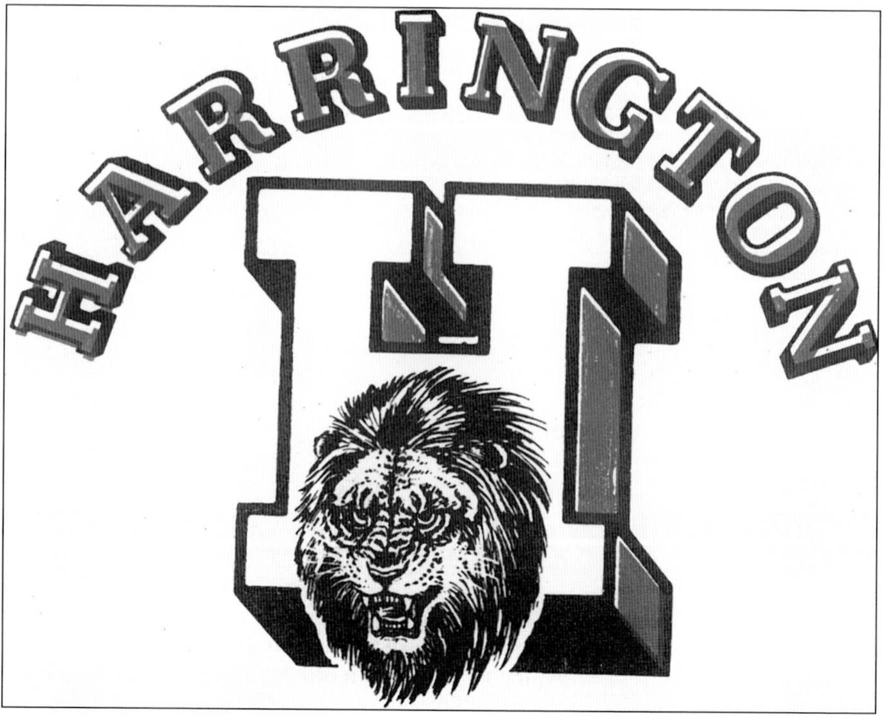

Five

A Small Town Becomes a Bustling City

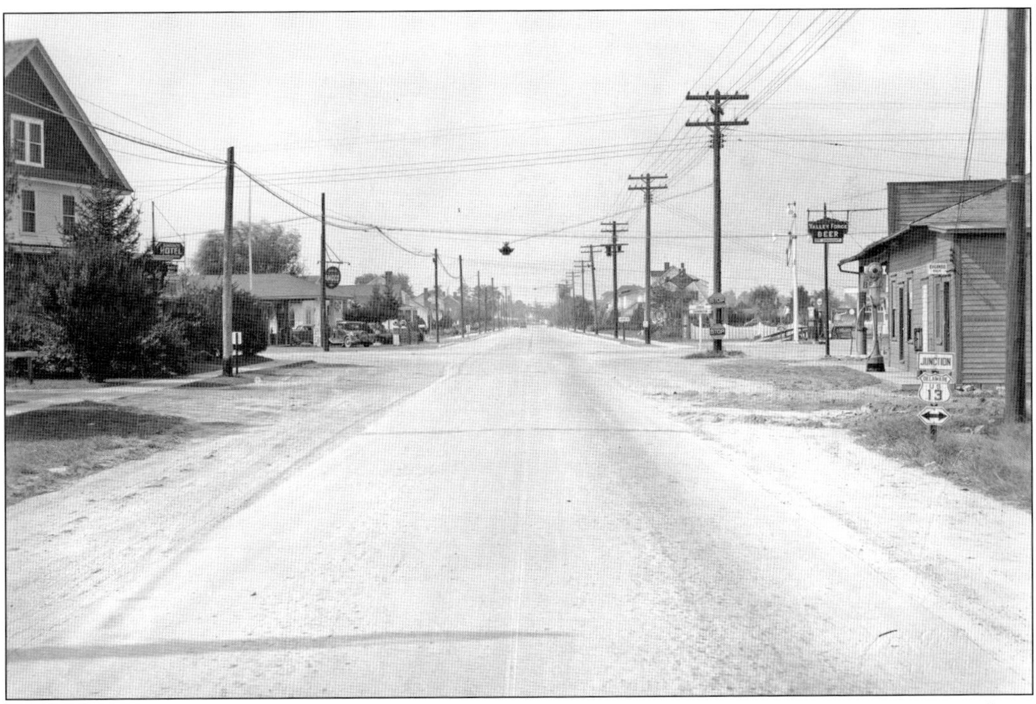

By 1923, a major highway had come to Harrington. Begun in 1911 at the Maryland-Delaware line, the concrete highway was slowly expanded northward to the Pennsylvania-Delaware line. The entire project was funded by Coleman DuPont and thus was named the DuPont Highway. This created a huge population boom in the lower part of Delaware. It also gave another method for goods to be shipped from towns all around the area. (Courtesy of the Delaware Public Archives.)

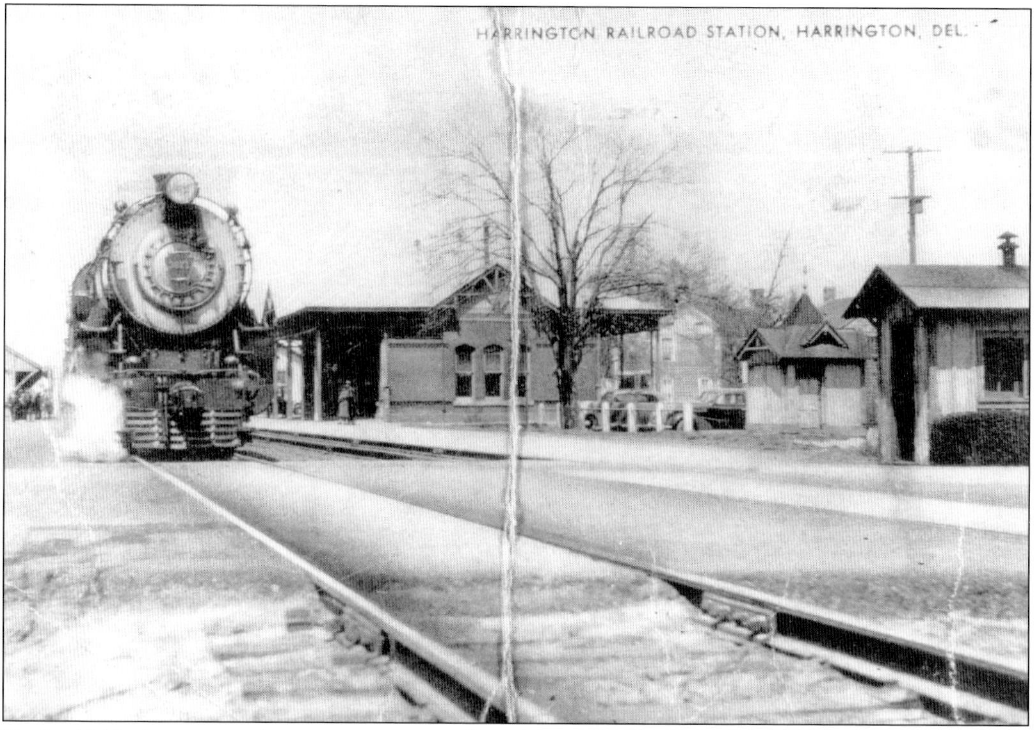

By the 1940s, large steam locomotives were pulling longer freight and passenger trains. On weekends, it was not uncommon to see as many as 12 passenger cars per train traveling through Harrington. Passengers would travel to Philadelphia to visit family or take in the sights, and families from the big city traveled to the end of the line at the Delaware beaches for vacation.

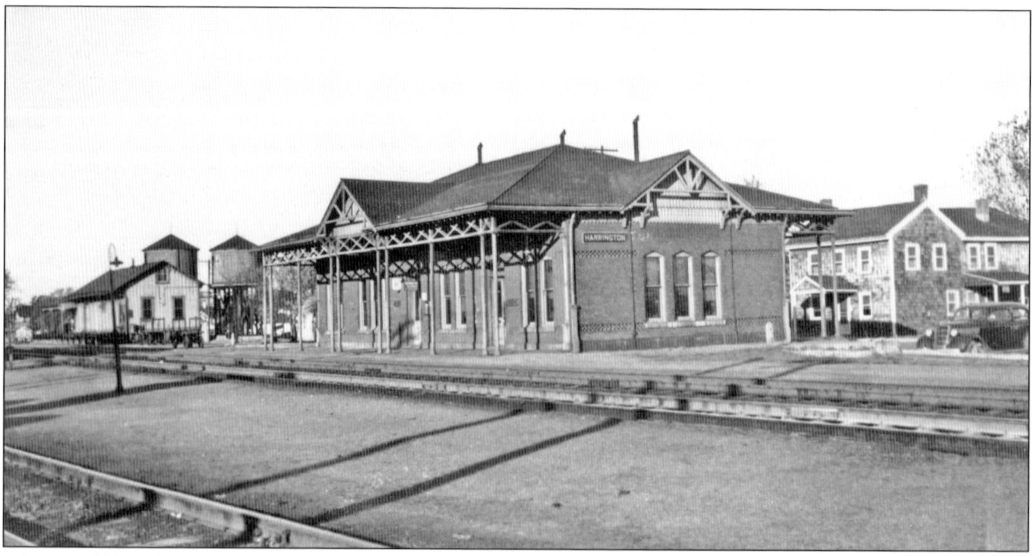

The small brick station in Harrington also underwent several enhancements. It was no longer lit by oil lamps and heated by potbelly stoves—electric lighting now illuminated the station inside and out. A boiler had been installed to provide heat to the station and hot water to the restrooms and to a kitchen, which allowed a lunch counter to serve meals to hungry travelers. (Courtesy of the Hagley Museum & Library.)

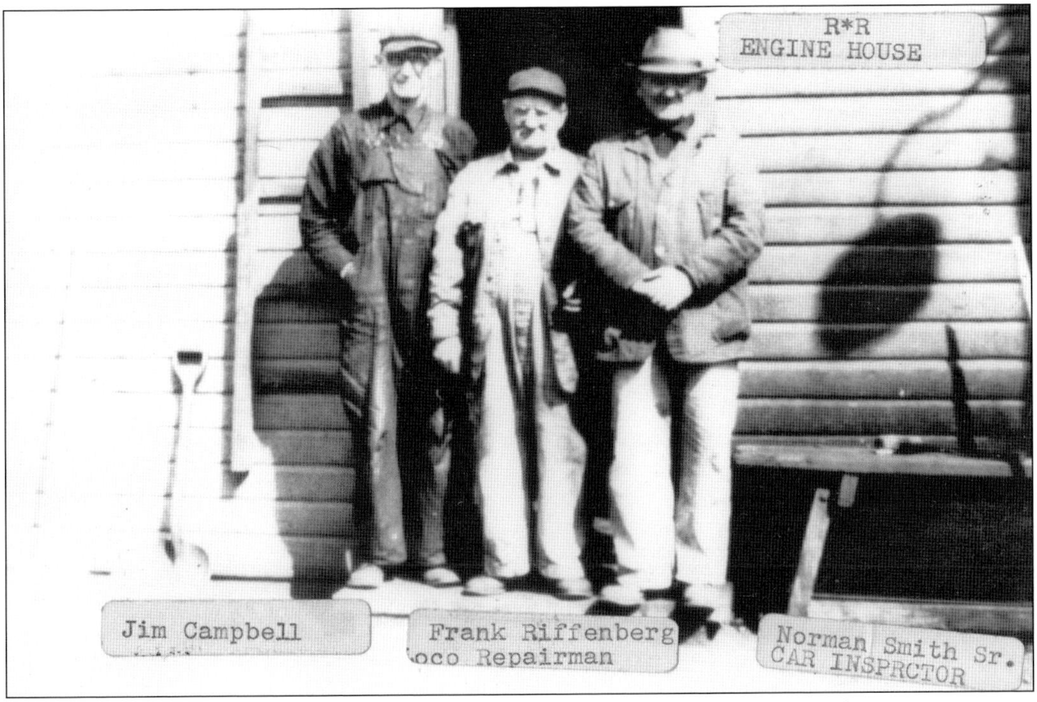

With larger and more frequent rail traffic, more workers were needed to keep the trains on time. During the 1940s, the Pennsylvania Railroad employed a large number of the town's population. More people moved to the area to seek employment on the railroad. The railroad workers pictured here are, from left to right, Jim Campbell, Frank Riffenberg, and Norman Smith Sr.

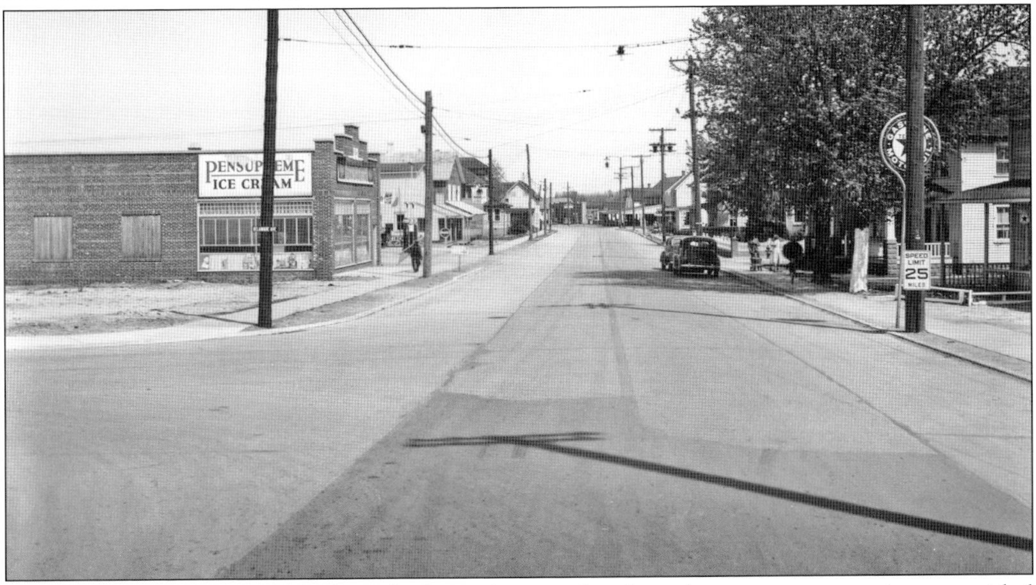

Replacing the livery and blacksmith shops that used to line the streets, gas stations provided services to citizens as the car became a household item. In the foreground, the new Penn Dairy Corporation plant was located here to take advantage of the numerous dairy farms in the area. The front of the plant housed a local restaurant that featured Pennsupreme Ice Cream, which quickly became a local favorite. (Courtesy of the Delaware Public Archives.)

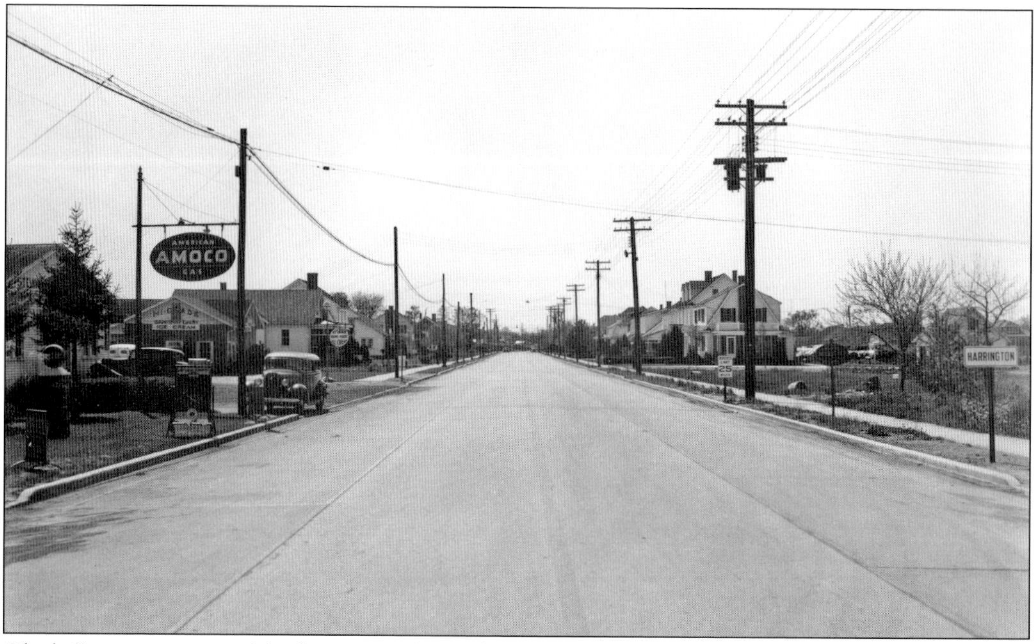

Clark Street is pictured looking west from the newly built DuPont Highway. Both sides of the street are lined with new homes. With a population of over 2,000 people by 1940, the town was busier than ever. Gone were the dirt streets and horses and buggies. As many as 10 service stations now served locals and travelers alike. (Courtesy of the Delaware Public Archives.)

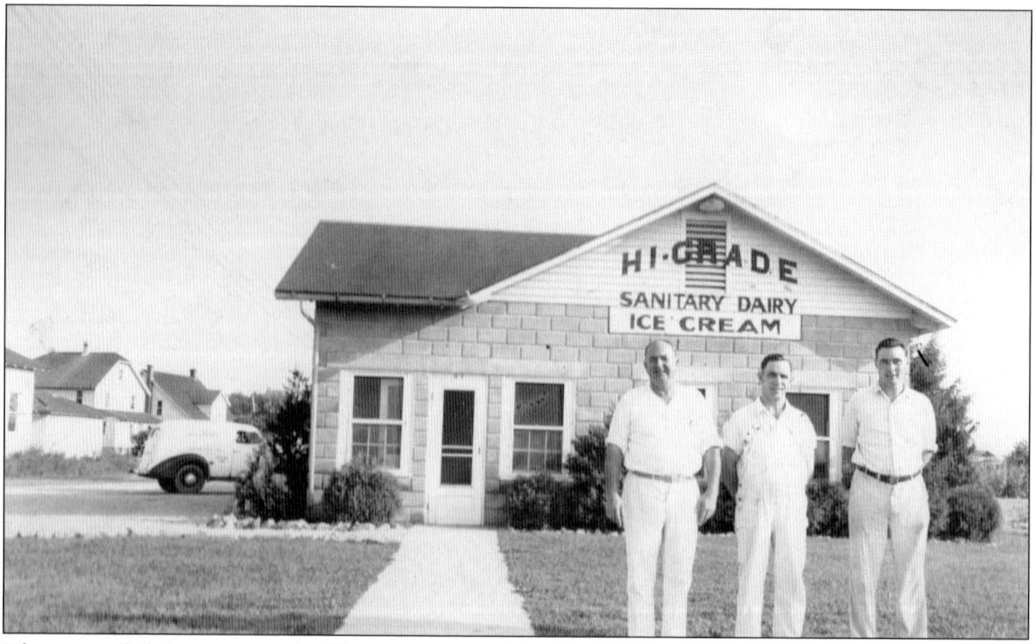

The second dairy to open in Harrington was Hi-Grade Dairy. When disease wiped out most of the peach trees in the area, farmers turned to livestock farming. With a large supply of fresh milk, these local plants had no shortage of raw ingredients. Benny Hughes was the owner during the 1950s and added a small lunch counter that served homemade ice cream, which locals ate by the gallon.

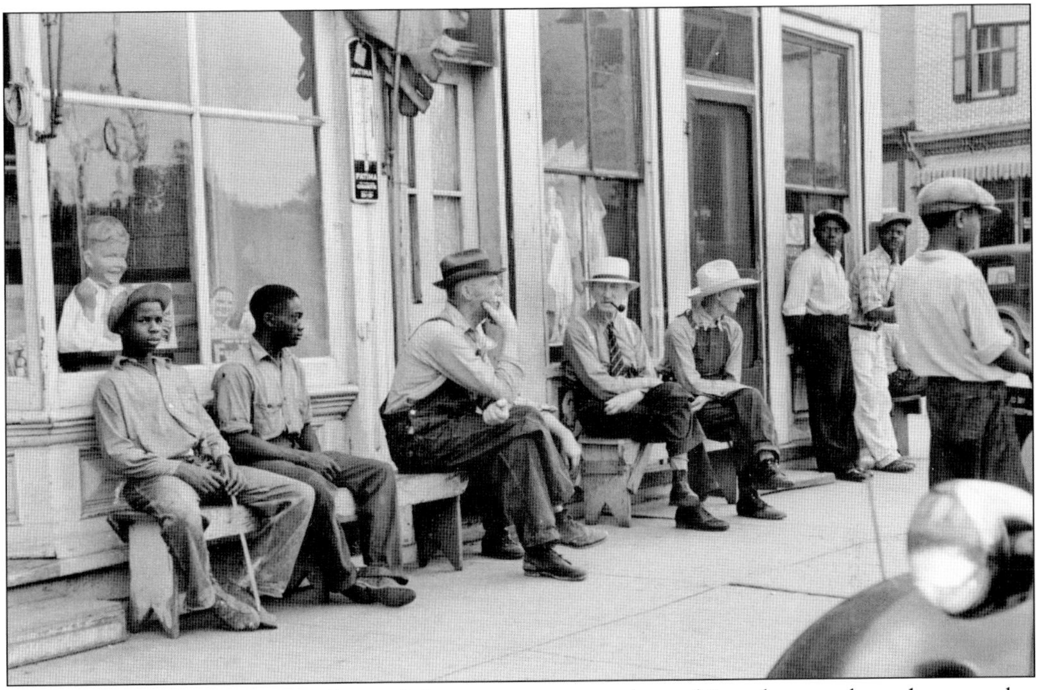

Locals enjoyed sitting out in front of the many stores and watching the people and cars go by. From young to old, this quickly became a pastime all enjoyed. On Saturday mornings, people would bring their cars to town, and they would carpool just to get a parking spot on a Saturday night. With several local restaurants, ice cream shops, dance spots, and taverns, there was something for all.

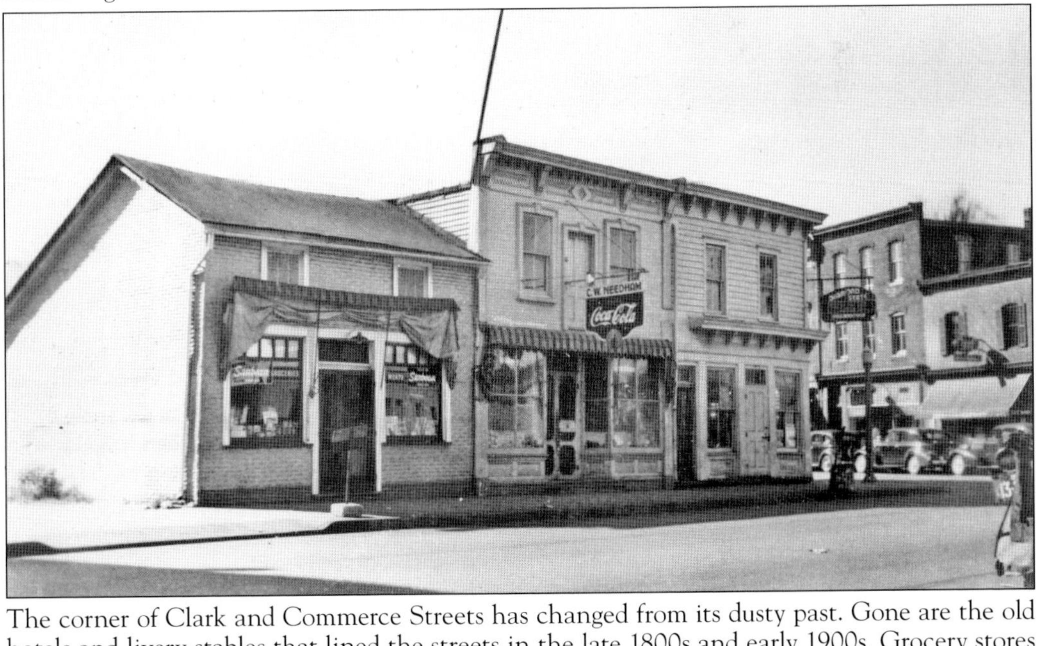

The corner of Clark and Commerce Streets has changed from its dusty past. Gone are the old hotels and livery stables that lined the streets in the late 1800s and early 1900s. Grocery stores and restaurants like those seen here now served the citizens. These storefronts changed purposes several times from the 1930s through the 1960s. (Courtesy of the Hagley Museum & Library.)

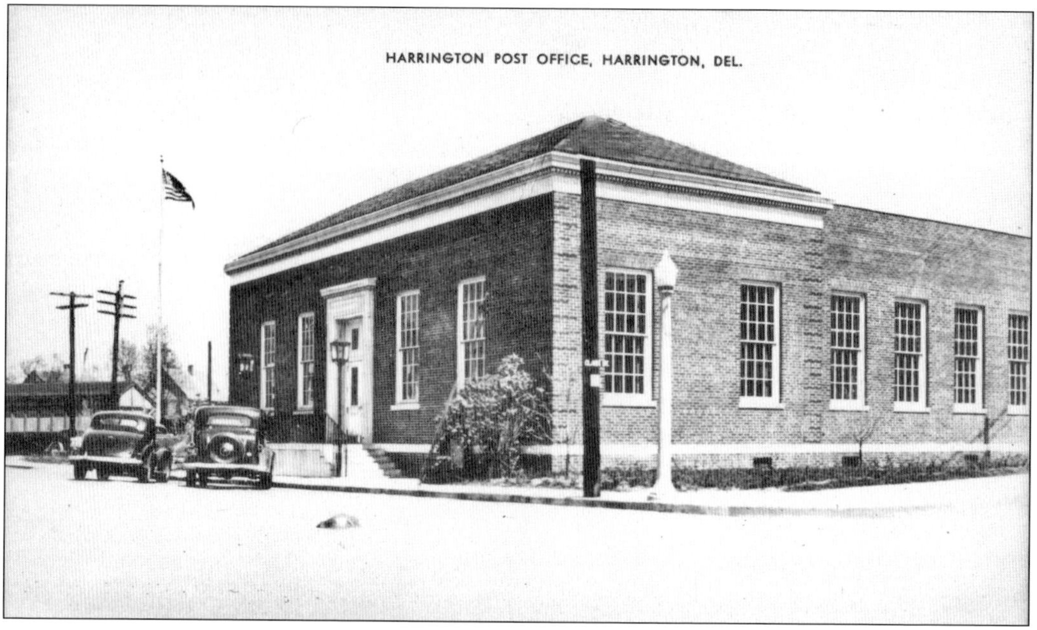

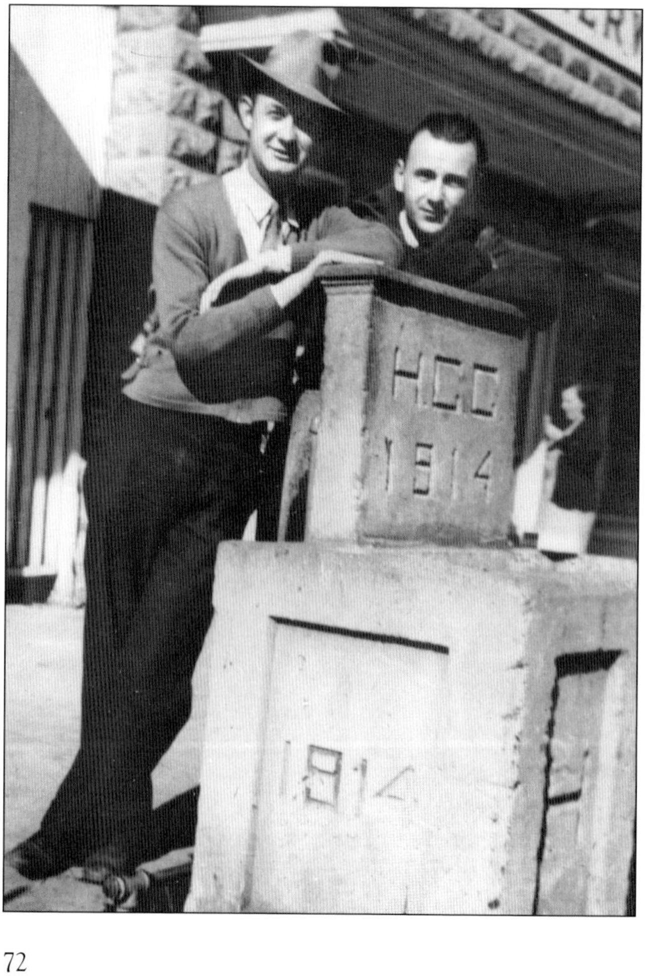

The Harrington Post Office was constructed in the mid-1930s. The old storefronts built in the mid-1800s were outdated and were torn down for the new post office. A wax tempera mural, *Men Hoeing*, was painted in 1941 by Eve Salisbury inside the post office. The program was funded by the US Treasury as a part of President Roosevelt's New Deal.

Installed in 1914 by a civic group called the New Century Club, the local water fountain across the street from the post office was not so much a cool drink of water on a warm day as it was another local hangout. Citizens would spend their spare time sitting around and telling stories and tall tales. Here, Clarence Collins (left) and William Reed swap the local chatter.

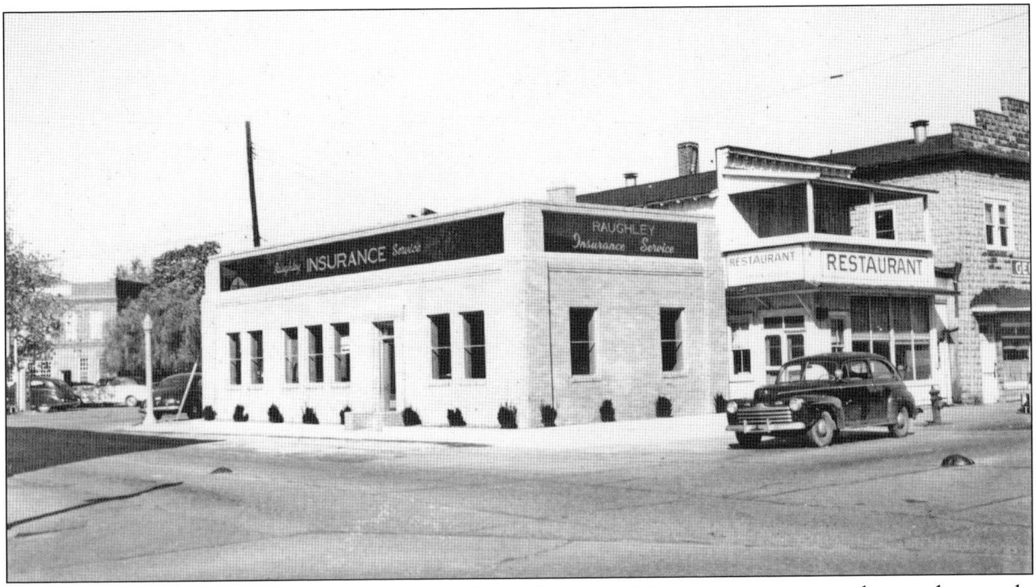

In the 1940s, Raughley Insurance was remodeled from an older gas station into the art deco style that was popular at the time. In 1969, the business was sold to Tom Parsons, who was one of the original founders of the Greater Harrington Historical Society. This was the first building to house artifacts collected by the organization. (Courtesy of the Hagley Museum & Library.)

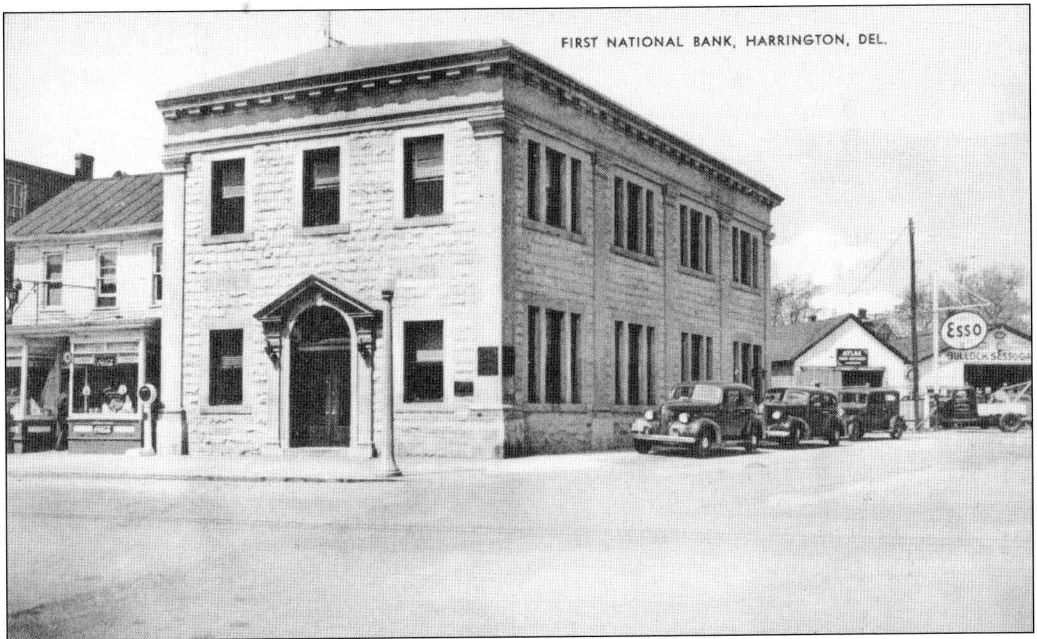

The new First National Bank of Harrington, constructed in 1927, was another building in the art deco style. An older wooden structure was demolished to make room for the more modern building; the city's streetscape was changing. The bank printed its own money until 1935. The adjacent store was later demolished to add a drive-through window.

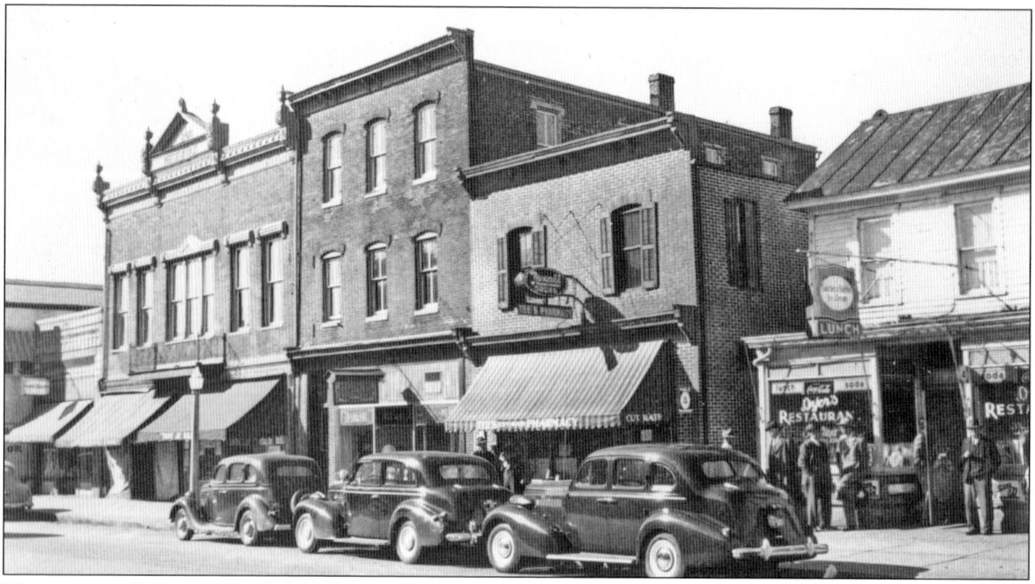

This view of the west side of Commerce Street shows the number of businesses serving locals and travelers in the 1940s. Dyler's Restaurant served local favorites like steak and chicken. Tee's Pharmacy was one of four pharmacies in town. Next door, Cupid's Ice Cream was the third such business serving sweet treats. It seems Harrington had a definite sweet tooth when it came to ice cream. (Courtesy of the Hagley Museum & Library.)

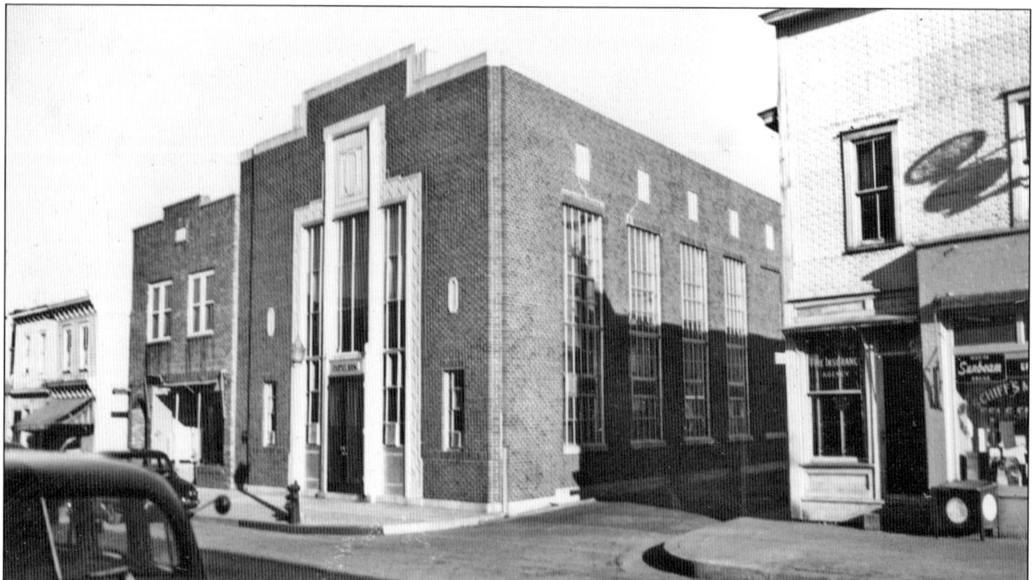

The Peoples Bank of Harrington, in business since 1904, also constructed a new art deco building in the 1920s. When it was built, the bank was hailed as one of the most modern banking facilities in lower Delaware. The bank remained at this location until the early 1970s. (Courtesy of the Hagley Museum & Library.)

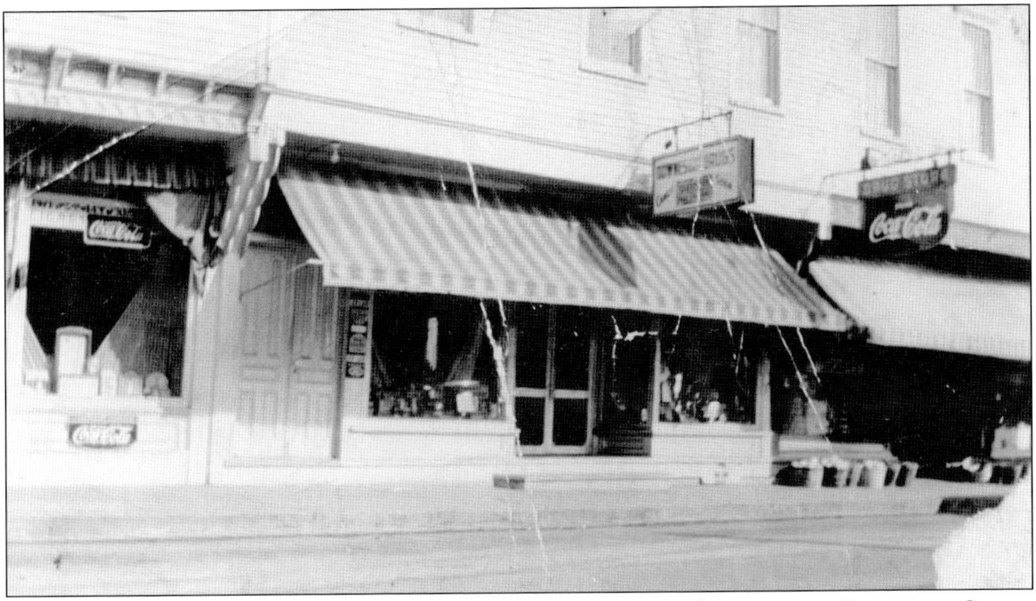

Downes Drug Store was one of the many businesses to occupy this space on Commerce Street. Downes Drugs was in business during the 1920s and 1930s. At that time, there were four drugstores in the town of only 2,000 people. These stores sold a variety of other dry goods in order to improve their sales.

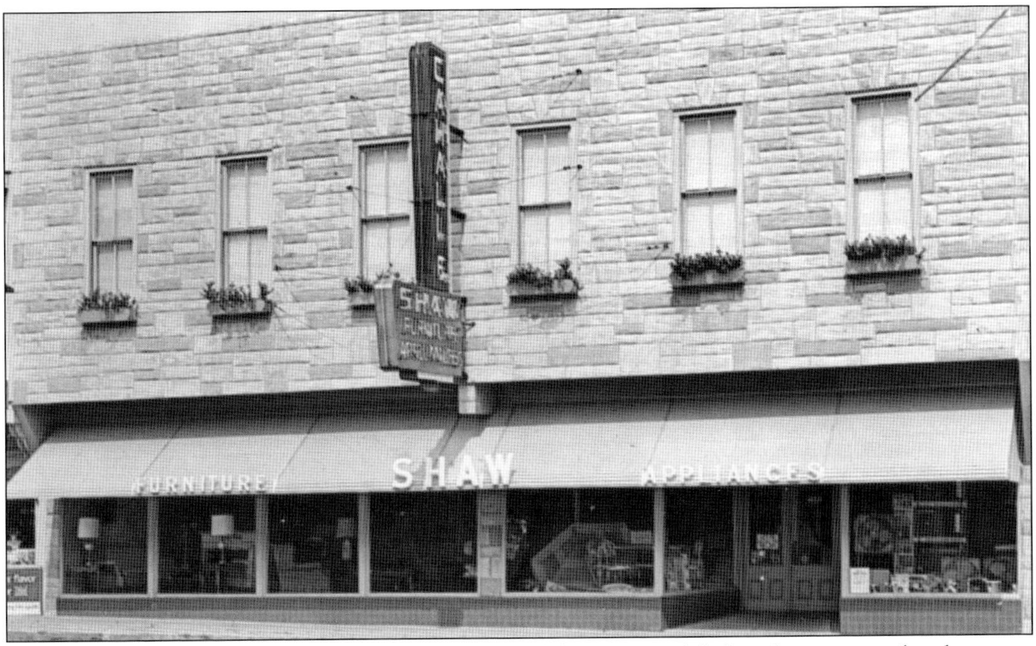

In the 1940s, the stores in the previous image had been remodeled and now served as home to Cahall and Shaw Furniture and Appliance. This was the first large retail store in Harrington, providing the newest furnishing and appliances. The citizens began to install refrigerators and radios, and a few even got the latest gadget, a television.

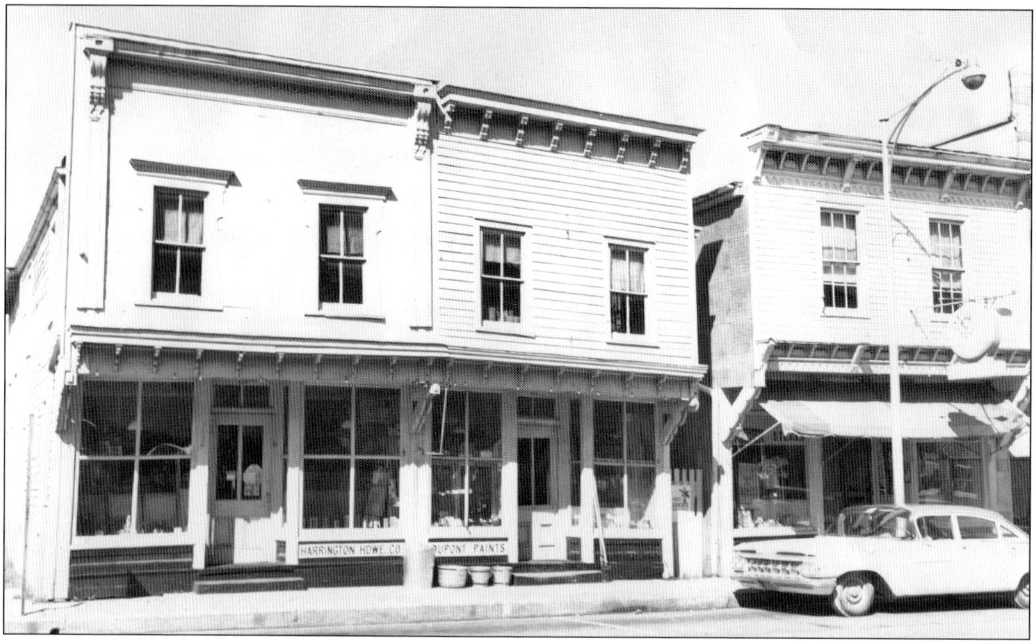

One of the iconic storefronts in Harrington is seen here on the left. Burton's Sports Shop was the place for teens from the 1940s through the 1980s. With old-fashioned fountain sodas, milkshakes, and a candy counter that sold a wide variety of items, this was the hangout for all. It had pinball machines, a jukebox, and a booth to snuggle in, and teens filled this hot spot day and night.

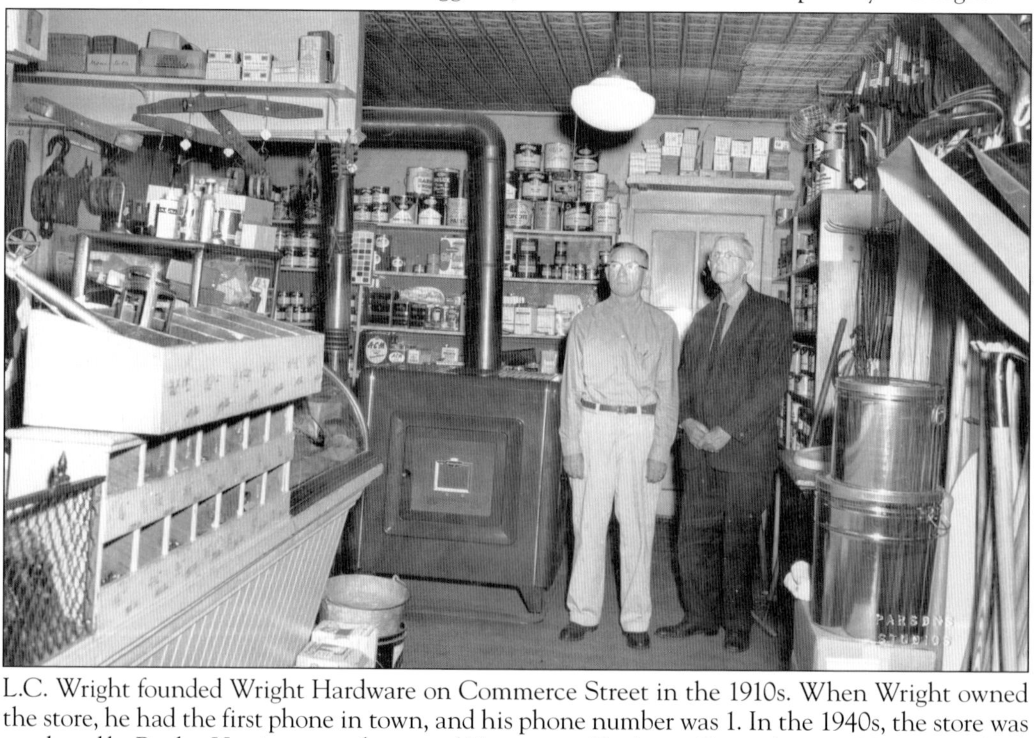

L.C. Wright founded Wright Hardware on Commerce Street in the 1910s. When Wright owned the store, he had the first phone in town, and his phone number was 1. In the 1940s, the store was purchased by Booker Harrington and renamed Harrington Hardware. Shown here are Harrington (left) and DeWitt Tatman. The store was well known to locals as the store that carried everything.

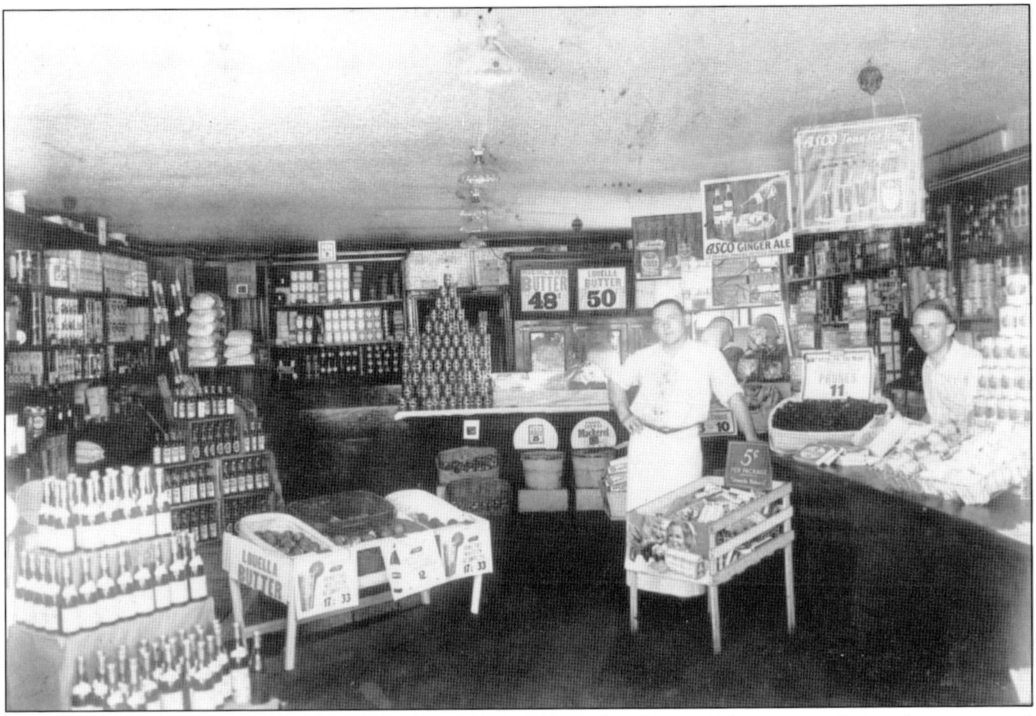

American Stores opened in Harrington in the 1920s. The former Harington School was moved to Commerce Street, and the first floor was converted into a grocery store. The store was later located on Clark Street and finally in Quillen's Shopping Center. The chain was based in Philadelphia and later became known as Acme. On the left is Miles Draper, and on the right is Gus Raughley.

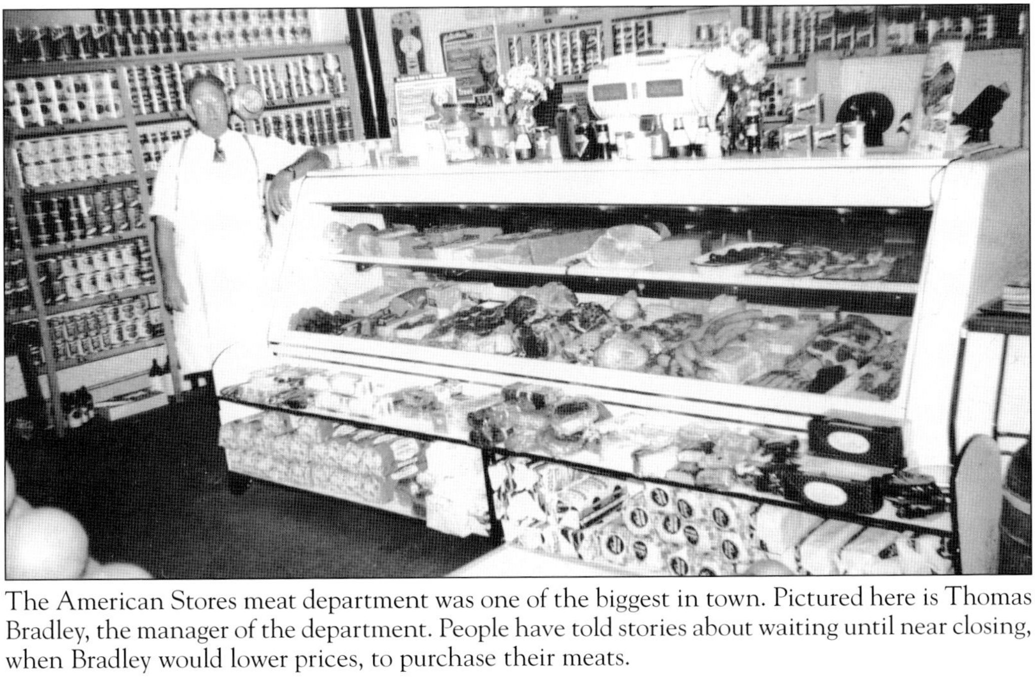

The American Stores meat department was one of the biggest in town. Pictured here is Thomas Bradley, the manager of the department. People have told stories about waiting until near closing, when Bradley would lower prices, to purchase their meats.

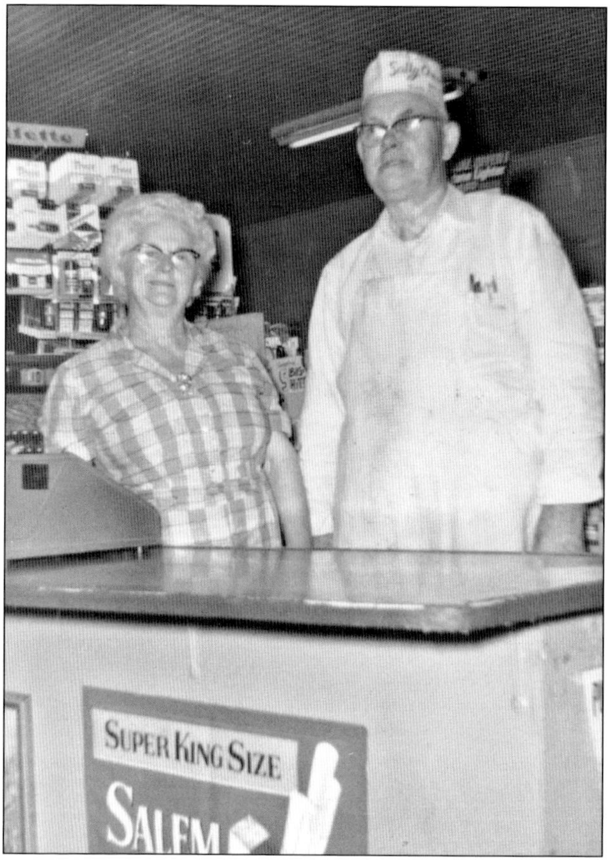

Sam Short and his wife, Ethel, owned one of the many small grocery stores in Harrington. Located on Center Street, the store was in operation from the 1940s to the 1970s. It then became an arcade and sub shop. During the time Short owned the building, the back room served a very different purpose than most storerooms did in a general store. During the 1950s, Short produced records under the Blue Hen label. Artists such as Rockabilly Hall of Fame member Jimmy Stayton, Honey Voshell, and Cecil Cline recorded songs at this studio. Sadly, Blue Hen Records turned down Patsy Cline.

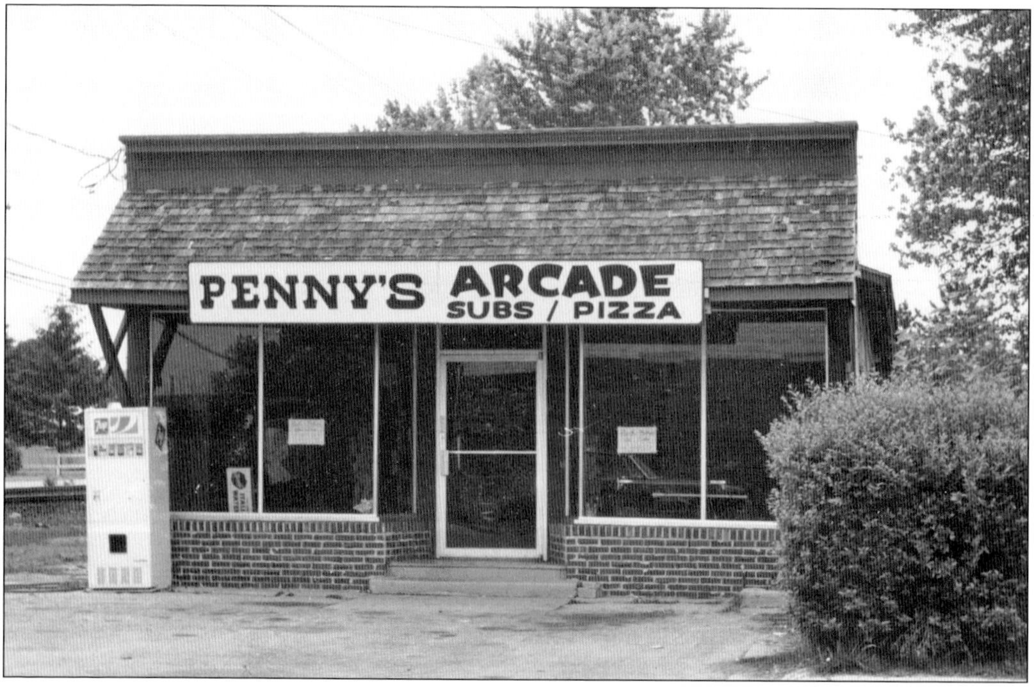

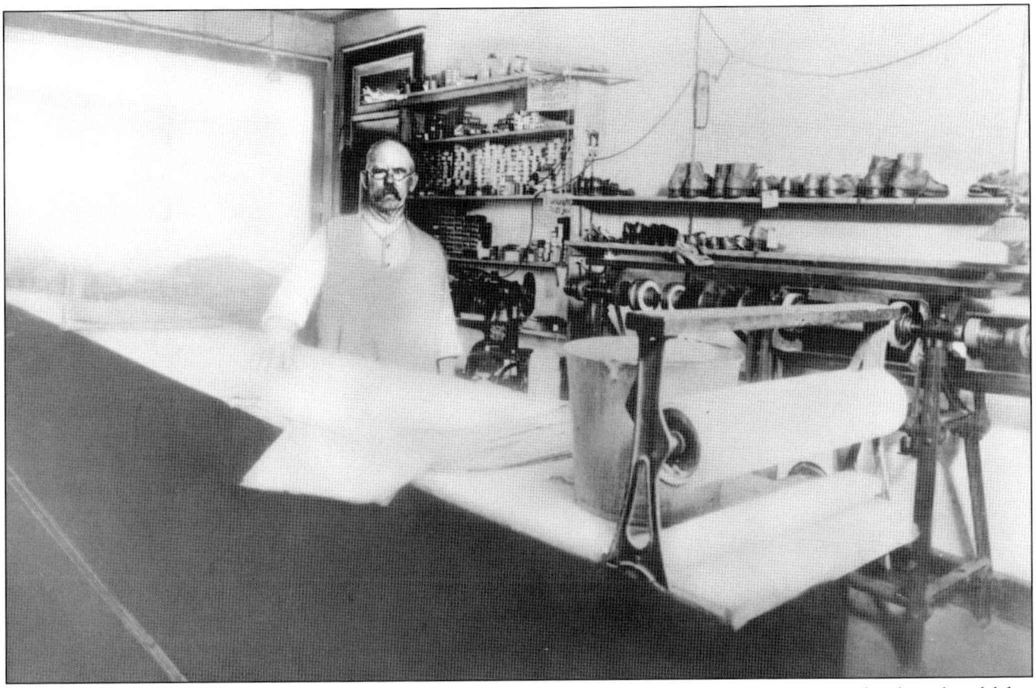

George E. Sullivan was among the first of the city's leather craftsmen. He was the local cobbler from 1926 through 1931. Prior to his leather business, he cut and milled his own timber to construct buildings in the area. Among his other occupations were furniture maker and wheelwright.

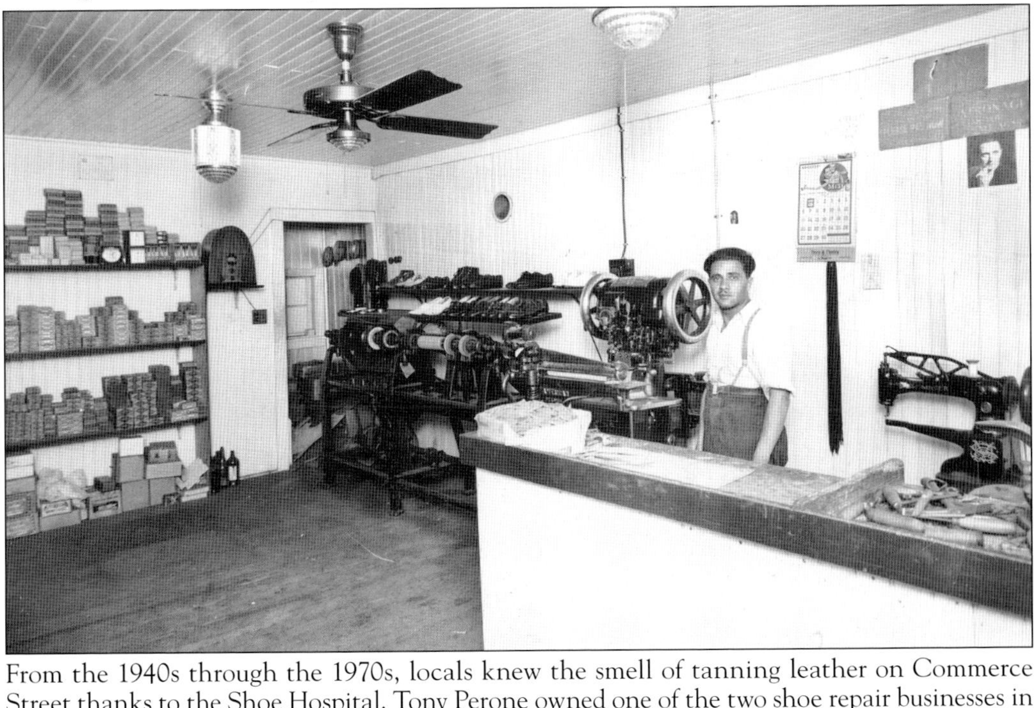

From the 1940s through the 1970s, locals knew the smell of tanning leather on Commerce Street thanks to the Shoe Hospital. Tony Perone owned one of the two shoe repair businesses in Harrington. Perone resoled and re-stitched leather shoes and repaired luggage, belts, and anything else locals asked him to.

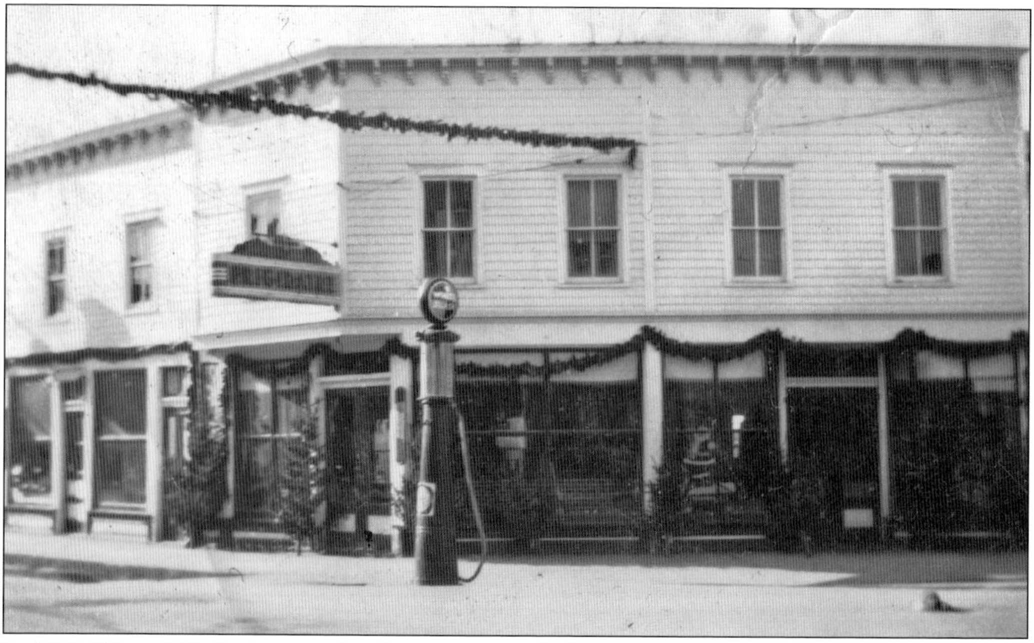

In 1935, Edward Taylor began a hardware store and John Deere dealership in Harrington. By the 1940s, the business had grown successfully. Taylor decided to renovate an abandoned mill to house the tractor dealership. In 1952, Walter Messick became a partner in the John Deere dealership. In the 1960s, Taylor sold his interest in the farm machinery business to Messick, allowing him to focus strictly on his hardware store. These two businessmen played several other roles in town. From banking leaders to very active roles with the Delaware State Fair, they were pillars of the community for decades. The John Deere dealership remains today and is operated by Walter's son Jimmy Messick, while the hardware store was closed in 2007 after it had been operated for several years by Bobby Taylor, Edward's son.

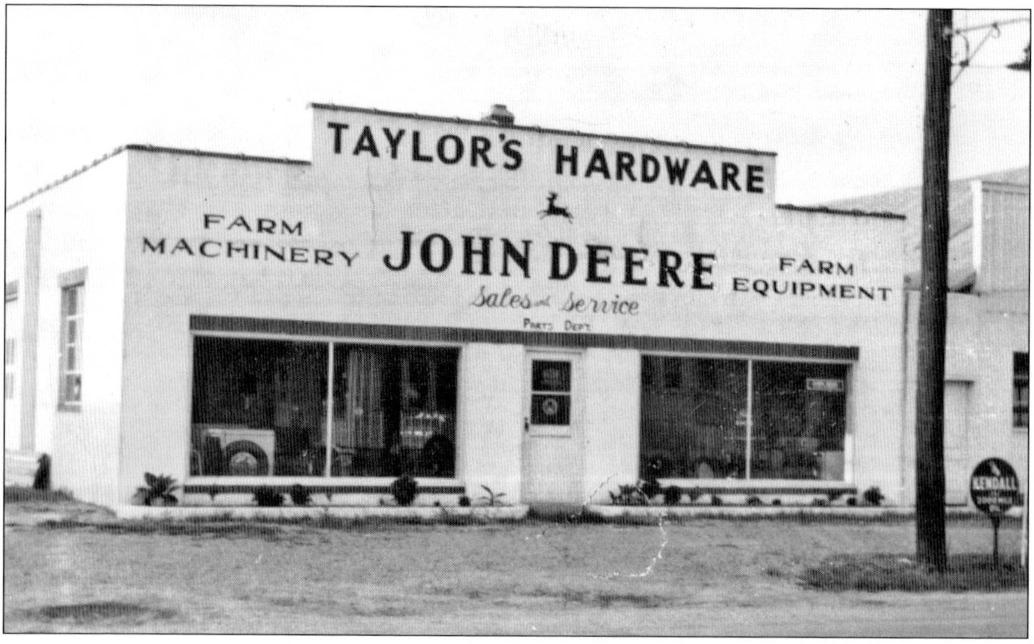

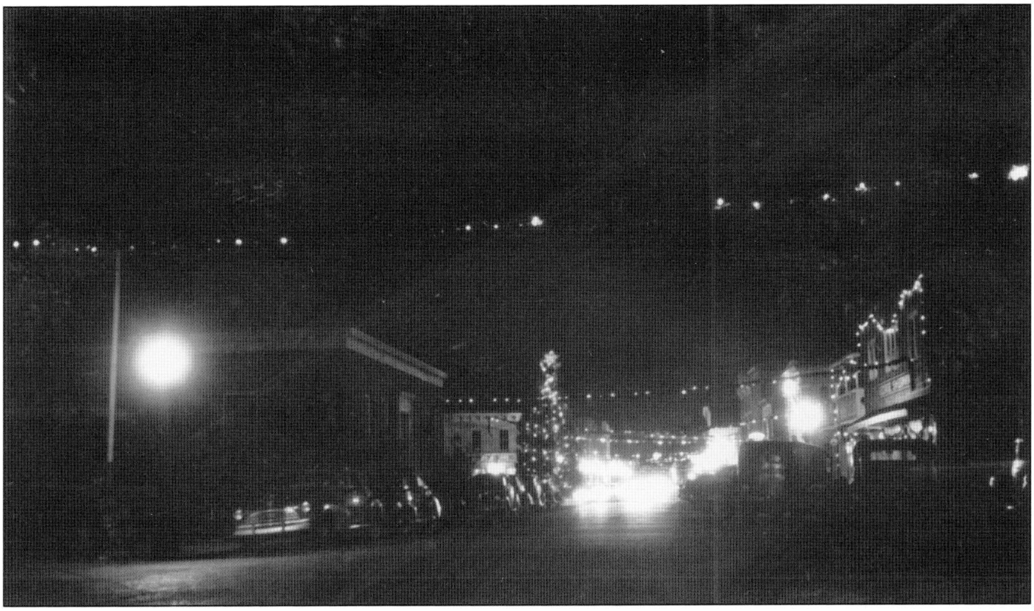

Christmas was a magical time of the year in Harrington. With a thriving business district, store owners sought multiple ways to attract customers during the holiday season. The merchants purchased decorations for the town, turning the streets into a picture postcard. An annual Christmas parade was held each year, with the chief elf, Santa Claus himself, being the guest of honor. Santa would then visit the children throughout the Christmas season at his house, set up again by the local business association. In 1957, the merchants came together to raffle off a pony that had been donated to them. Sylvia Outten of Harrington was the winner of the raffle. (Both, courtesy of the Hagley Museum & Library.)

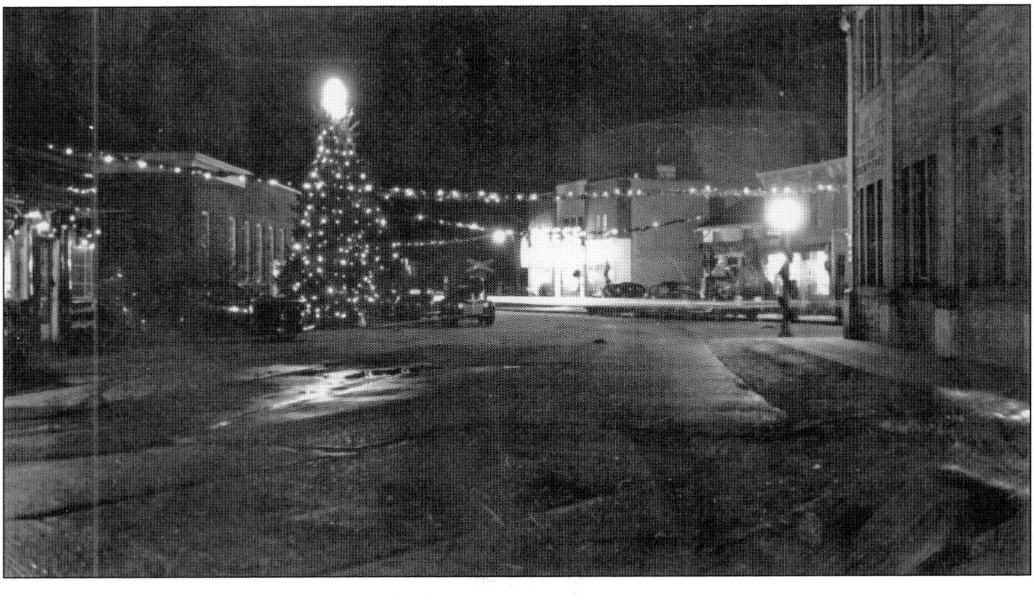

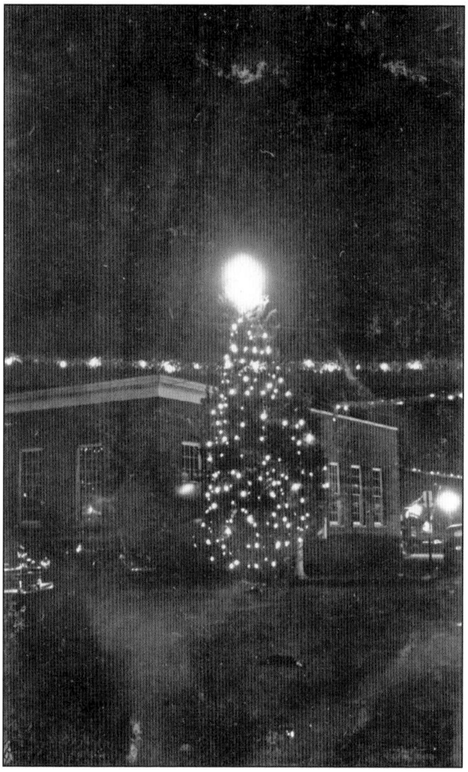

The town Christmas tree, located by the post office, was the site of many holiday events during the season. The local newspaper printed a supplement filled with Christmas carols, and locals and church choirs would then gather around the tree for the special lighting ceremony and sing carols, filling the street with the sounds of the season. (Courtesy of the Hagley Museum & Library.)

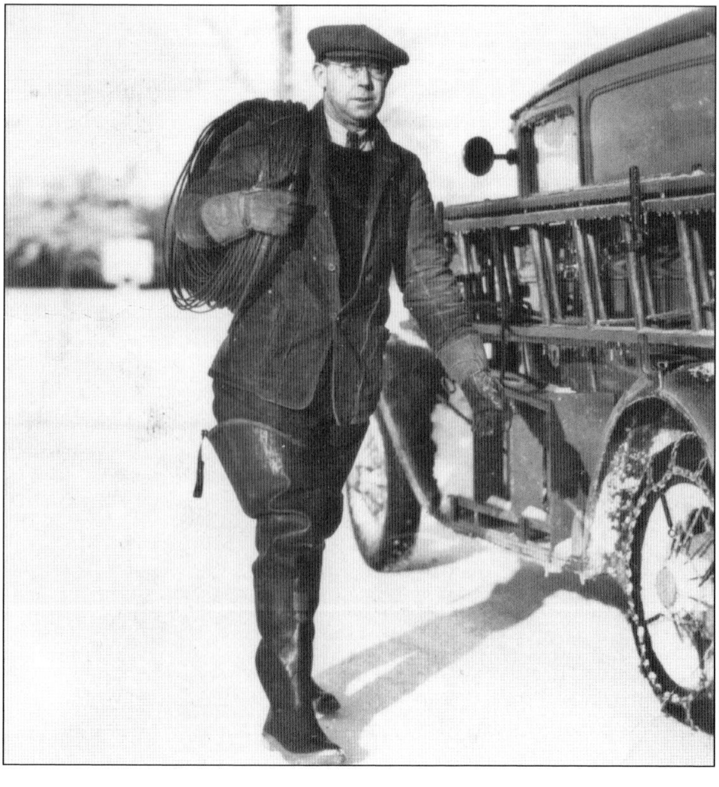

Wintertime was not a wonderland for everyone in Harrington. Just as with the postal service, through rain, snow, and dark of night, other services had to be maintained as well. Winder Massey of Harrington was a one-man band for the Diamond State Telephone Company, responsible for maintaining all the phone lines in the Harrington area.

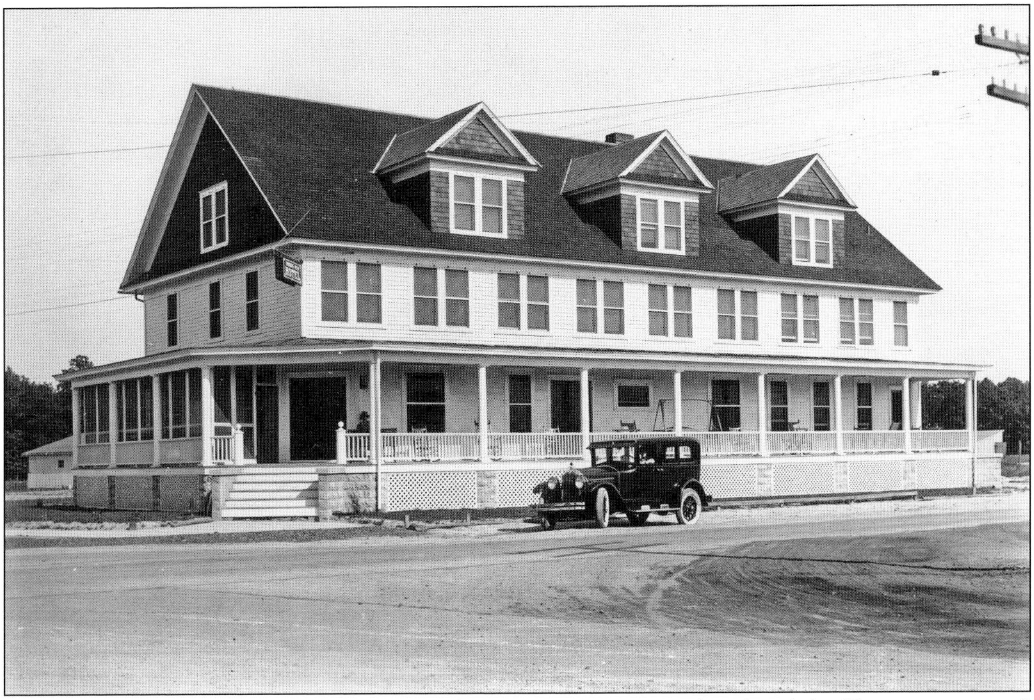

By the 1950s, the old hotels were gone from the city. New, more modern hotels had been constructed to serve the weary road and rail travelers. Swains Hotel was built at the intersection of the new dual highway on the edge of Harrington. The three-story facility housed a banquet room, restaurant, and over 30 rooms and suites. (Courtesy of the Delaware Public Archives.)

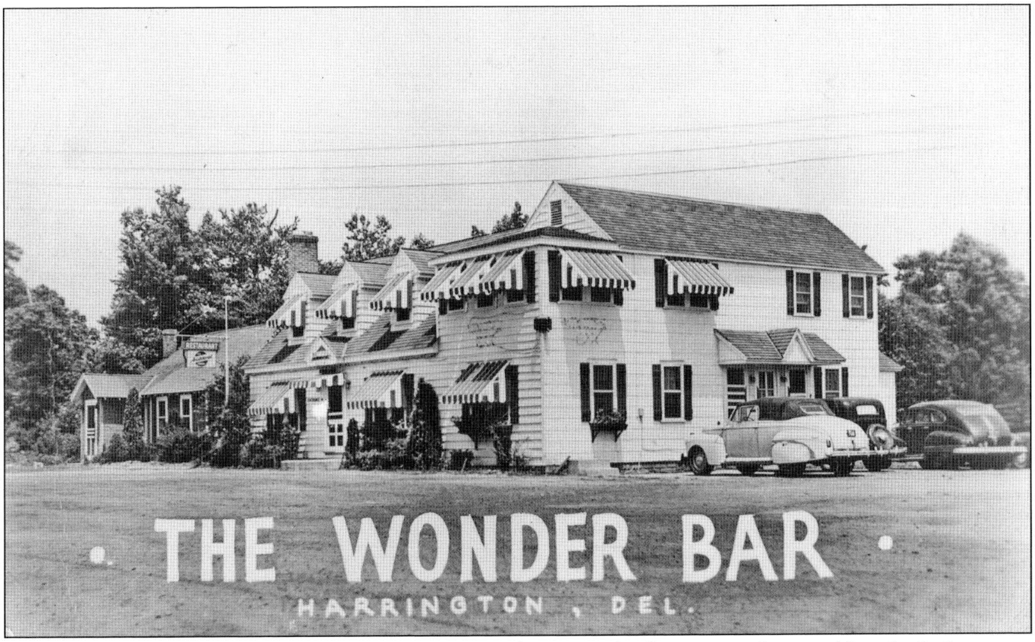

The Wonder Bar was another facility constructed to serve highway travelers and locals. In business from the 1940s to the 1970s, when it was destroyed by fire, the restaurant served warm meals and cold drinks to all who came.

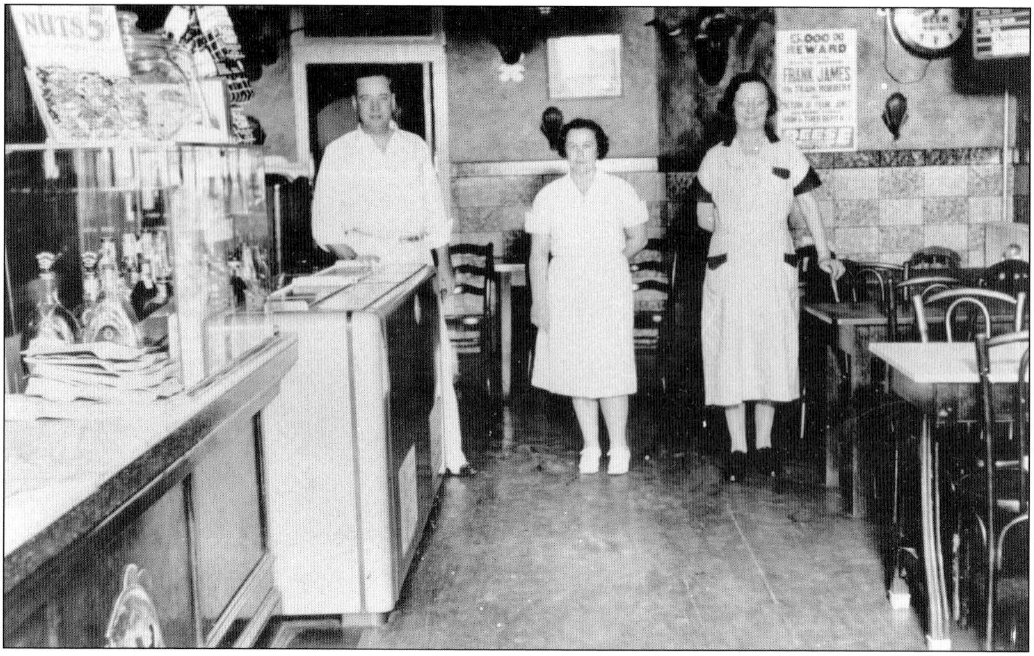

Stones Hotel and Bar was built in the late 1800s as two separate buildings and later combined into the hotel and bar. A favorite watering hole among the locals, the bar has had many owners and been renovated many times throughout its existence. Pictured from left to right are Lindsey McVey, Ann Collins, and Roby Flowers in the 1940s.

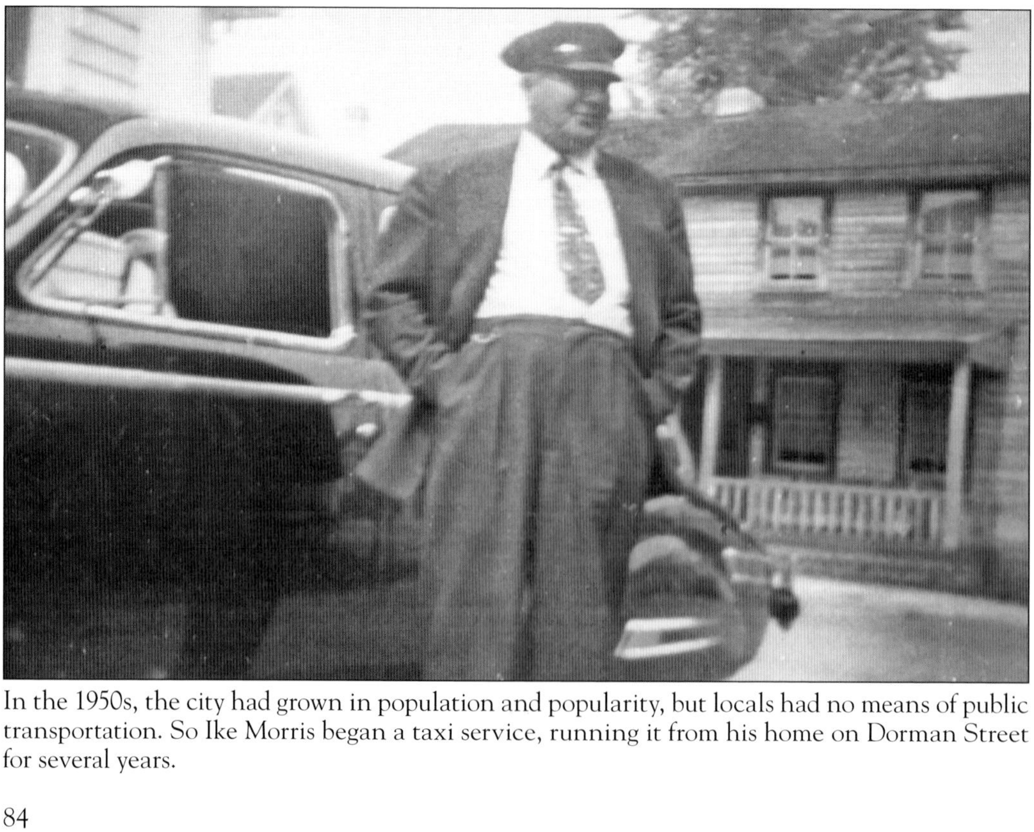

In the 1950s, the city had grown in population and popularity, but locals had no means of public transportation. So Ike Morris began a taxi service, running it from his home on Dorman Street for several years.

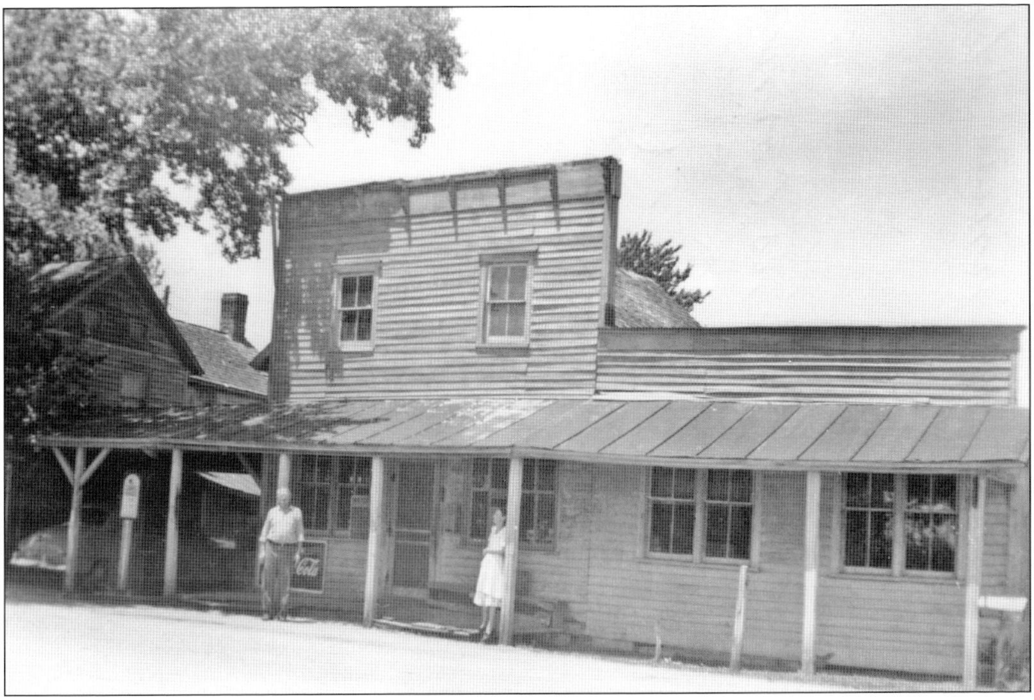

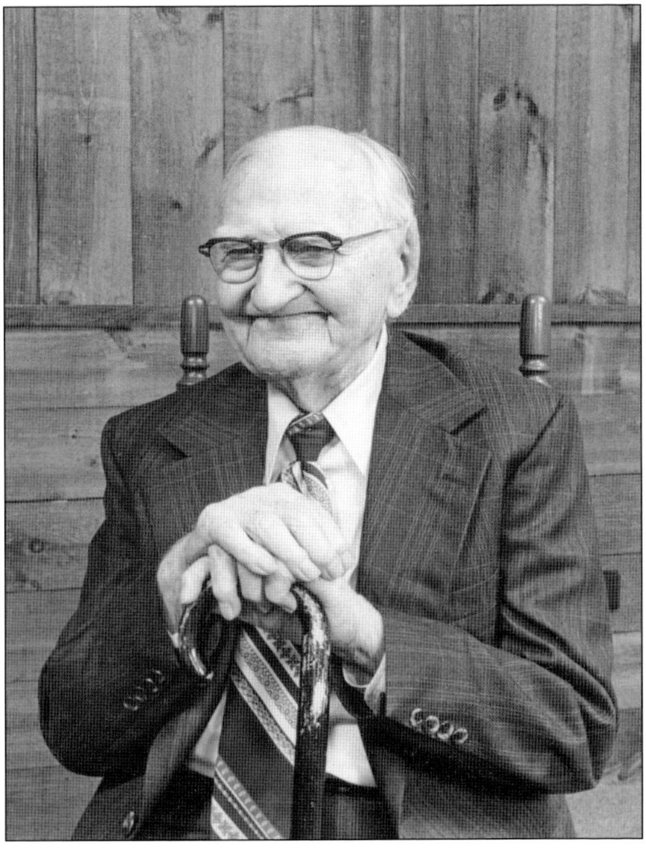

Outside of Harrington, the farmers and country families still required the daily essentials, such as bread and milk. General stores filled this void from the 1920s to the 1970s, when transportation became more available. Amos Minner opened a store at Masten's Corner that served locals for 70 years. Not only did he provide customers with groceries and other needs, but his store also served as a gathering place where news and local events would be discussed around the old coal stove. Minner lived to be 99 years old, and upon his death, locals still remembered those days of him sitting and listening by the hour to their stories. (Above, courtesy of the Delaware Public Archives.)

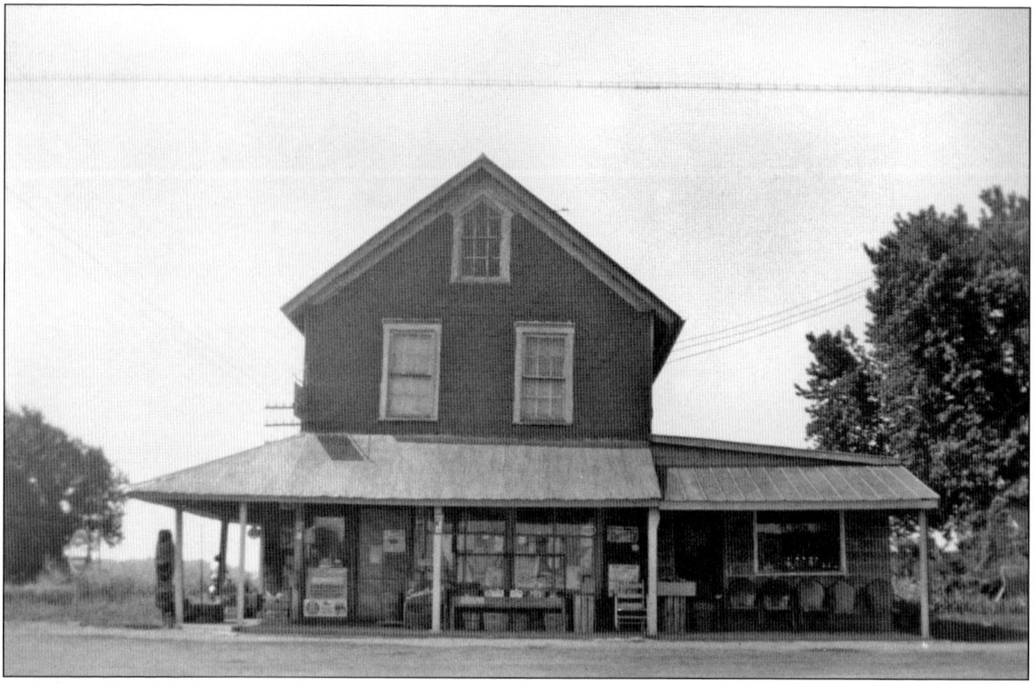

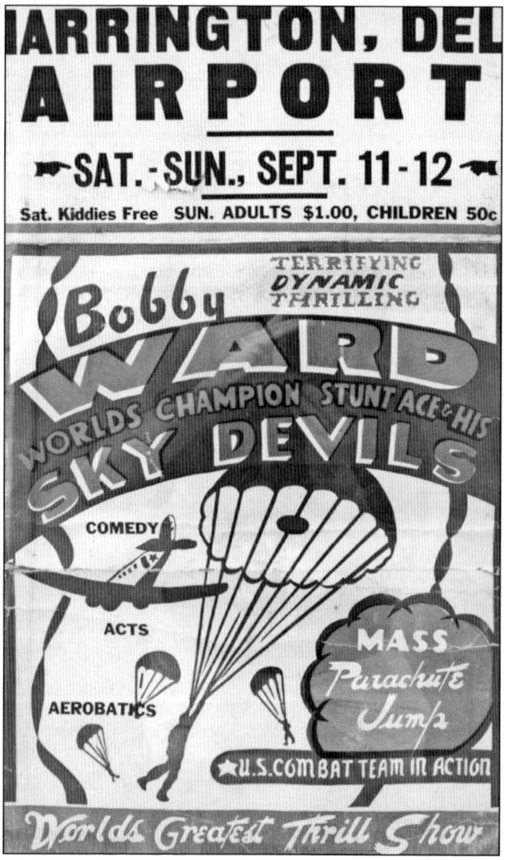

Other country crossroads had their own general stores. Whiteleysburg, Burrsville, and Andrewsville each had their own places to shop, gather, and exchange the events of the day. The Andrews store, in Andrewsville, was open from the 1930s until the 1980s. (Courtesy of the Delaware Public Archives.)

Several small airports sprang up in the area, most of which were used in the crop dusting industry. Harrington Airport, east of town, served as a landing strip for locals and some light commercial aircraft as well. It also hosted thrilling skydiving and stunt flying events.

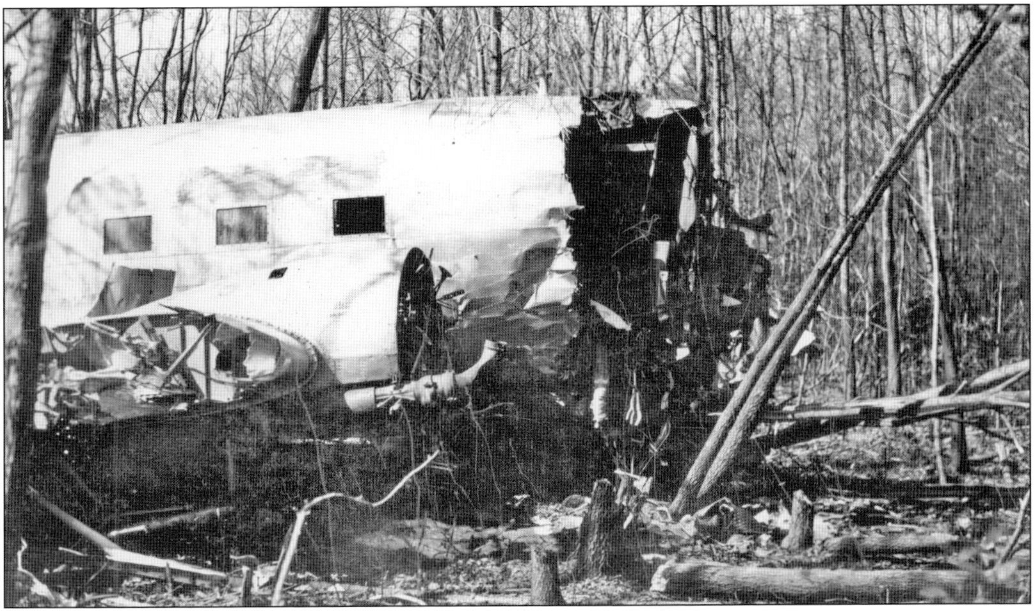

Sadly, not all the events at the Harrington Airfield were family fun. On February 5, 1947, a cargo plane en route to Raleigh, North Carolina, from New York was diverted to Harrington after one of its two engines malfunctioned. Aboard were three crewmembers and cargo from a New York manufacturer. The plane was rapidly losing altitude, so it had to land downwind, causing the aircraft to overshoot the runway and crash into the nearby woods. One of the crewmembers was killed in the crash. A second fatal crash occurred on August 30, 1953, when Noble Chipman Minner and his passenger Lela Macklin were killed when his single-engine plane crashed. The airport closed on March 16, 1956. (Both, courtesy of the Hagley Museum & Library.)

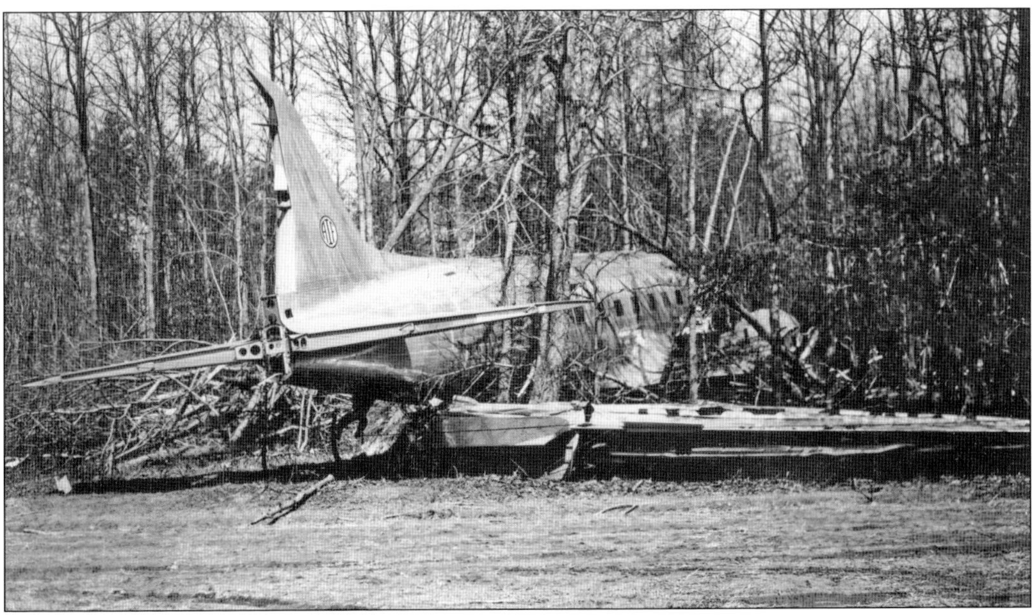

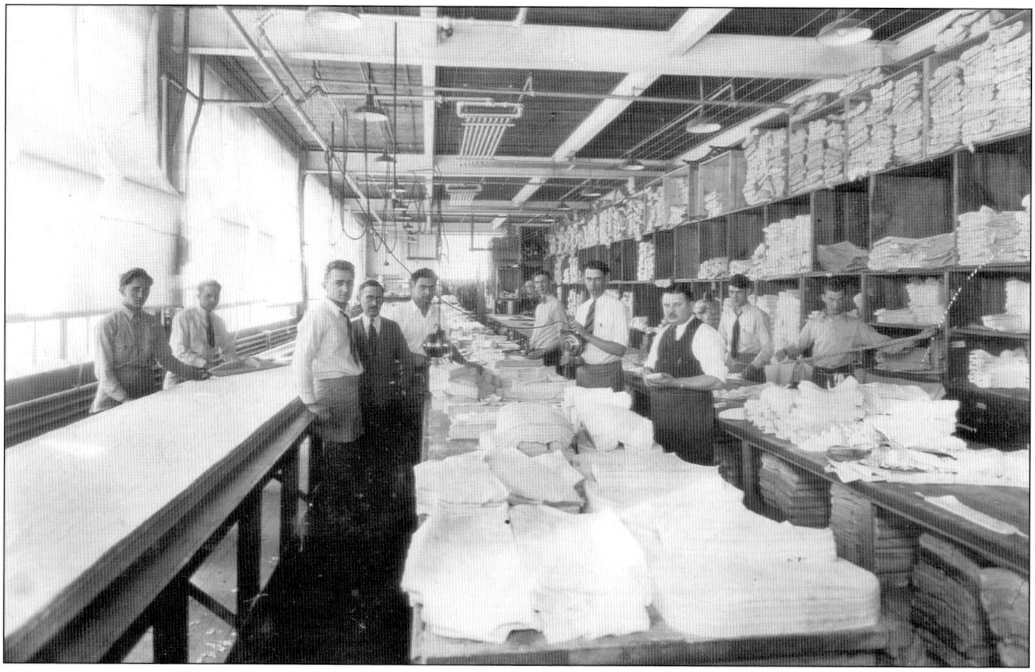

The garment industry continued strong in Harrington into the early 1970s. Harrington Shirt Factory, on Clark Street, made clothing for the Aetna Shirt Company. At its peak, the plant employed nearly 100 workers. When the factory began, it employed mostly men, but with World War II, it changed to a mostly female workforce.

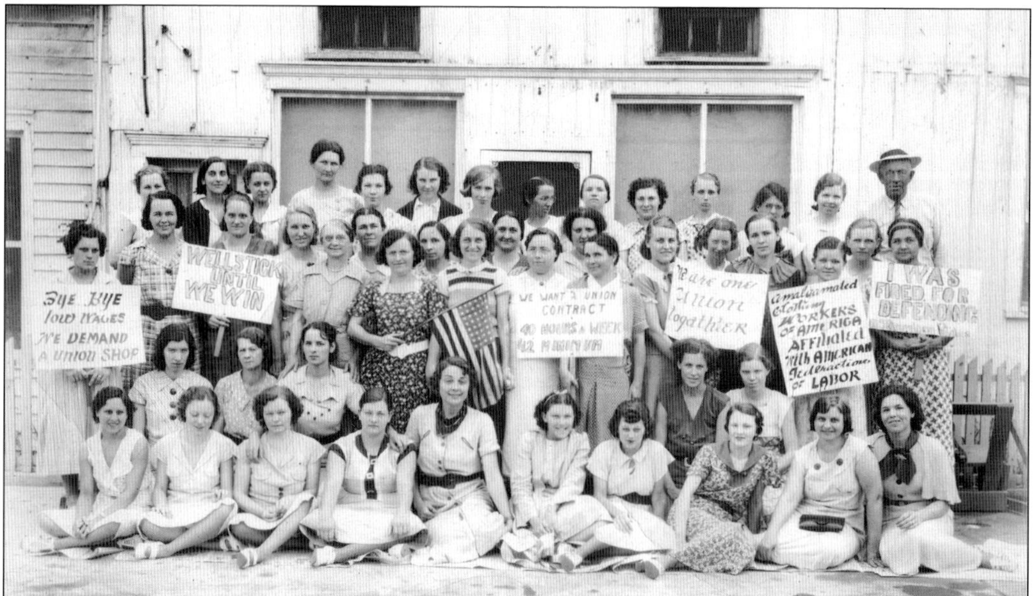

Both before and after World War II, garment workers fought for better working conditions and wages. Here, workers at the Ace Manufacturing Company are on strike demanding just such benefits. Garment strikes were common among the factories in Harrington. The last of the garment factories closed in the 1970s.

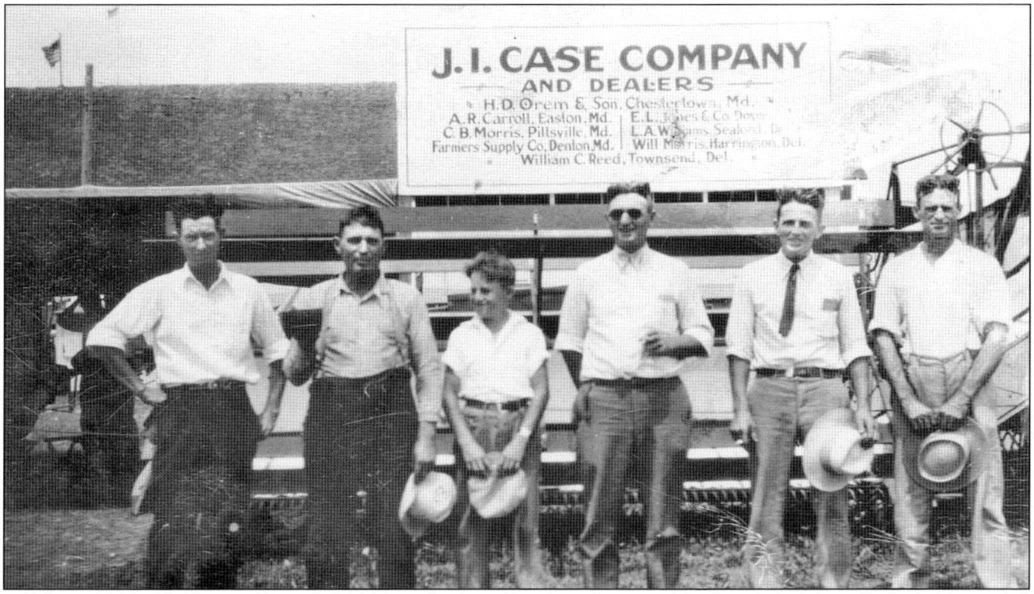

Despite the growing industries in Harrington and the surrounding area, farming was still very much a way of life. The businesses that supported the industry also found the area an ideal location to establish shops and retail space. Case tractor dealers from the area gathered for this photograph to advertise their businesses.

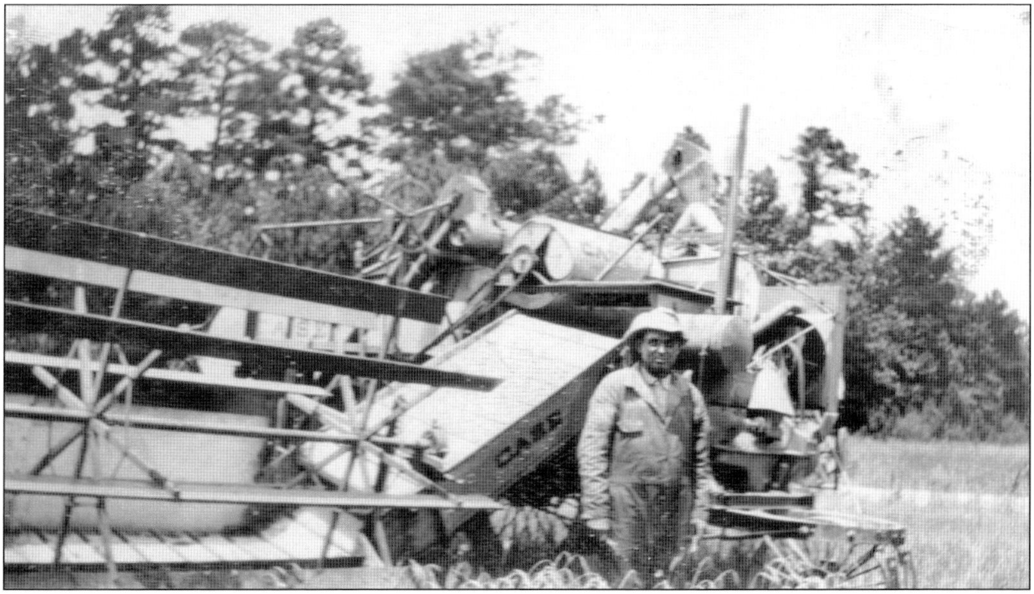

Farmers purchased newer and more modern machinery for greater crop yields and increases in acreage farmed, all while reducing cost and the number of hours they had to spend working in the fields. What took days to be harvested by horse-drawn machinery could by the 1930s be accomplished in just hours.

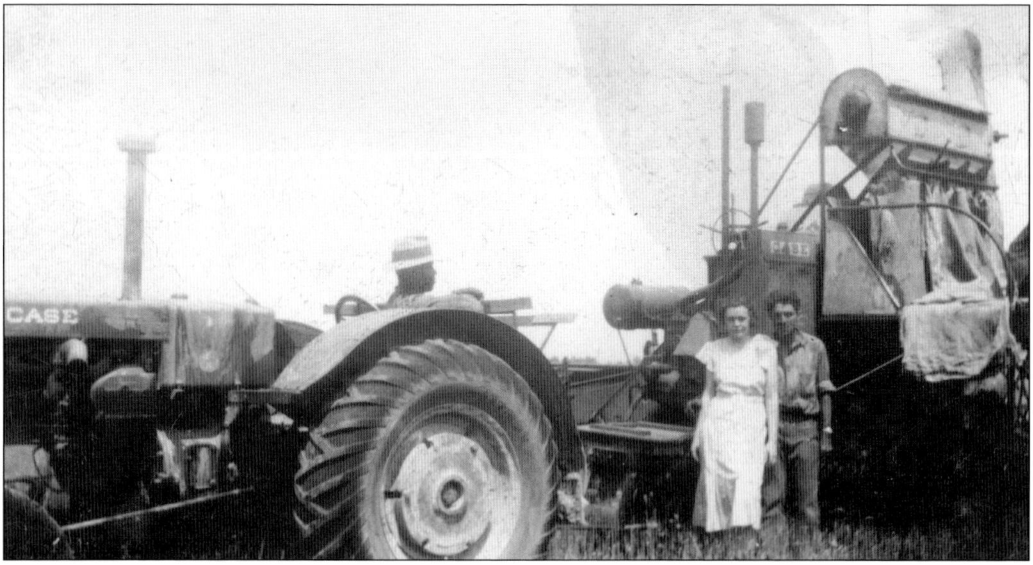

Machinery also reduced the need for milling companies. In days gone by, seed cleaning had to be done by a hand-cranked machine. In the 1950s, harvesting and cleaning seeds could be accomplished by one piece of machinery. This allowed farmers to harvest and bag their product, reducing cost and saving time.

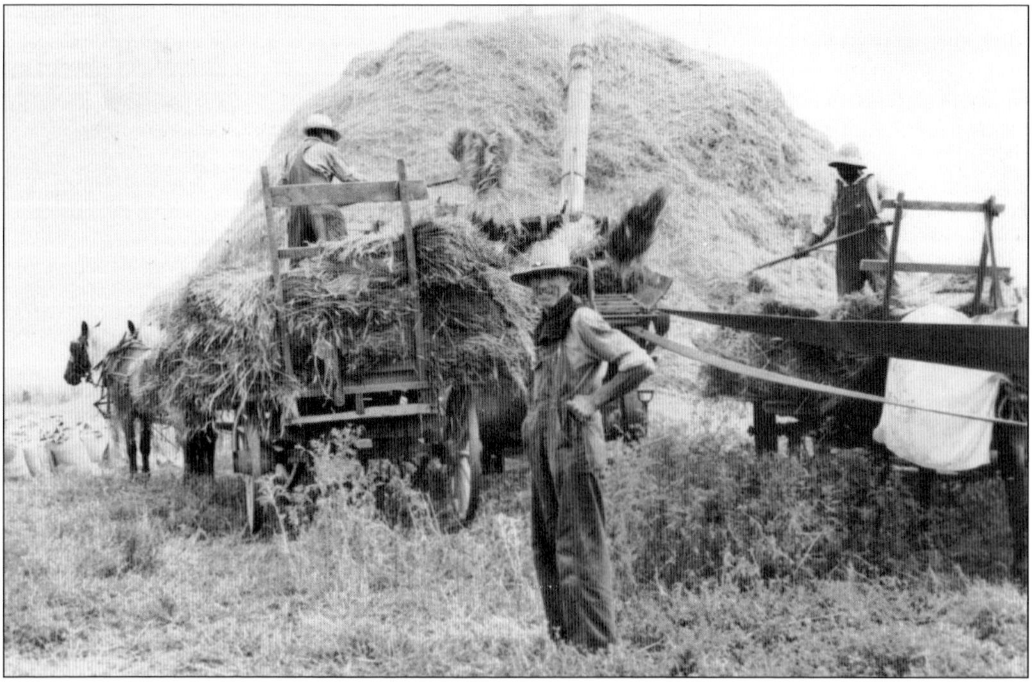

Even the farmers who slowly adapted to machinery found ways to cut time and cost. A wheat threshing machine driven by a steam engine could reduce the project of separating the wheat from the husk and straw from hours or days down to minutes. Prior to the advent of such machines, it would take an hour to separate a single bushel of wheat.

From the mid-1800s on, Harrington had at least one local doctor. Each of these men was the image of the true country doctor. Black bags and house calls were common. The first known doctor in the area was Frederick J. Owens, who settled in Harrington in 1857. Dr. Owens later served as the assistant surgeon to the 1st Regiment, Delaware Volunteer Infantry, during the Civil War. Appointed just before Gettysburg, he served on the front lines with the regiment until the close of the war. Next to come to town was Dr. James D. West in 1881. The third doctor to call Harrington home was Terrence Gustavus Riley, pictured at right, who hung his shingle up in 1895. He practiced from his home on Dorman Street. (Below, courtesy of the Delaware Public Archives.)

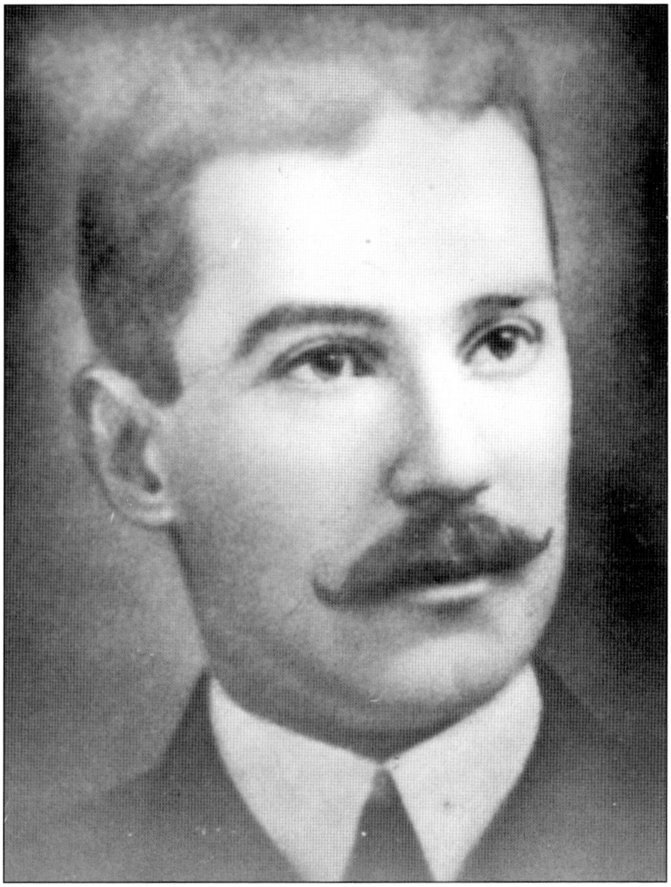

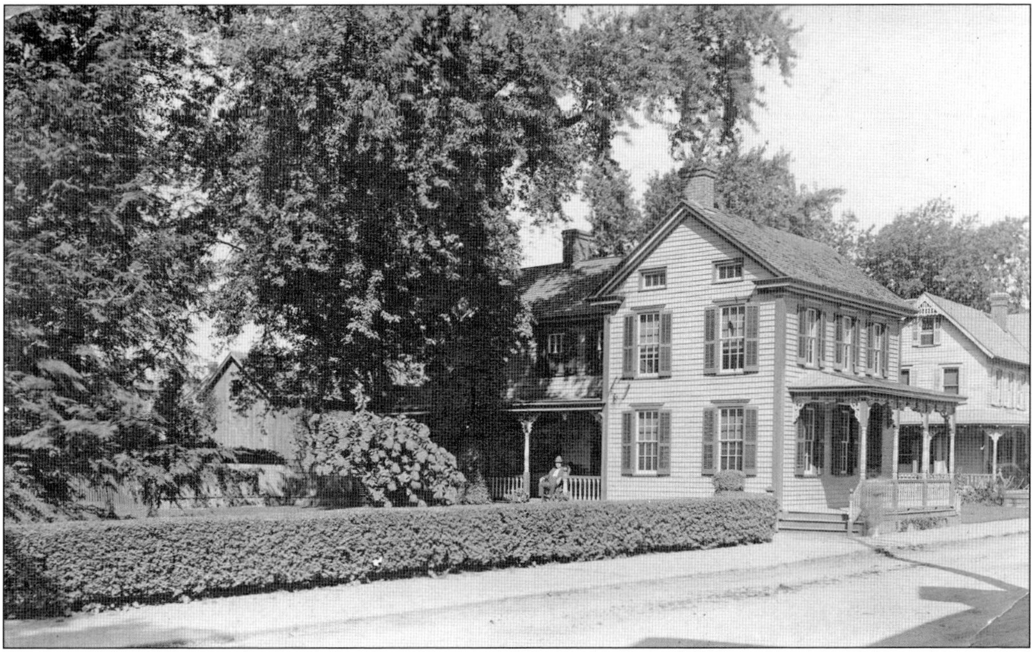

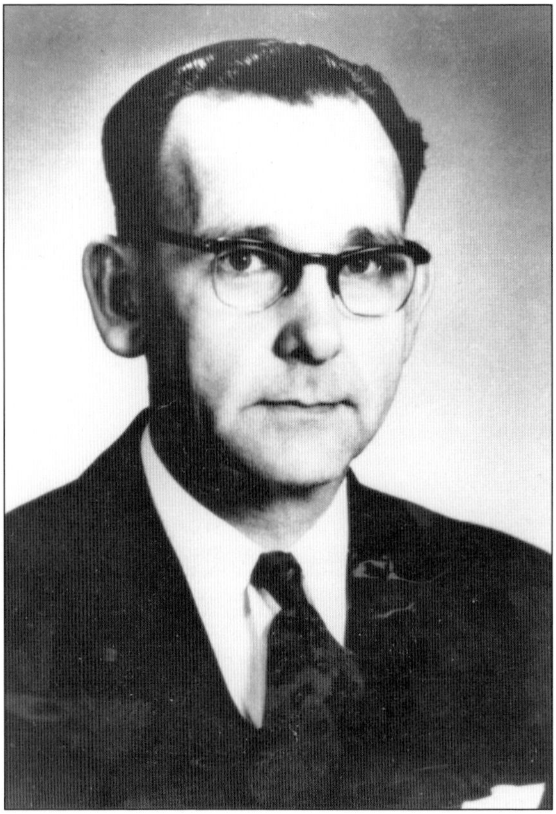

Dr. Hewitt Smith came to Harrington in the 1920s. His house and office were on Fleming Street. As with the other doctors before him, Dr. Smith made house calls frequently to those who could not make it in to his office. Dr. Smith was not the only member of his household to make house calls. During World War II, manpower for the local fire company was low. Since their house was next door to the firehouse, his wife, Martha Smith, volunteered to drive the fire engine. The windshield on the truck was added just for her. After the war, she was not allowed to join the fire company because it had a policy of not allowing women.

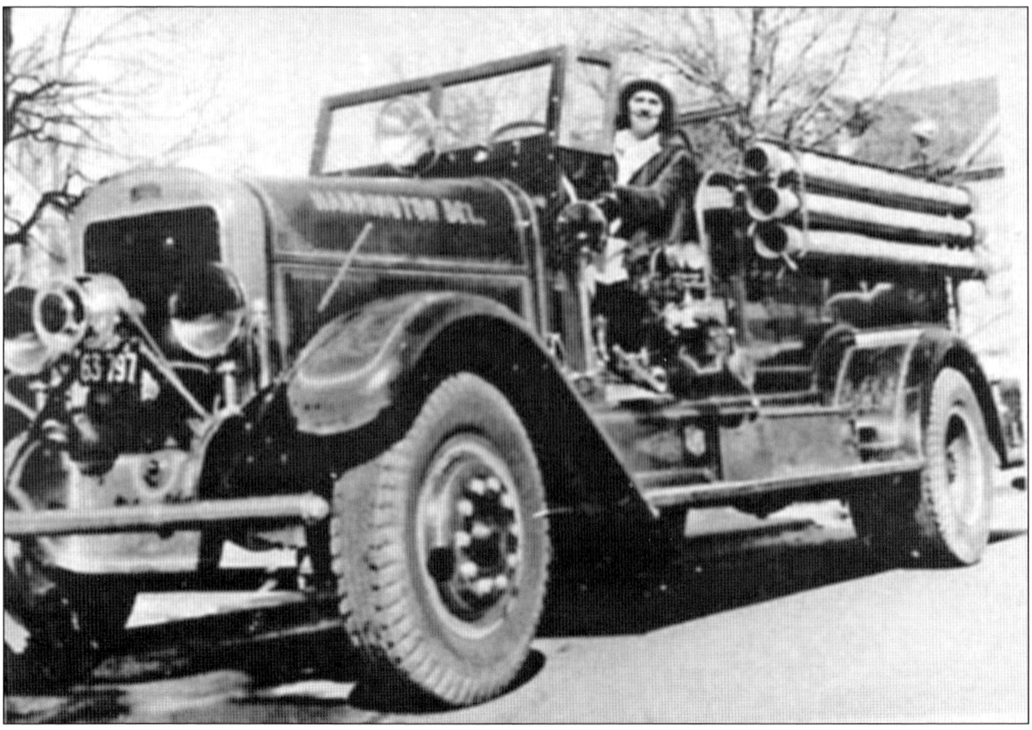

Perhaps the most legendary of the local physicians was Dr. William Thomas Chipman. Born in Delaware, he returned to the state he loved after he graduated. He was one of the founding physicians at Milford Emergency Hospital in 1921. Settling in Harrington, his home and practice were located on Clark Street. Many tall tales about his driving to patients' houses and the hospital are still told today. Dr. Chipman became involved in all aspects of his community. He served for several years as a member of the Delaware House of Representatives, even rising to speaker of the house in 1949. Today, the former high school in Harrington bears his name as the W.T. Chipman Junior High School. The Boone-Chipman Society also still serves as a fundraising wing for the Bayhealth Medical Center, Milford Memorial Hospital Campus.

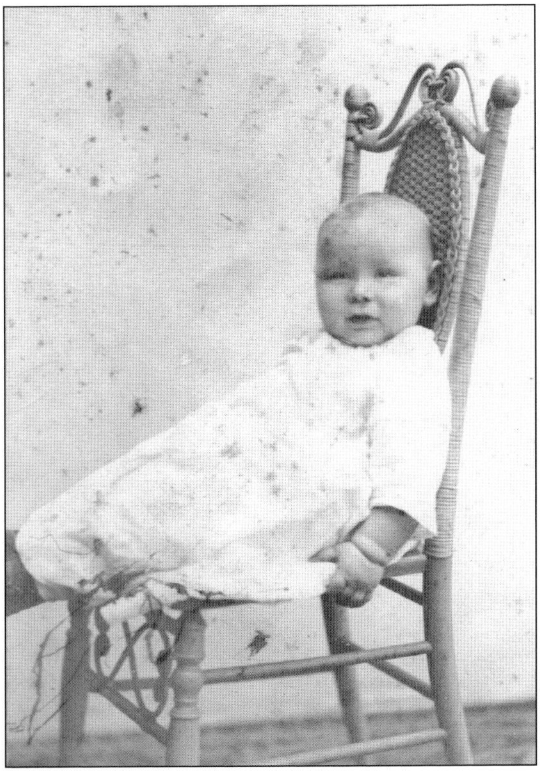

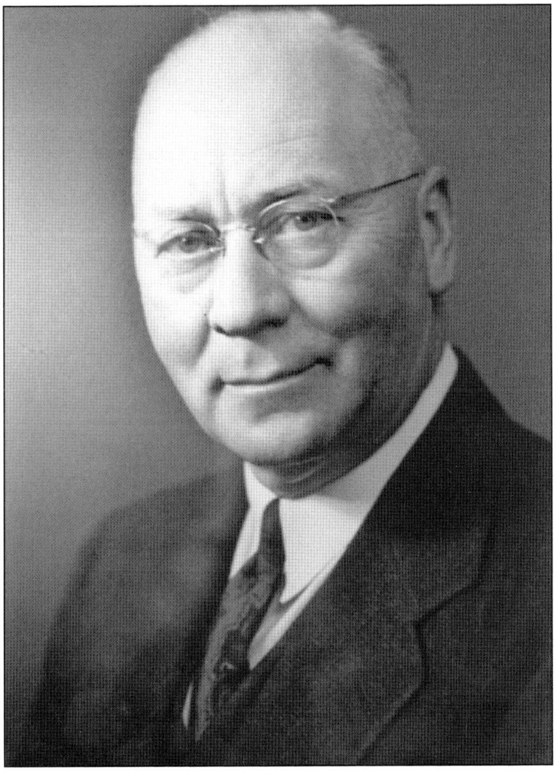

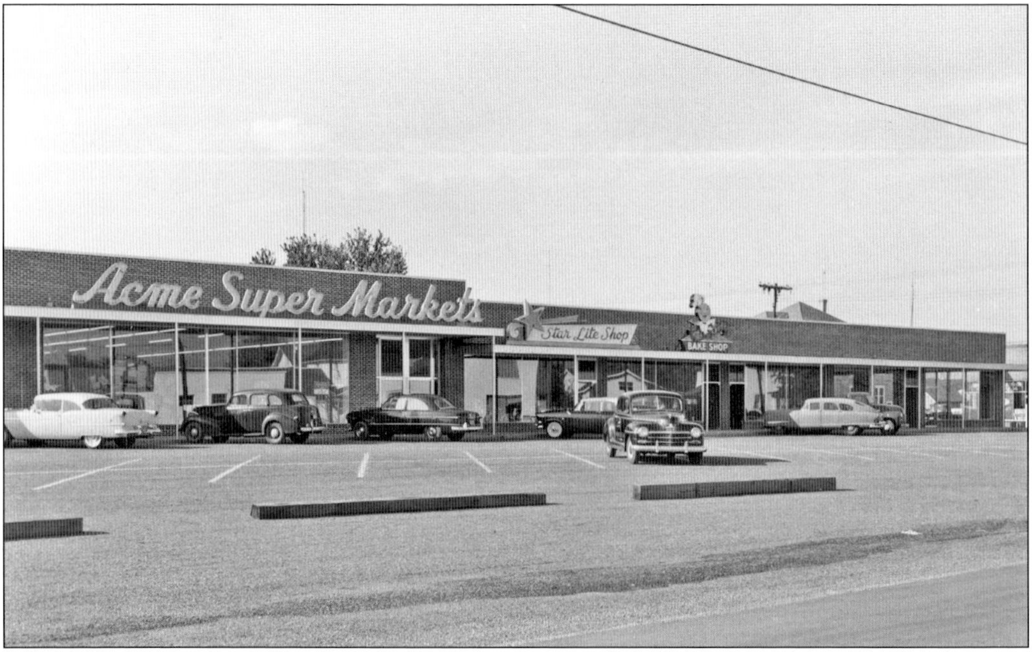

As the town grew bigger, larger storefronts were needed, and Quillen's Shopping Center was constructed on Clark Street in the 1950s. The center became home to a larger Acme Super Market, a National Five & Ten Cent Store, and local shops such as a bakery, pharmacy, and giftshop. (Courtesy of the Delaware Public Archives)

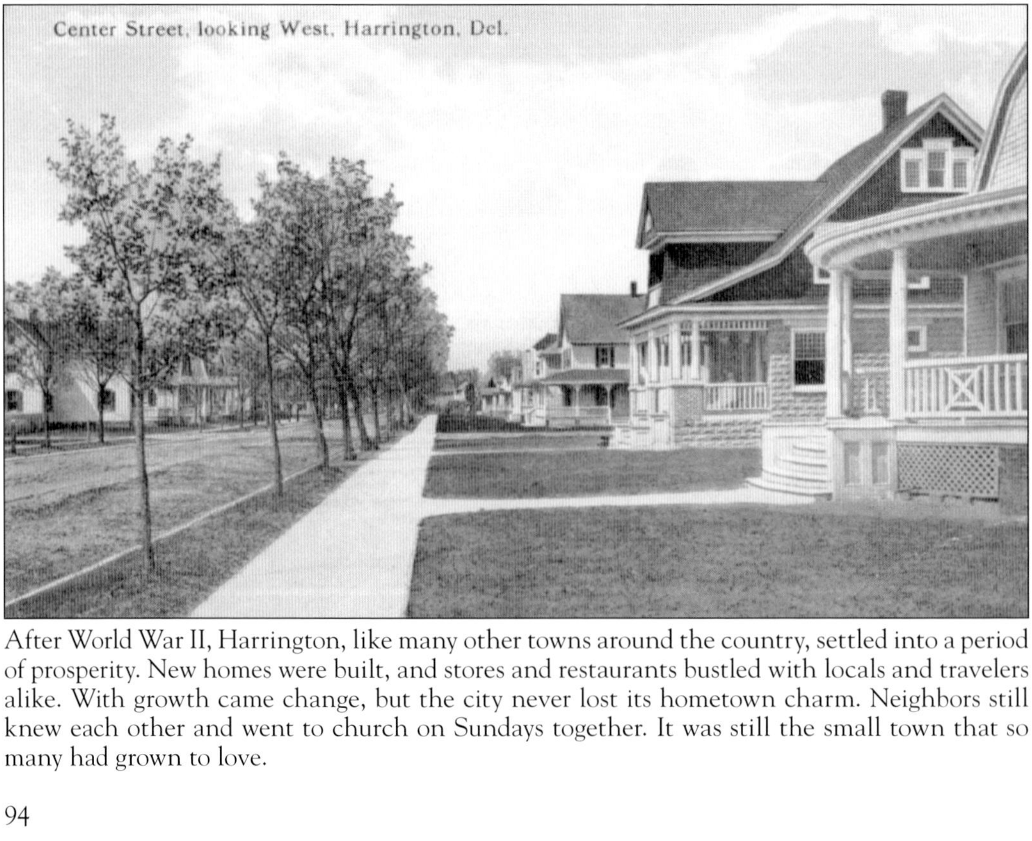

After World War II, Harrington, like many other towns around the country, settled into a period of prosperity. New homes were built, and stores and restaurants bustled with locals and travelers alike. With growth came change, but the city never lost its hometown charm. Neighbors still knew each other and went to church on Sundays together. It was still the small town that so many had grown to love.

Six

From a Day at the Park to a Night on the Town

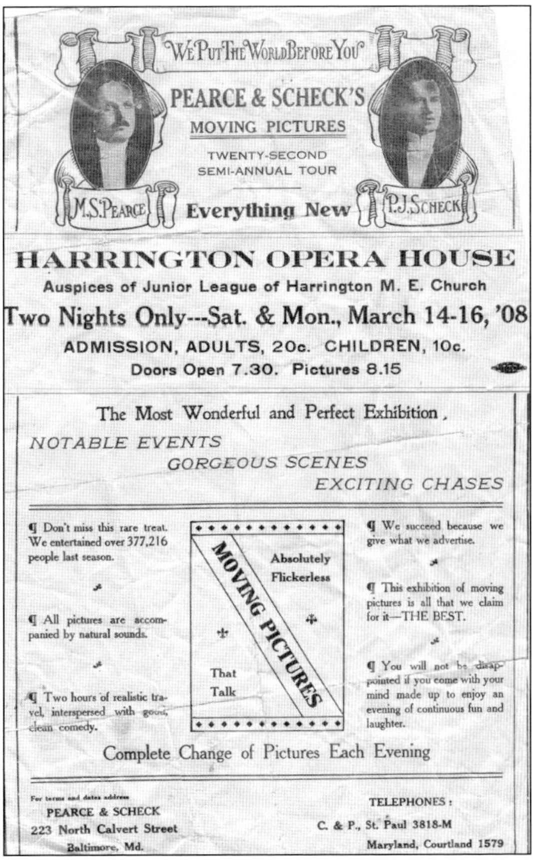

Harrington Opera House was in business from the 1900s through the 1920s. It was actually the second opera house in the town. It had a small stage used for traveling vaudeville shows, and although it did not have a movie projector of its own, the owners hired traveling movie companies to show the latest movies.

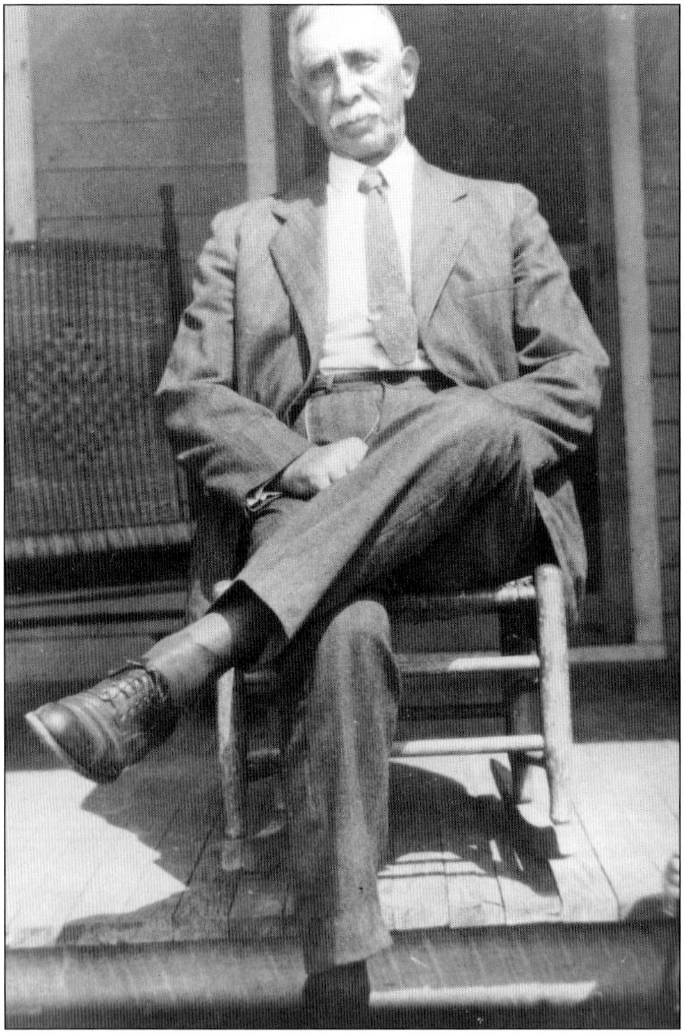

The first truly successful entertainment venture in Harrington was opened by E.C. Reese in 1903. Located on Commerce Street, it had a large stage and a projector for silent motion pictures. Finally, locals could enjoy entertainment every evening. On May 19, 1916, the most famous silent movie star of Hollywood, Charlie Chaplin himself, paid a visit to the opera house. In 1913, E.C. Reese's grandson Reese Booker Harrington became manager of the opera house at the age of just 10. But according to all accounts, Reese had a head for business and a passion for the entertainment industry.

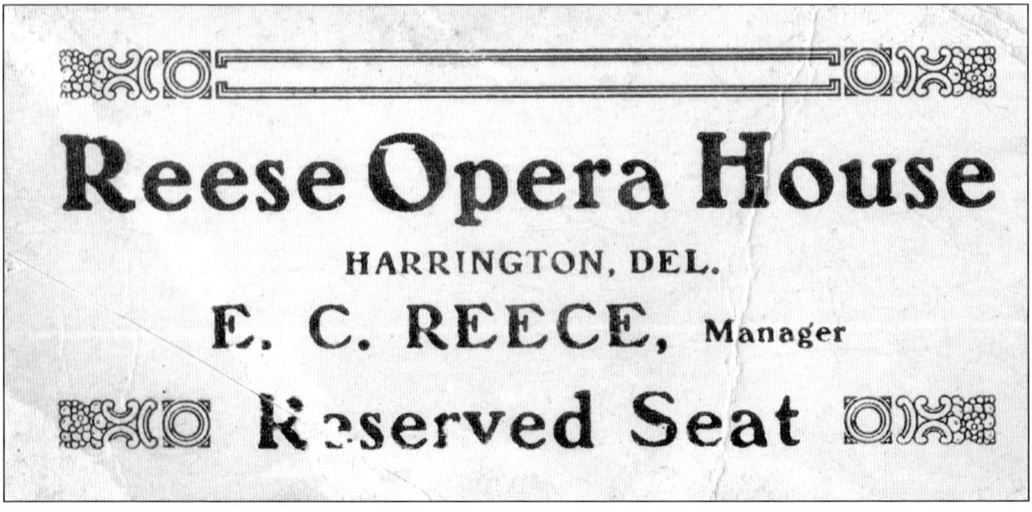

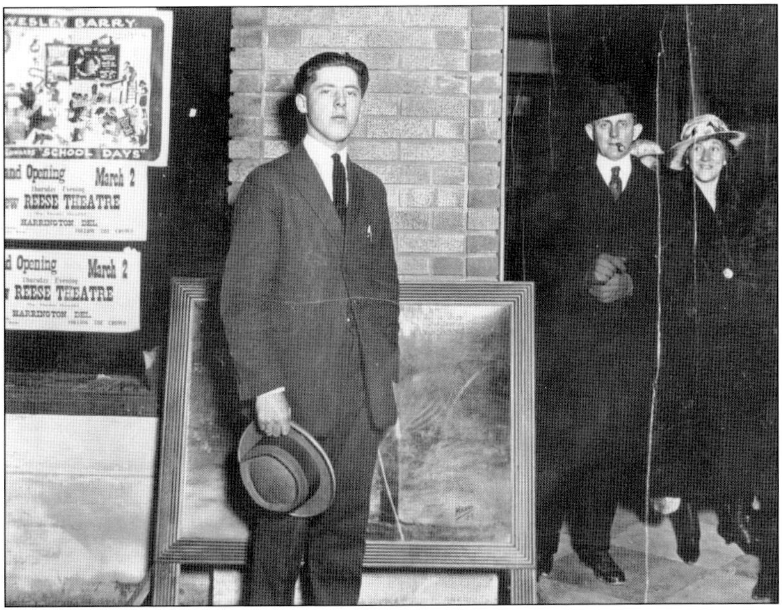

After he had managed his grandfather's opera house, Reese Booker Harrington attended Columbia University, where he fell in love with the New York theaters and vaudeville. When he returned home, he set about creating a version of those theaters in Harrington. In 1922, he started the Reese Theatre.

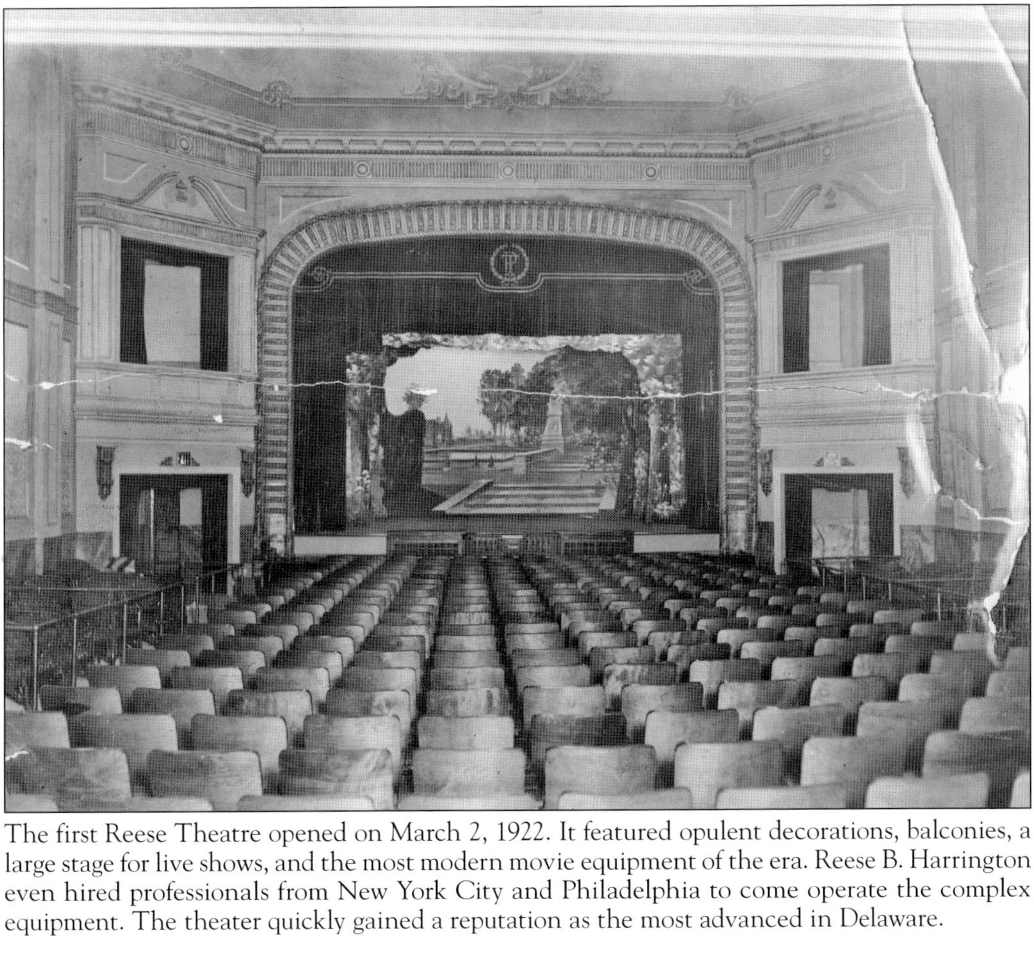

The first Reese Theatre opened on March 2, 1922. It featured opulent decorations, balconies, a large stage for live shows, and the most modern movie equipment of the era. Reese B. Harrington even hired professionals from New York City and Philadelphia to come operate the complex equipment. The theater quickly gained a reputation as the most advanced in Delaware.

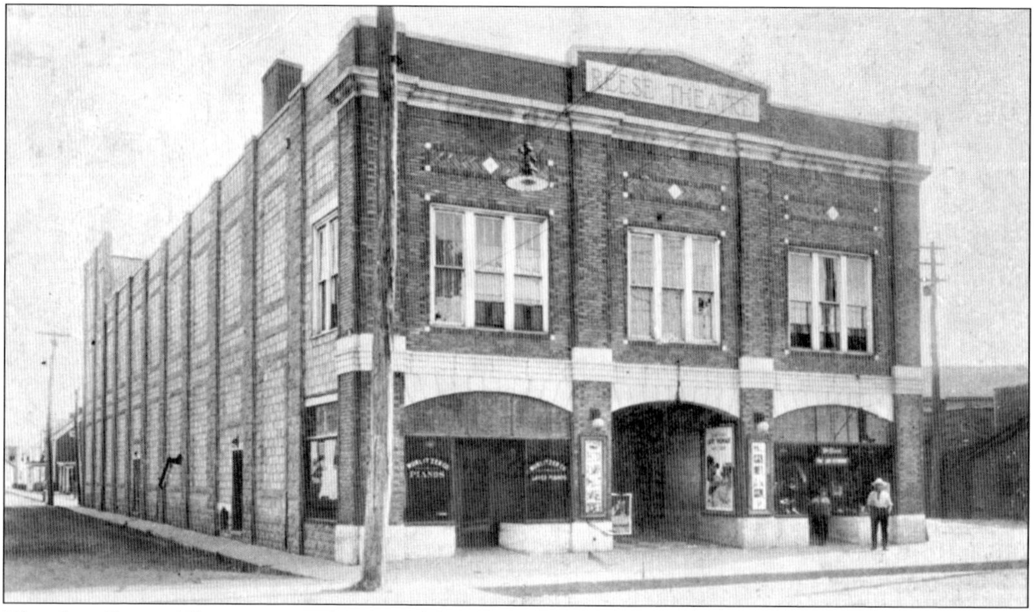

The first Reese Theatre was destroyed by fire on November 15, 1943. On May 23, 1944, the newly constructed Reese Theatre opened its doors. The building was filled with even more modern conveniences and again operated the latest cinema technology. Reese B. Harrington had traveled the country during the construction to ensure his theater had the absolute best equipment available.

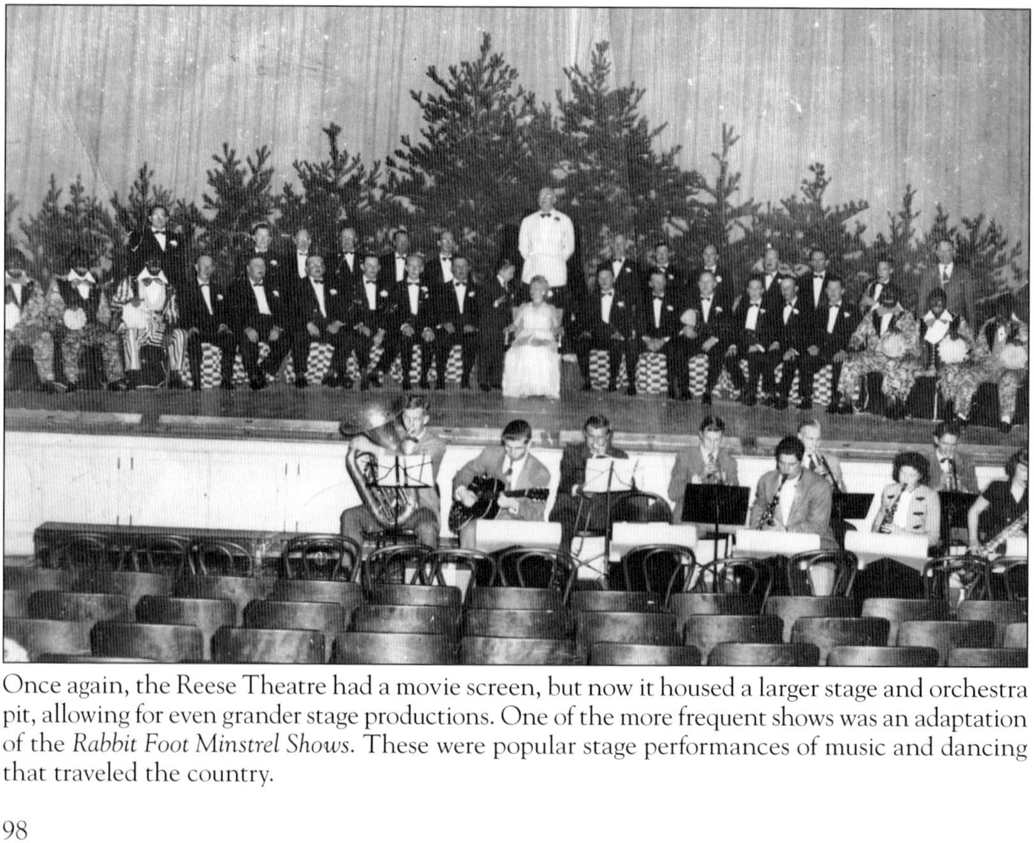

Once again, the Reese Theatre had a movie screen, but now it housed a larger stage and orchestra pit, allowing for even grander stage productions. One of the more frequent shows was an adaptation of the *Rabbit Foot Minstrel Shows*. These were popular stage performances of music and dancing that traveled the country.

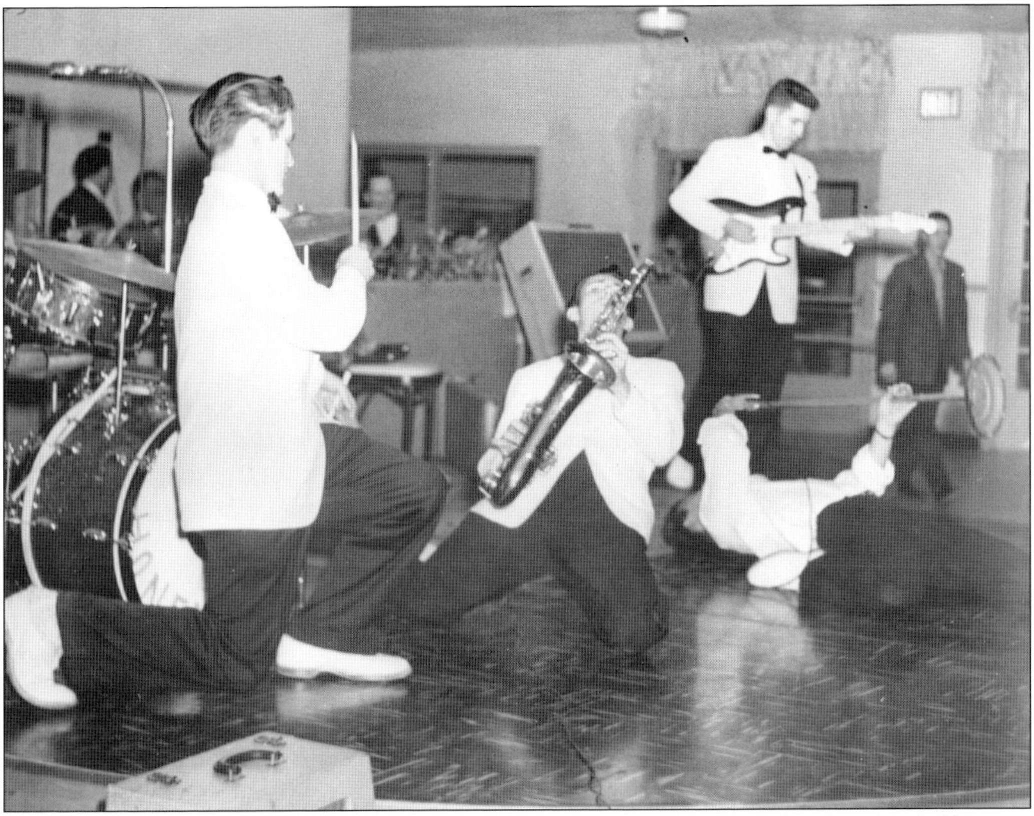

Local teens enjoyed the latest dance crazes at events around Harrington. The churches held events for teens at the National Guard Amory and other venues. Honey Voshell and the Honeycombs were a local group that often played these events. Other acts or disc jockeys would spin tunes through the evening as teens twisted to the latest dance music.

For the younger kids in Harrington, organized sports were a part of their youth. Organizations such as Little League baseball and Pop Warner football gave them the chance to play on fields under adult supervision while learning the proper ways to play their favorite sports and the lessons of teamwork and fair play. These activities not only gave them something to do but also created bonds that would last a lifetime.

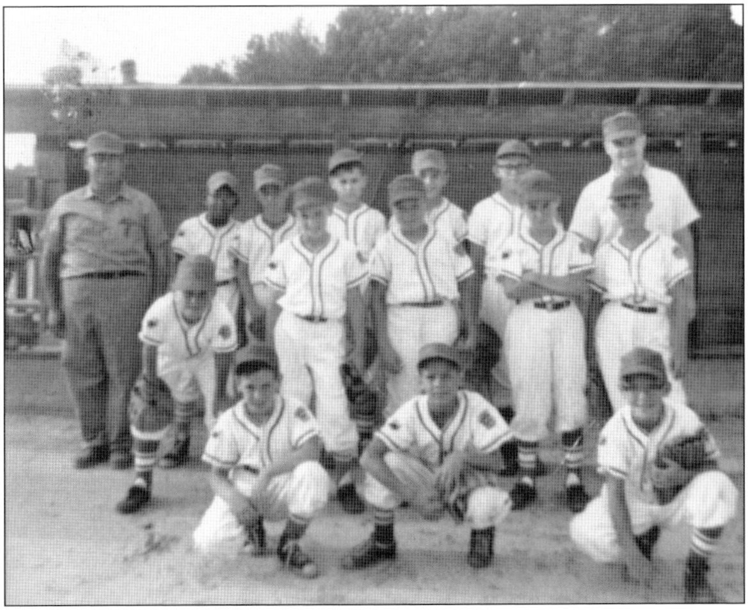

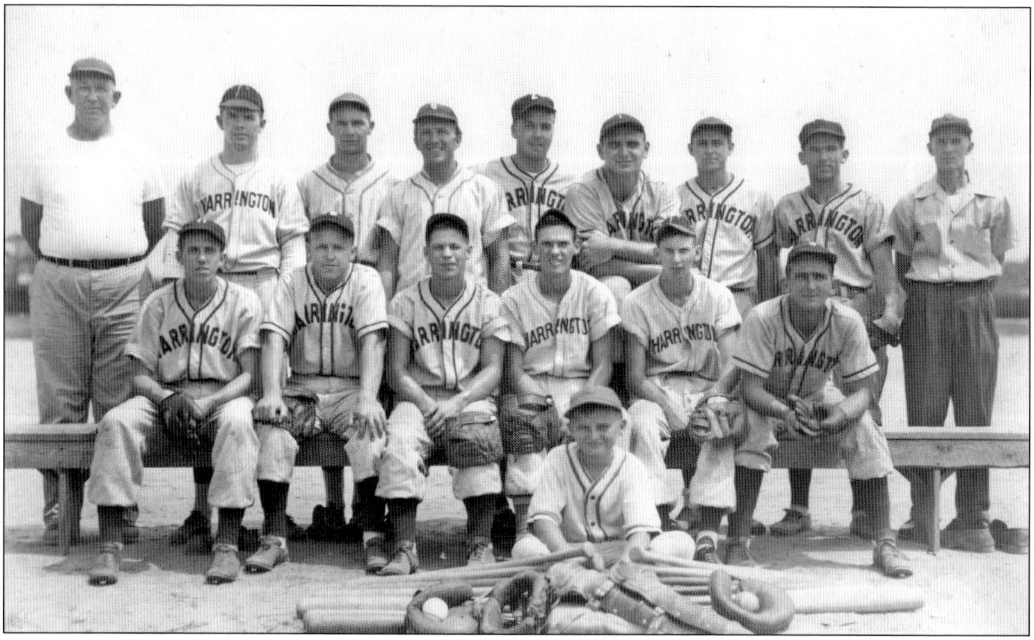

Baseball was not only America's pastime but Harrington's as well. The Eastern Shore and Mid Del Baseball Leagues were established in 1922 and lasted until 1950. Teams from small towns all over the Delmarva Peninsula played in the leagues at various times. The Harrington team played on a field between the railroad tracks and the fairgrounds. Other teams were from Masten's Corner, Felton, Staytonsville, Viola, and Milford. Even a few companies such as Playtex fielded teams made up of employees. At times, professional teams would be paid to play exhibition games against these local players. Baseball was more than a game, it was a community event for these small towns. Such famous players as Jimmy Foxx and Satchel Paige played in these leagues.

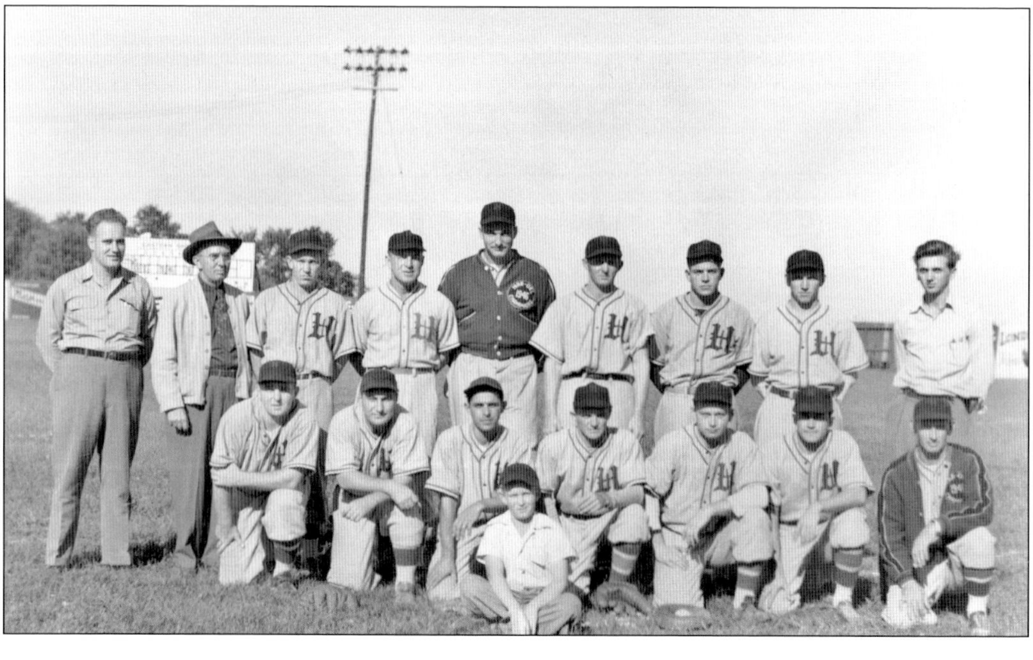

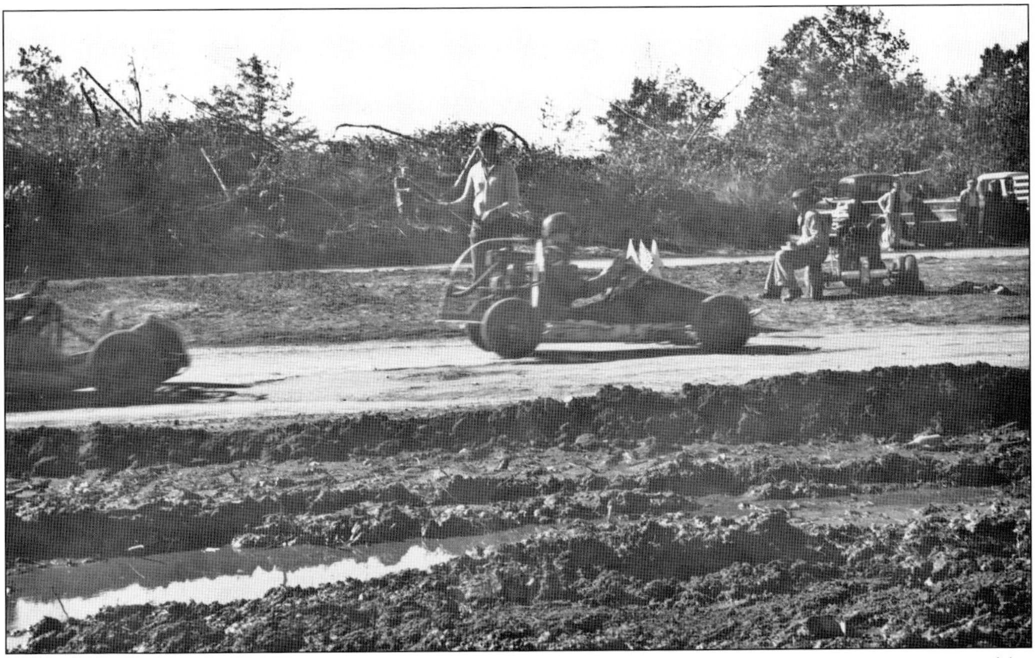

Blue Hen Racing was another amateur sporting group that came about in the 1950s. Formed by a group of seven local men, it rented a track from Benny Brownstein for a dollar a year. To create the Blue Hen Speedway out of a field of mud, the group paid $70 for the needed dirt, and local businessman John Satterfield donated the clay needed to finish the racing surface. The men worked on cars for each other at Joe's Night Shop, a local garage that belonged to Joe Gray, one of the seven members. They ran weekly events, had sponsors for trophies and prize money, and an announcer to keep race fans up on the action. Locals came out to enjoy the races, and a snack bar was set up to sell concessions.

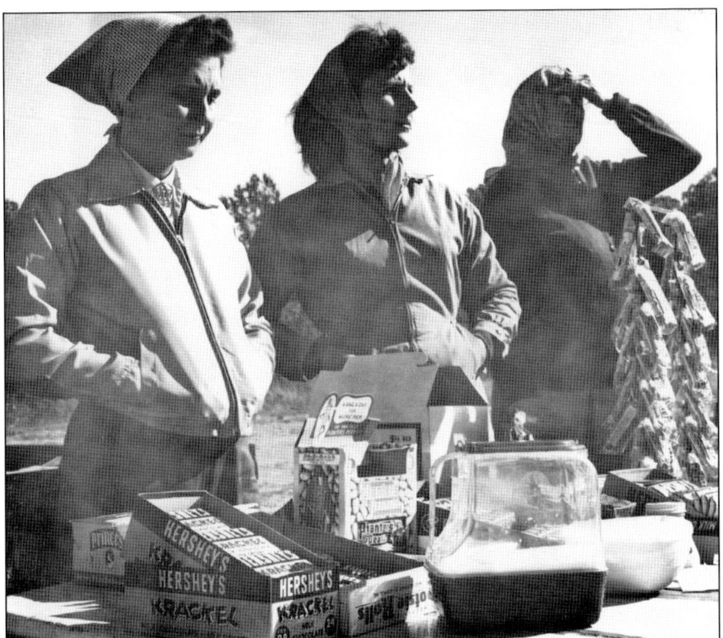

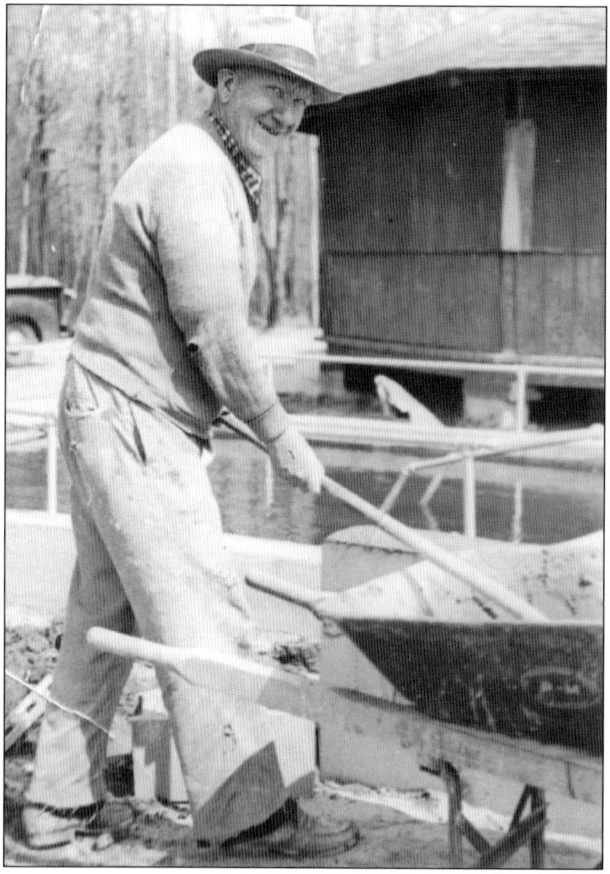

Perhaps there are no better memories of childhood in Harrington than those created by William Wheeler. Beginning in 1947 and lasting until 1978, Wheeler's Park was more than just a small playground where kids could hang out—for many, it was Harrington's version of Disneyland. For just 10¢ admission, a child could spend hours on the swings, Tarzan ropes, and monkey bars, and swim in either the small concrete pool or the stream nearby, all under the watchful eyes of Wheeler and his wife, Lillian. To the Wheelers, the park was more than a business, it was a way to give back to their community.

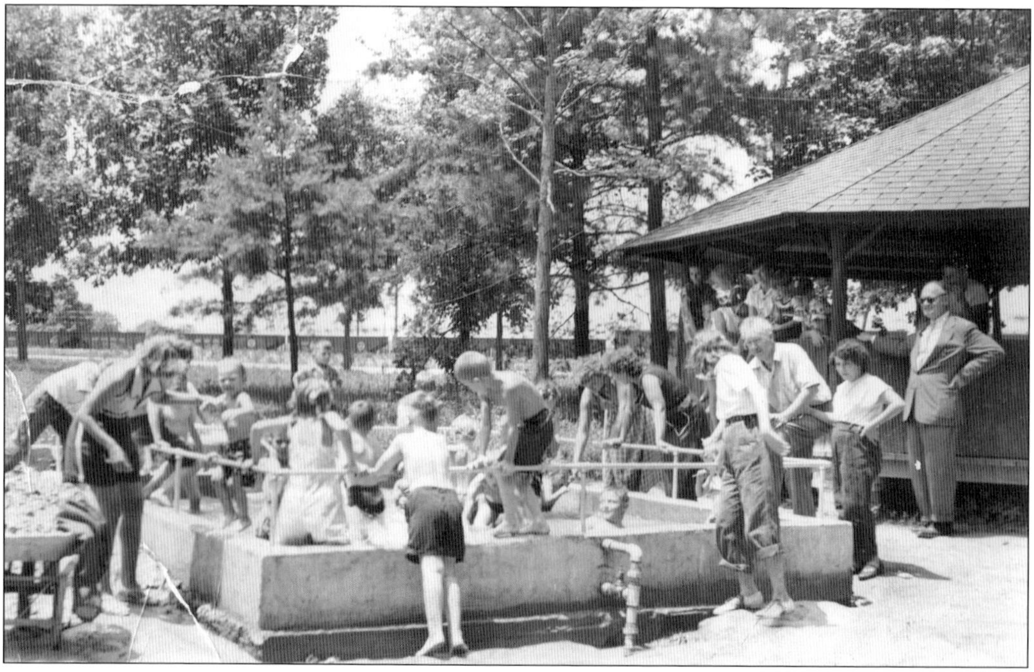

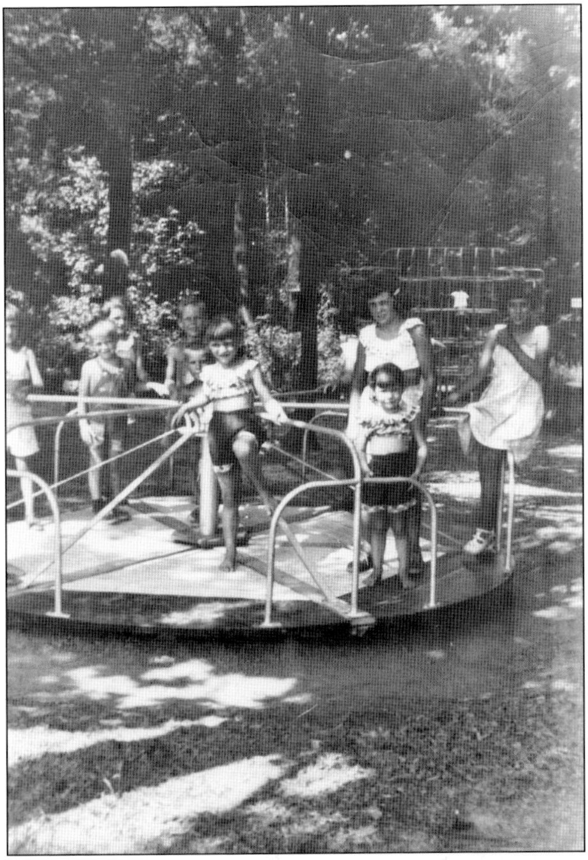

The merry-go-round was one of the favorite rides at Wheeler's Park. Kids would spin themselves dizzy trying to be the last one standing, all the while giggling and laughing till their sides hurt. Then they would line up to have their picture taken sitting on the horse tree. They could buy snacks and drinks at the small concession stand or sit and watch the monkeys play in their cage. The park even boasted a bandstand where on Saturday and Sunday local bands would play free concerts. Locals used the stand and the nearby picnic tables as a place to hold many family reunions.

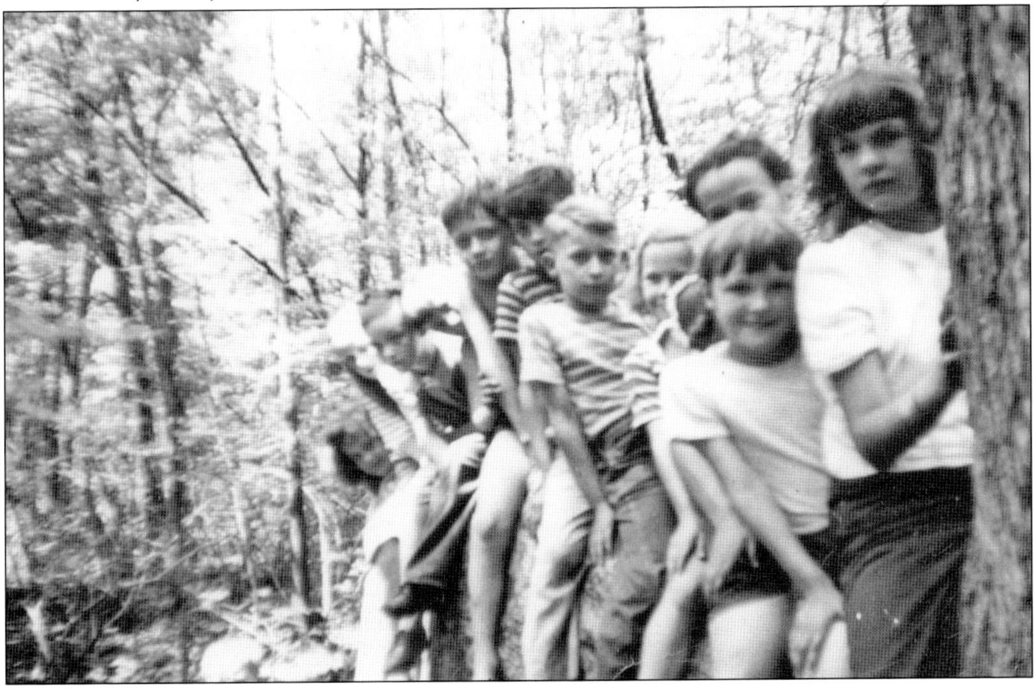

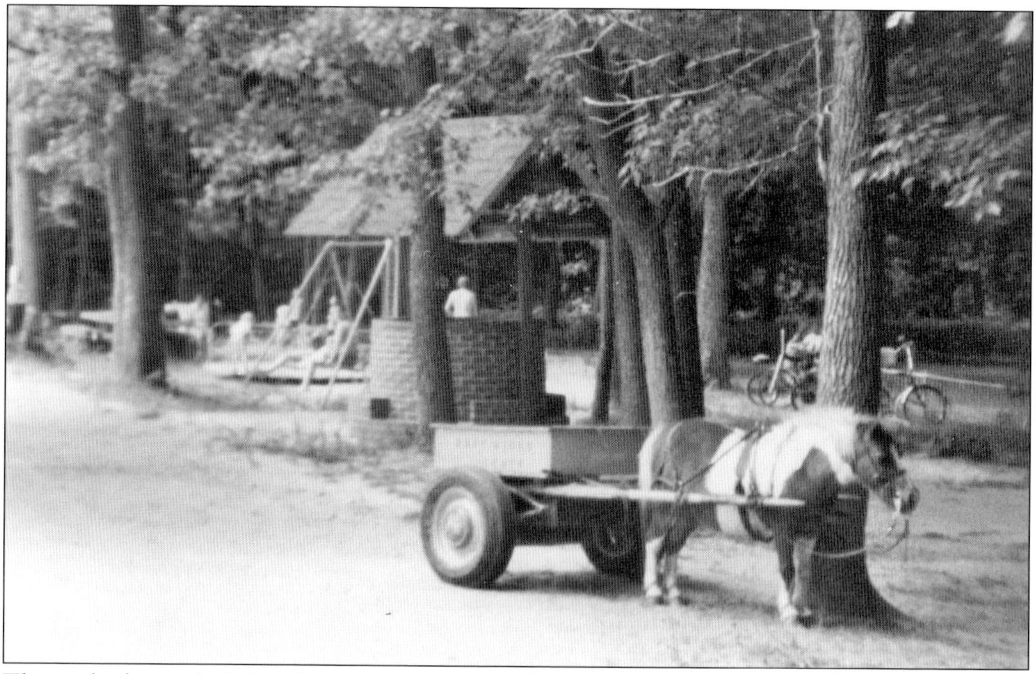

The park also included perhaps everyone's two favorite rides. For an additional 10¢, Wheeler would give a ride around the grounds in a pony cart. It was a great way to enjoy the trails while getting a short rest from all the activities. And without a doubt the icon of Wheeler's Park was the gas-powered train. For 10¢, children could ride the small train around an oval track. As the train sped through the concrete tunnel, the passengers would scream to hear their echoes. And all the while, Wheeler himself would beam with a smile, because in his heart he too was that same kid screaming in the tunnel.

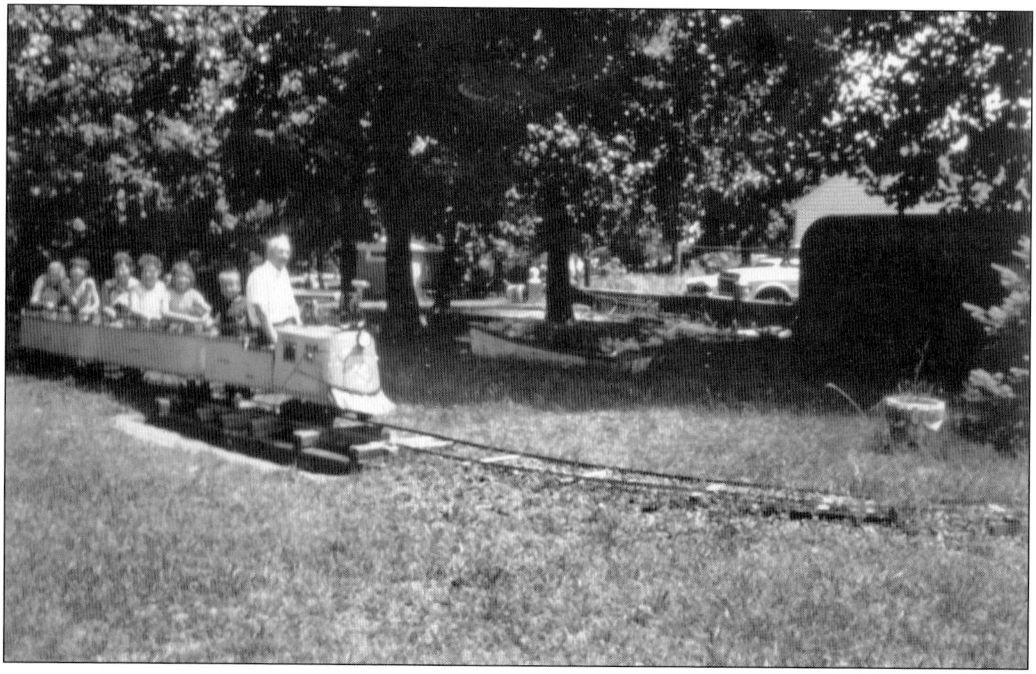

Seven

Take Me to the Fair

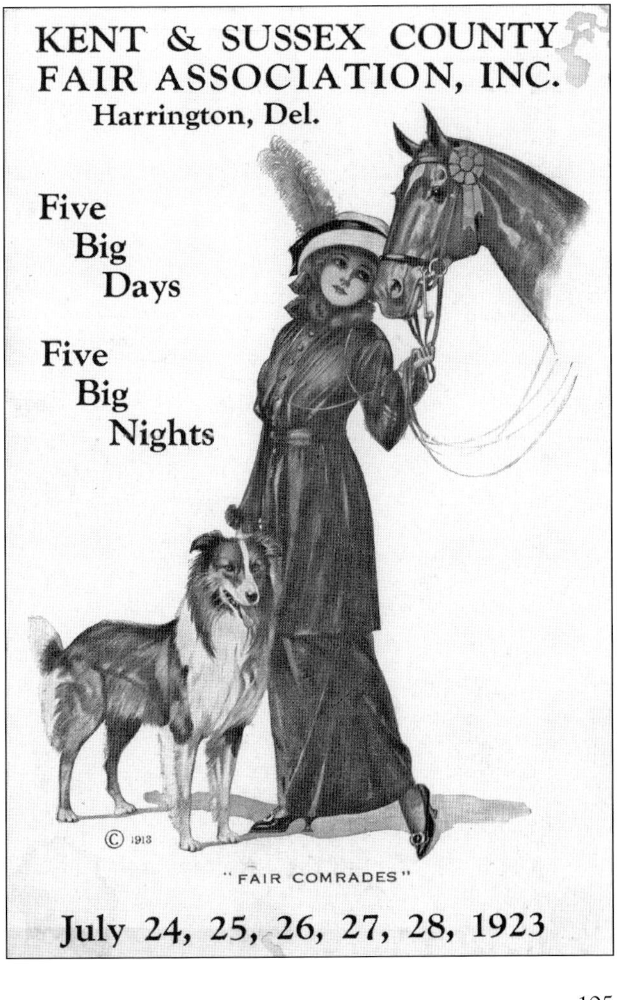

January 12, 1920, was a date that not only affected the citizens of Harrington but has come to draw hundreds of thousands to the area each year. On this date, a group of local businessmen gathered to discuss the formation of a fair. The Kent and Sussex Fair Association was created, and the month of July in Harrington would never be the same. (Courtesy of the Delaware Public Archives.)

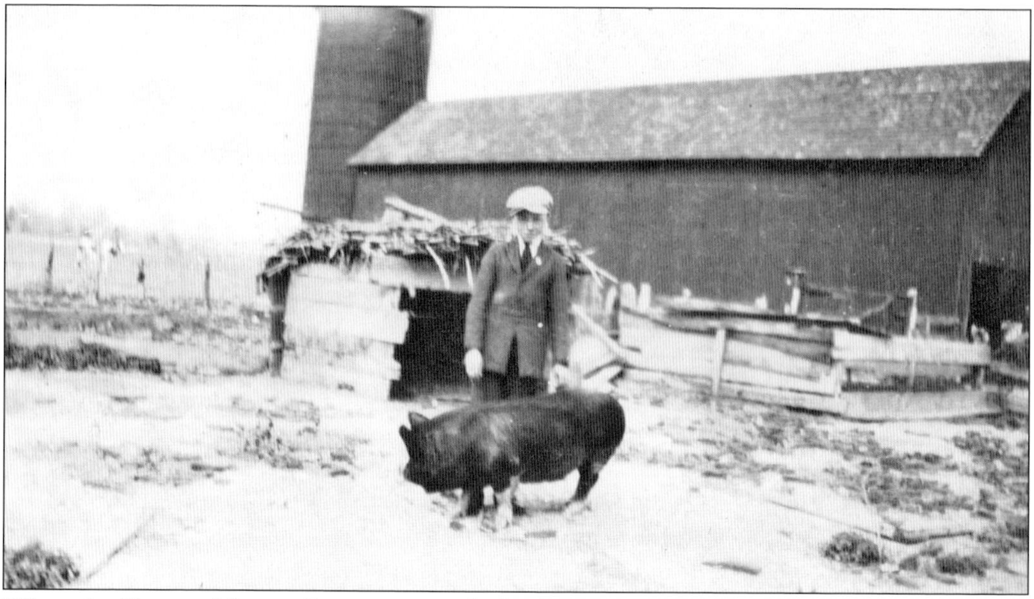

When the Kent and Sussex Fair was created, the decision was made to highlight the area's rich agricultural heritage. Shown here is the grand champion pig from the 1920 fair and his young owner. From its first days, youth would play a central role in the farm displays during the fair.

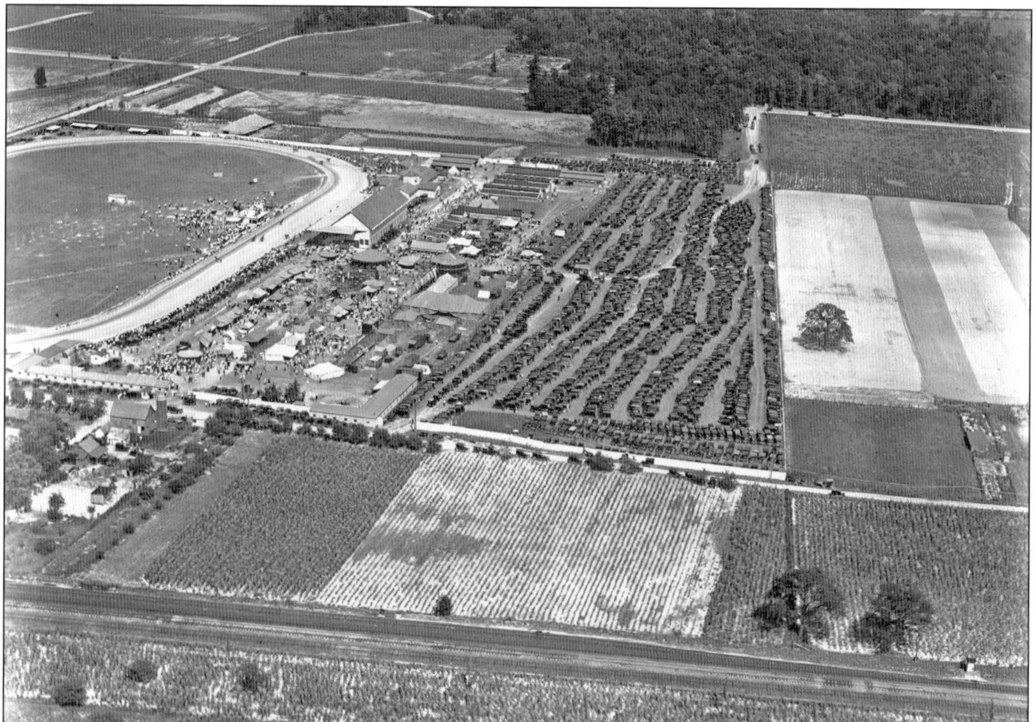

This aerial photograph shows the fairgrounds in the early 1920s. The fair board of directors contracted with Krause Greater Shows to provide rides, games, and entertainment for the patrons to enjoy. At the time, Krause was the leading traveling carnival show on the East Coast. (Courtesy of the Hagley Museum & Library.)

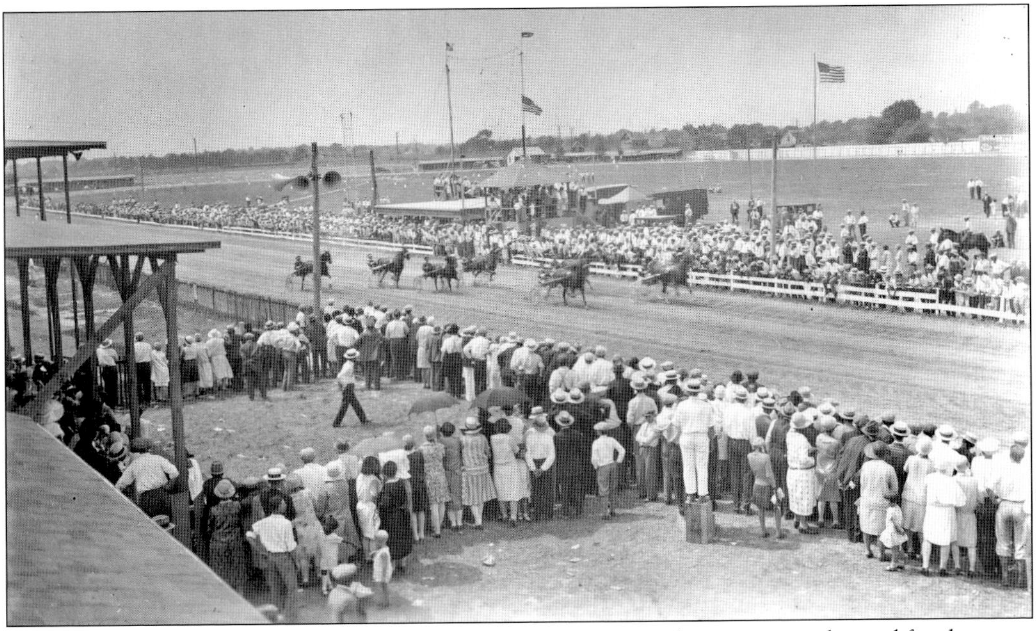

Harness racing became a staple of the Kent and Sussex Fair. Admission was charged for the races as well as for vaudeville stage acts added to the five-day event. With the proceeds from these events, the sale of stock certificates in the fair corporation, and other revenue sources, the fair continued to grow. In just five short years, it had become a week-long event. (Courtesy of the Delaware Public Archives.)

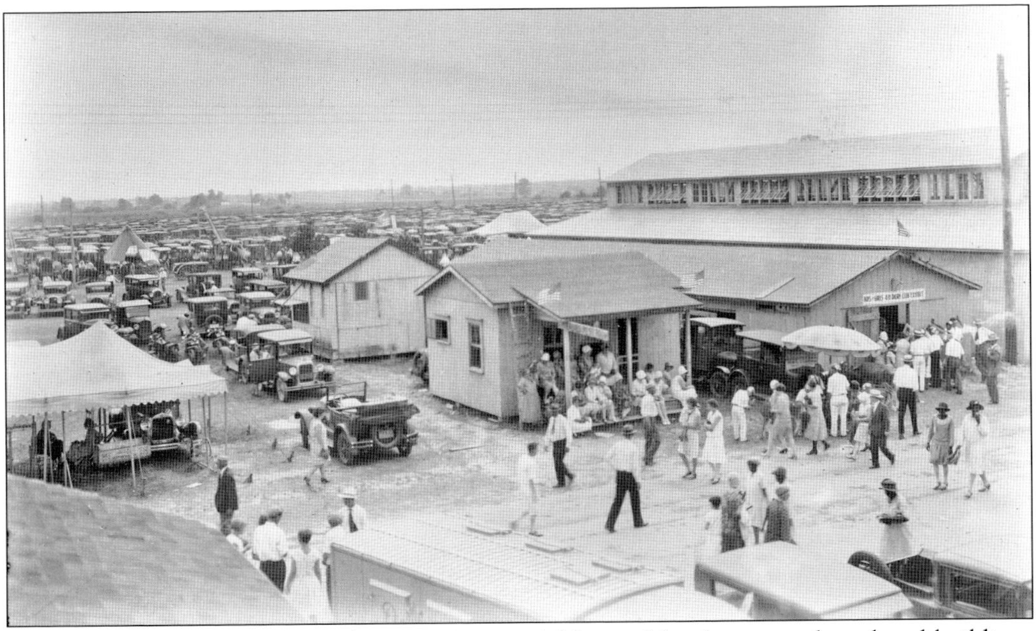

As the fair grew in length, it also grew in size. Additional land was purchased and buildings constructed to house other exhibits. A floral department, a boys and girls club department, and a poultry department were added, with premiums being paid to the prize winners in each category. The fair kept to its roots as first and foremost an exhibition of local agricultural products. (Courtesy of the Delaware Public Archives.)

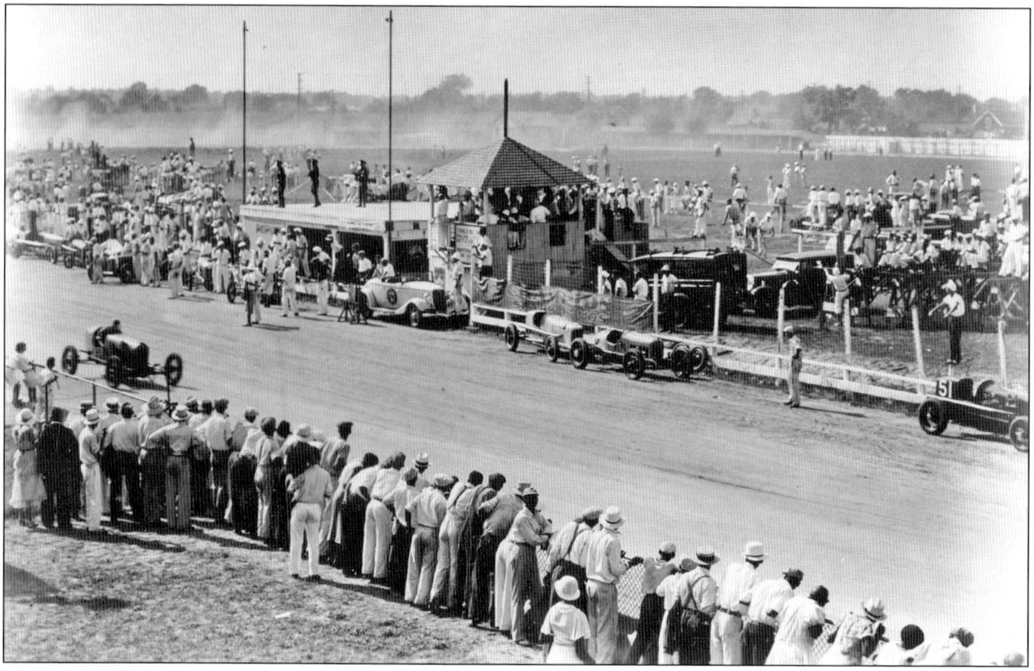

Henry Ford was quoted as saying "auto racing began five minutes after the second car was built." And so it was at the Kent and Sussex Fair. Beginning in 1921, two nights of auto racing were held on the harness track in front of the grandstands. Scores of people would come out for heat races and all the excitement leading up to the feature race. The Harrington Fire Company sponsored the auto races for decades, and for a while, the races were even sanctioned as point-earning events by NASCAR, increasing the number of drivers and cars entering. (Below, courtesy of the Delaware Public Archives.)

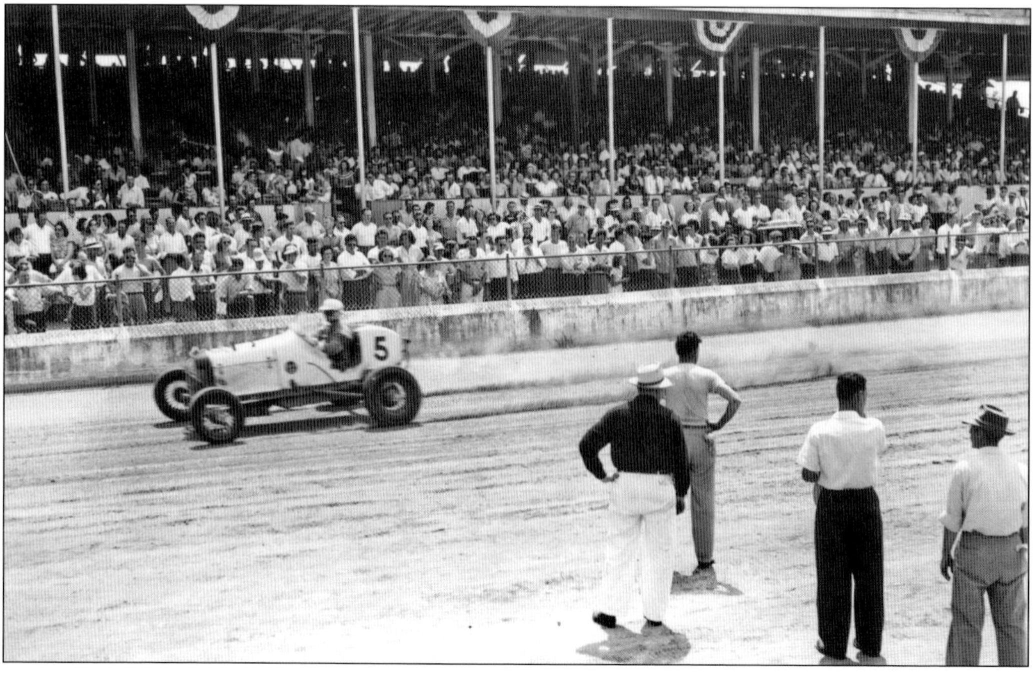

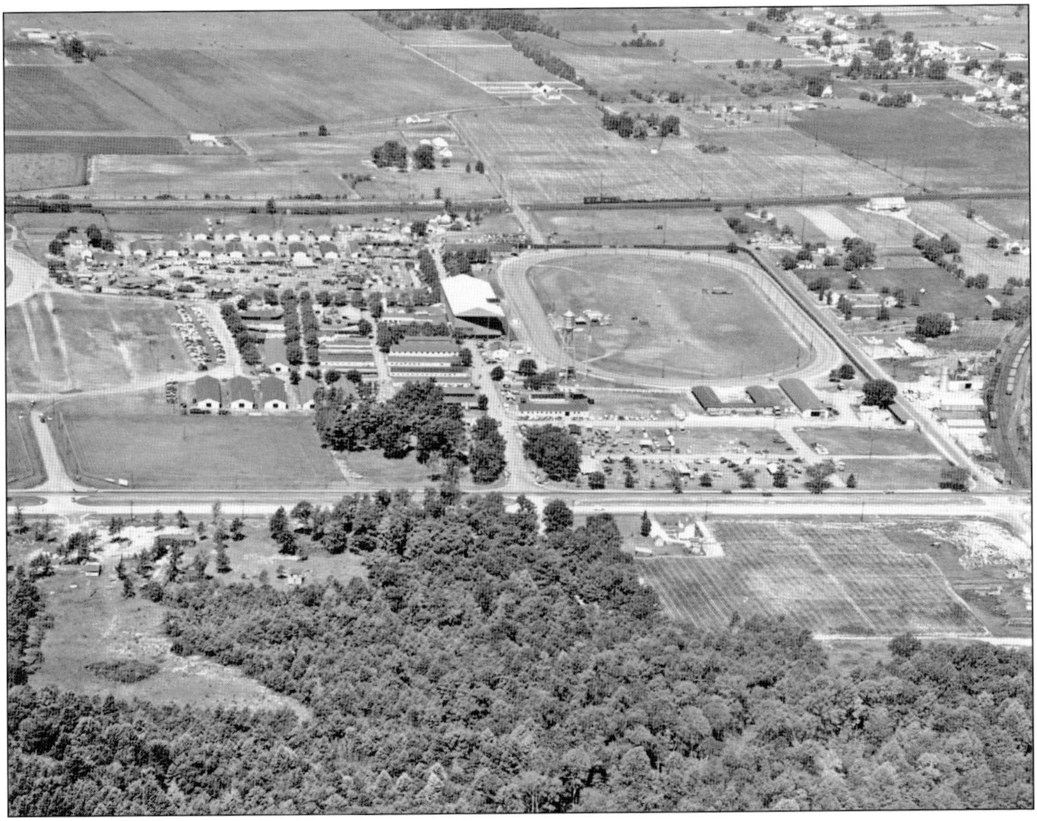

By the 1950s, the fair had grown even larger. In 1950, an onsite water tower was constructed to meet the growing demands of vendors and patrons. A new grandstand was constructed in 1955 to allow for larger crowds to witness such acts as the world-famous Rockettes, the Lone Ranger, and Johnny Cash. (Courtesy of the Delaware Public Archives.)

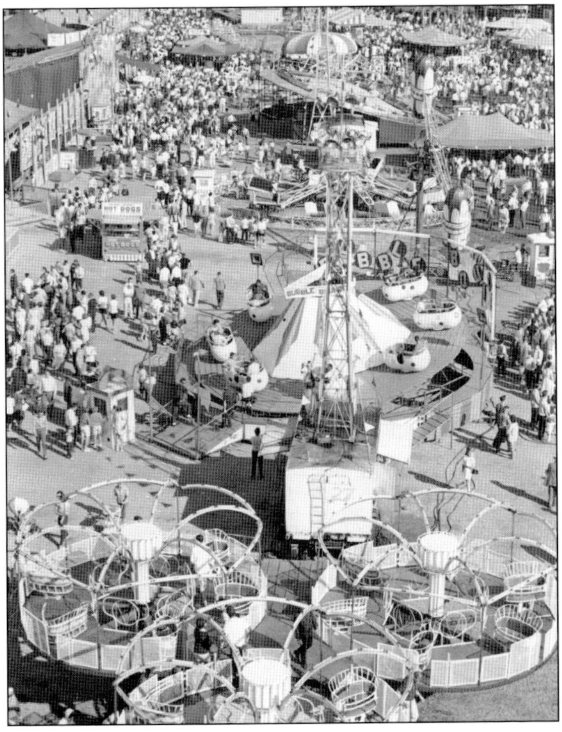

The midway of rides and games grew dramatically as well. The James E. Strates shows provided carnival rides and games of chance. When the midway first opened in 1920, there were only three rides, but by the 1950s, the midway was home to more than 30 amusement rides, from small rides for the kids to larger and more exciting rides for adults.

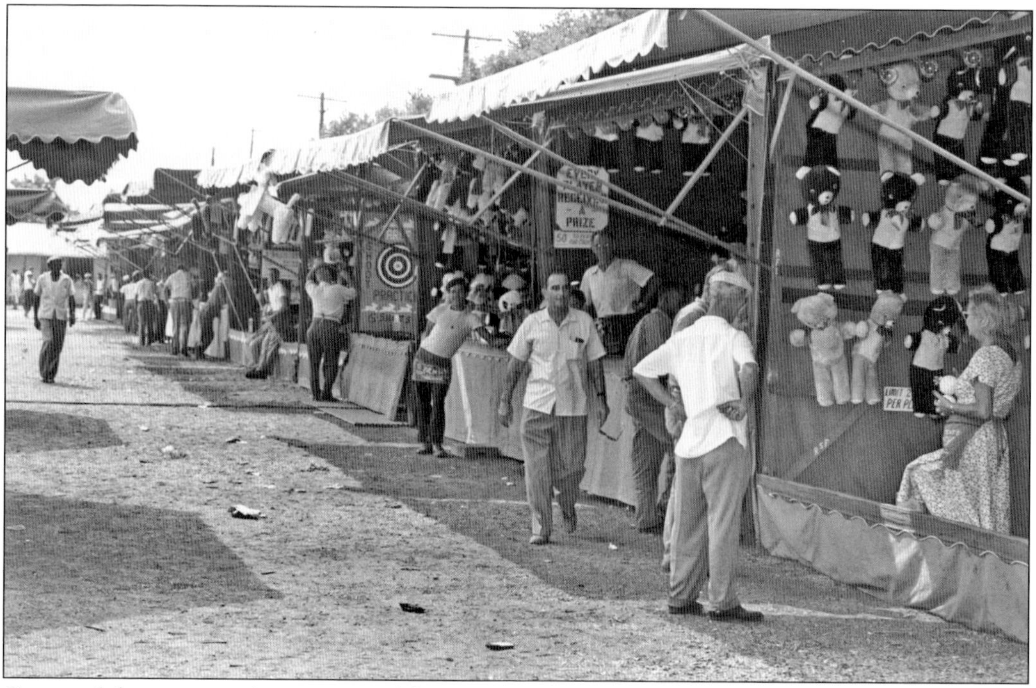

Games of chance were always a part of the carnival. From knocking over milk bottles and shooting clay pipes and ducks to pitching pennies to win dishes, locals flocked to these games for the chance to win prizes, and the guys wanted to show off their skills to impress their favorite gal. (Courtesy of the Delaware Public Archives.)

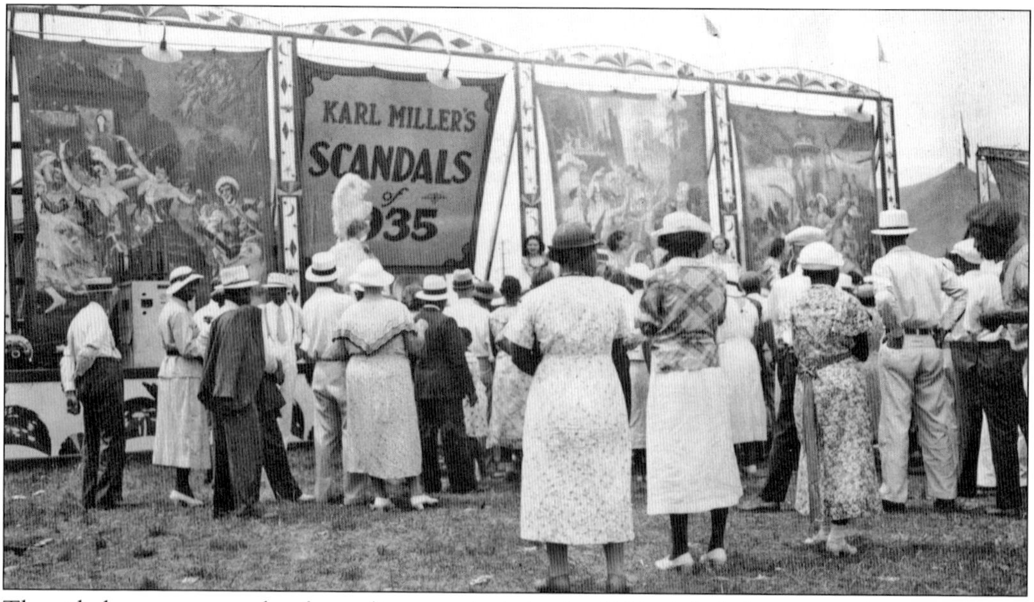

The sideshow was a staple of traveling carnivals in the 1900s. Made famous in America by P.T. Barnum, soon every carnival had its own acts. From the snake charmer to the tallest or smallest person, patrons would pay 10¢ to see the oddities of the sideshow. The "girlie shows" were also a part of these traveling caravans—ladies would dance in an adults-only show. (Courtesy of the Hagley Museum & Library.)

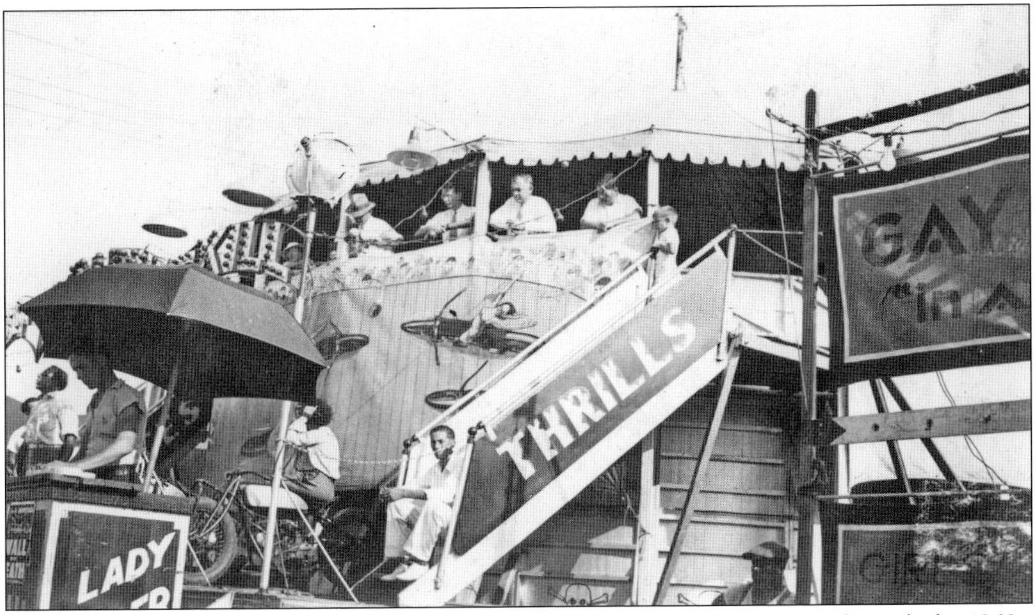

The Wall of Death was another sideshow act that was popular from the 1930s through the 1960s. Daredevils would climb aboard their motorcycles and begin to build up speed, slowly climbing the walls while driving faster and faster. As many as four riders at a time would weave in and out, thrilling onlookers with spine-chilling action. (Courtesy of the Hagley Museum & Library.)

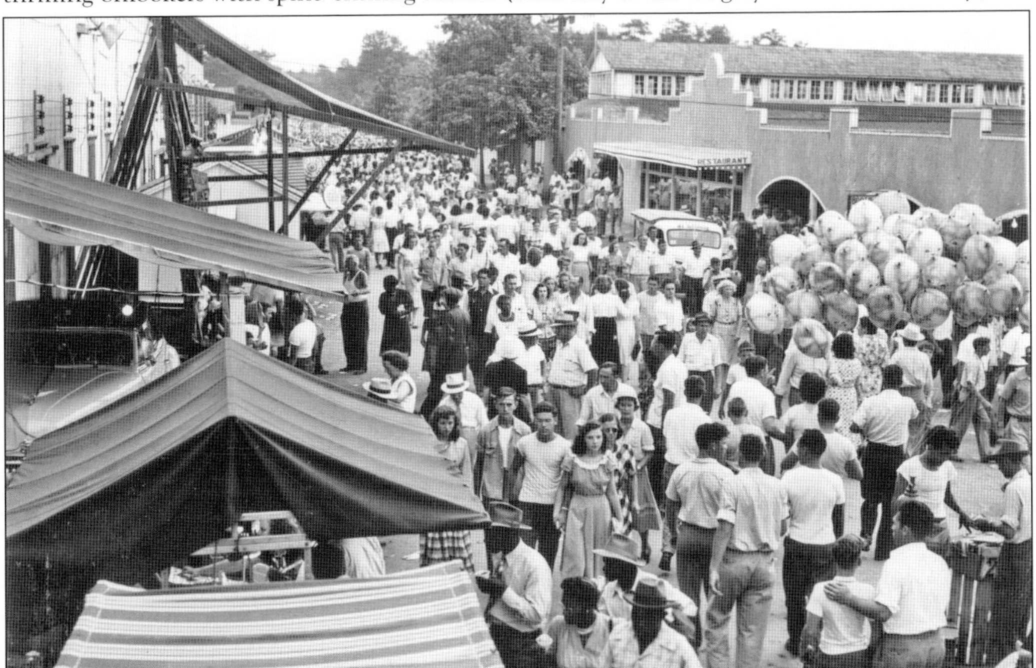

By the mid-1950s, the fair was booming. Each year's crowds set new records for attendance. Larger and more permanent structures replaced older ones. Some had been constructed by German prisoners of war, as the fairgrounds had housed prisoners in 1945 and 1946. During these years, no fair events occurred due to security reasons. (Courtesy of the Delaware Public Archives.)

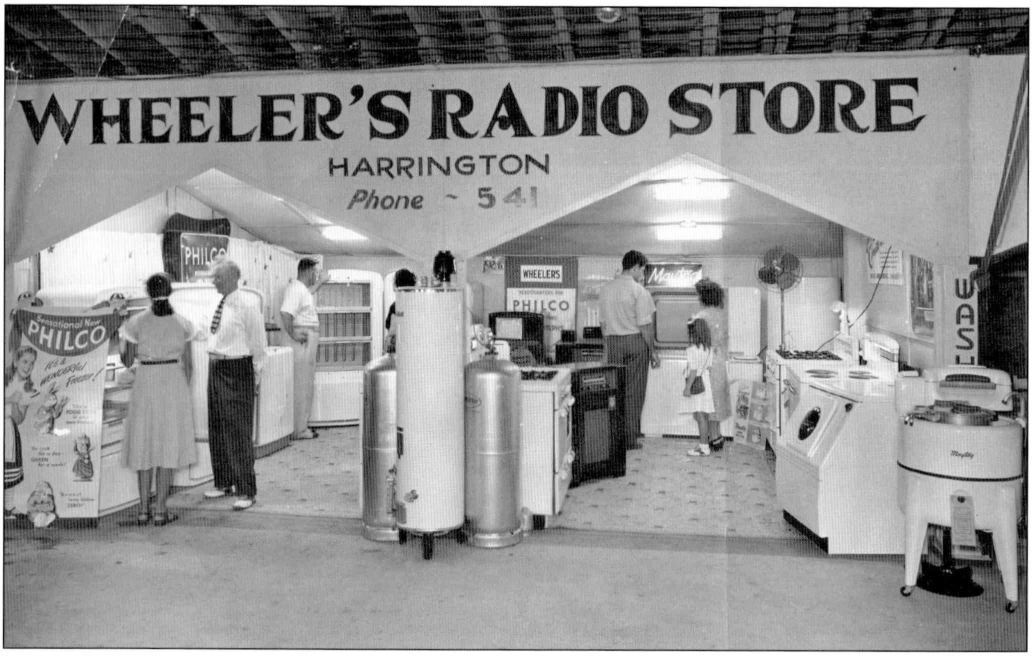

Local and regional businesses came to the fair to display and sell their latest products. Wheeler's Radio store, operated by William Wheeler of Harrington, set up a large venue under the grandstand displaying the newest in appliances, radios, and the new fad in America, television. Patrons would stop by and browse the deals being offered at the fair.

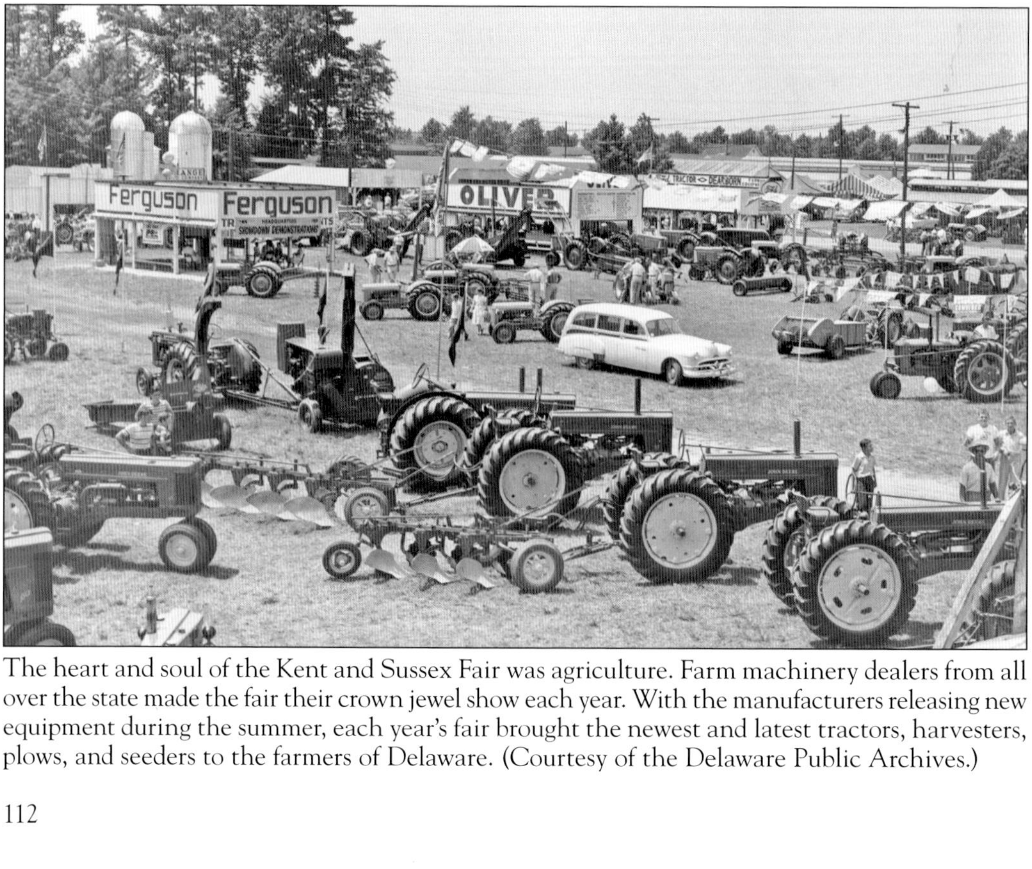

The heart and soul of the Kent and Sussex Fair was agriculture. Farm machinery dealers from all over the state made the fair their crown jewel show each year. With the manufacturers releasing new equipment during the summer, each year's fair brought the newest and latest tractors, harvesters, plows, and seeders to the farmers of Delaware. (Courtesy of the Delaware Public Archives.)

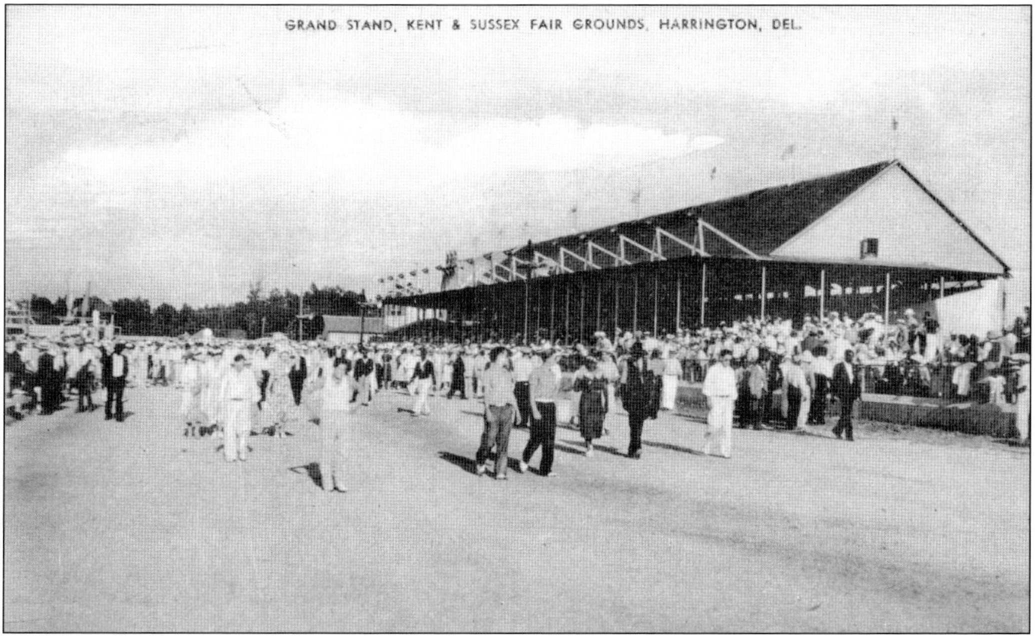

In 1955, with the new grandstand in place, fairgoers paraded in front of the grandstands for various reasons. From dressing up their cows and participating in the prettiest cow contest to simply putting on their Sunday finest and walking the harness track, everyone wanted to take in the new all-metal grandstand as it gleamed in the sunshine.

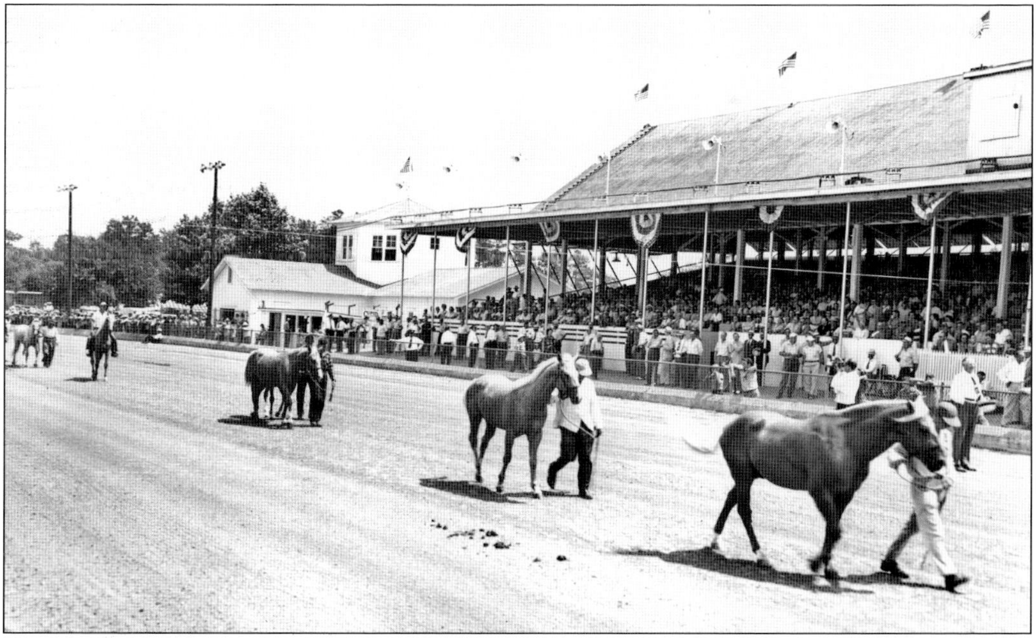

The grandstand allowed harness racing to thrive at the fairgrounds. In 1945, the State of Delaware passed legislation to allow pari-mutuel betting on the harness racing industry. On August 15, 1946, a 15-day harness racing meet was scheduled. The event was a huge success, actually lasting 18 days. This event was the first on the Maryland-Delaware circuit and one of the first on the East Coast. (Courtesy of the Delaware Public Archives.)

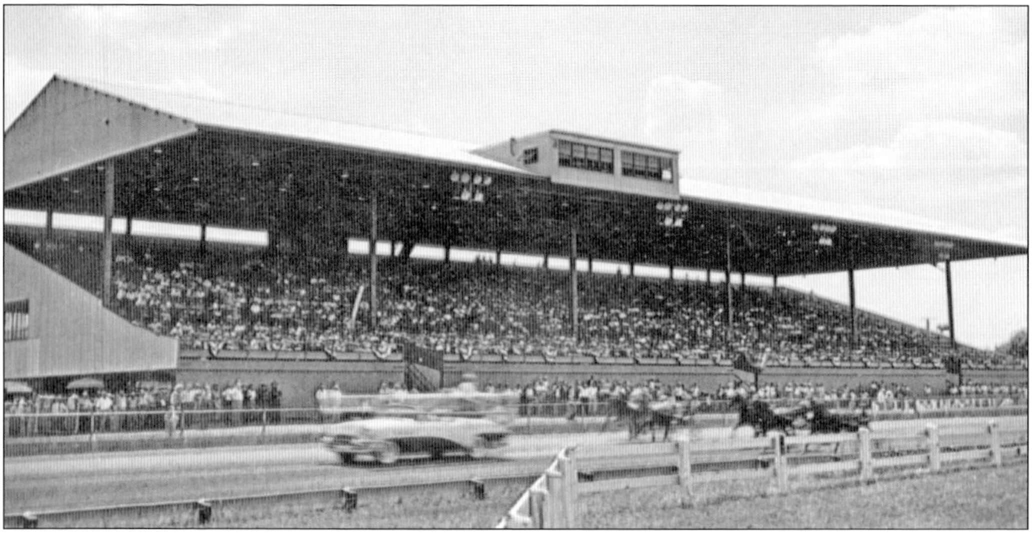

When pari-mutuel betting began, the harness racing portion of the fair had to create a separate organization. In order to maintain its close relationship with the association, the group chose the name Kent-Sussex Racing Association. The name changed again in March 1967 to the Harrington Raceway. Crowds would stream into the grandstands to watch and bet on their favorite horses. Perhaps the most famous horse to ever run the half-mile track at Harrington was Adios Harry. Owned by J. Howard Lyons of Harrington and trained and driven by son Luther Lyons, he won the 1954 Little Brown Jug, setting a new three-heat record for three-year-old pacers. At five, Adios Harry held 12 world pacing records at distances ranging from a mile to a mile and a half. He was featured on the front cover of the July 23, 1956, issue of *Sports Illustrated* magazine. (Below, courtesy of the Delaware Public Archives.)

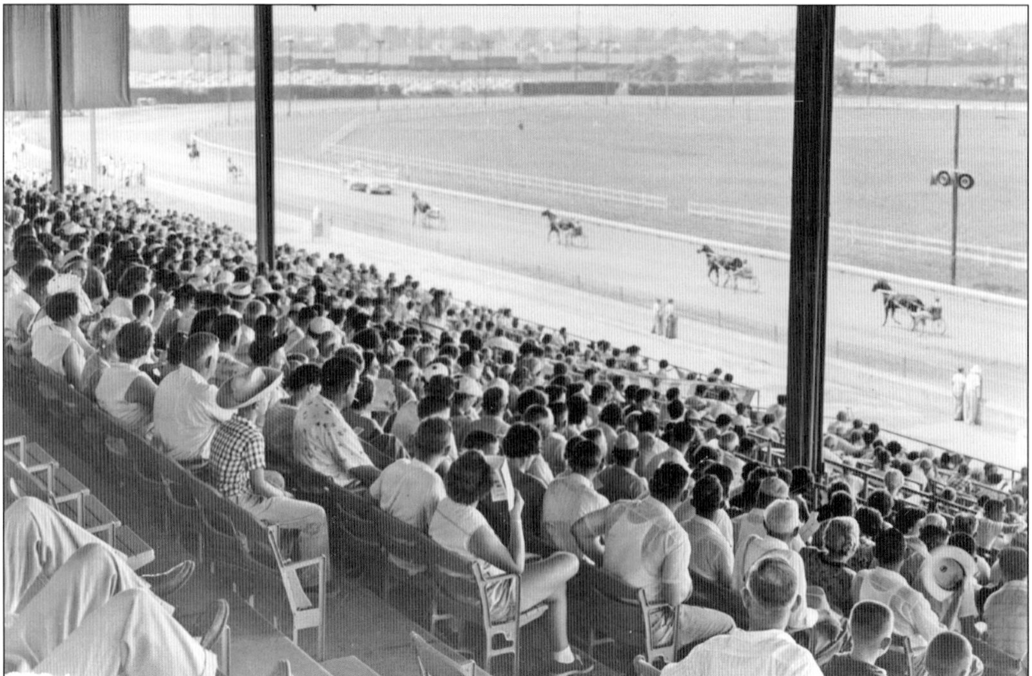

Eight

Showing Our Civic Pride

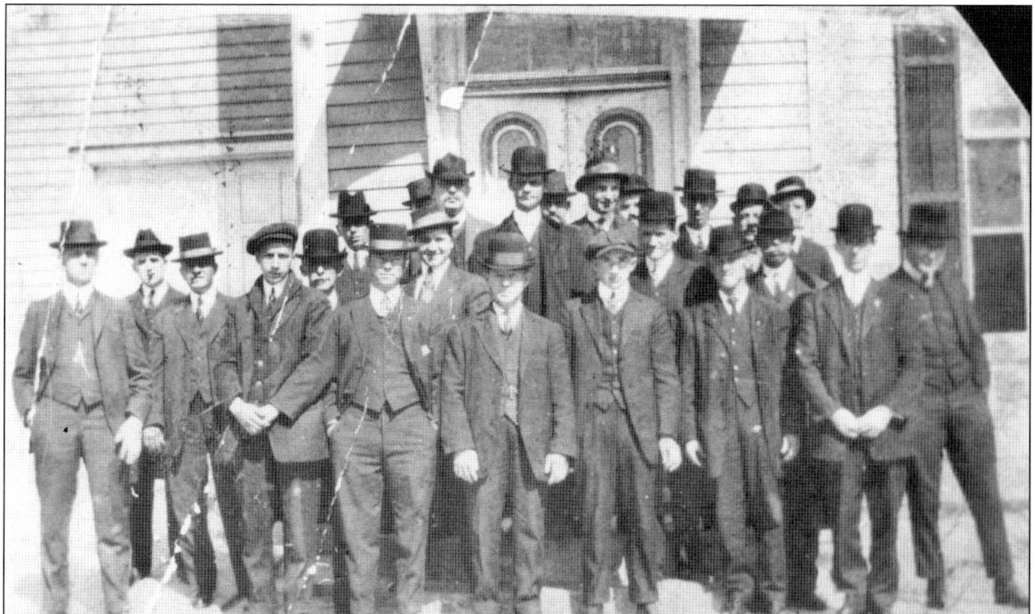

On August 15, 1905, a special meeting of the citizens of Harrington was called to organize a volunteer fire company. A committee was formed to write a constitution and bylaws, and on September 15, 1905, the Harrington Fire Company Inc. was born. The former Methodist Episcopal church served as the fire hall.

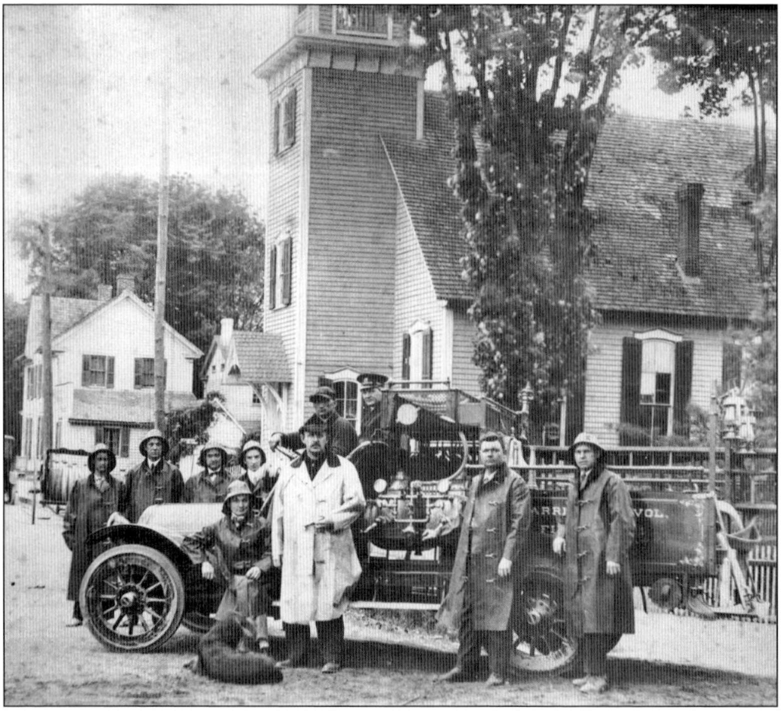

From 1908 until 1913, the fire company was inactive, mostly due to a lack of a fire engine. On March 1, 1915, a movement was begun to purchase a chemical engine for the fire company. Chances were sold on a Ford Model T car, with the man holding the winning ticket donating the car back to the fire company. The engine was delivered on January 2, 1916.

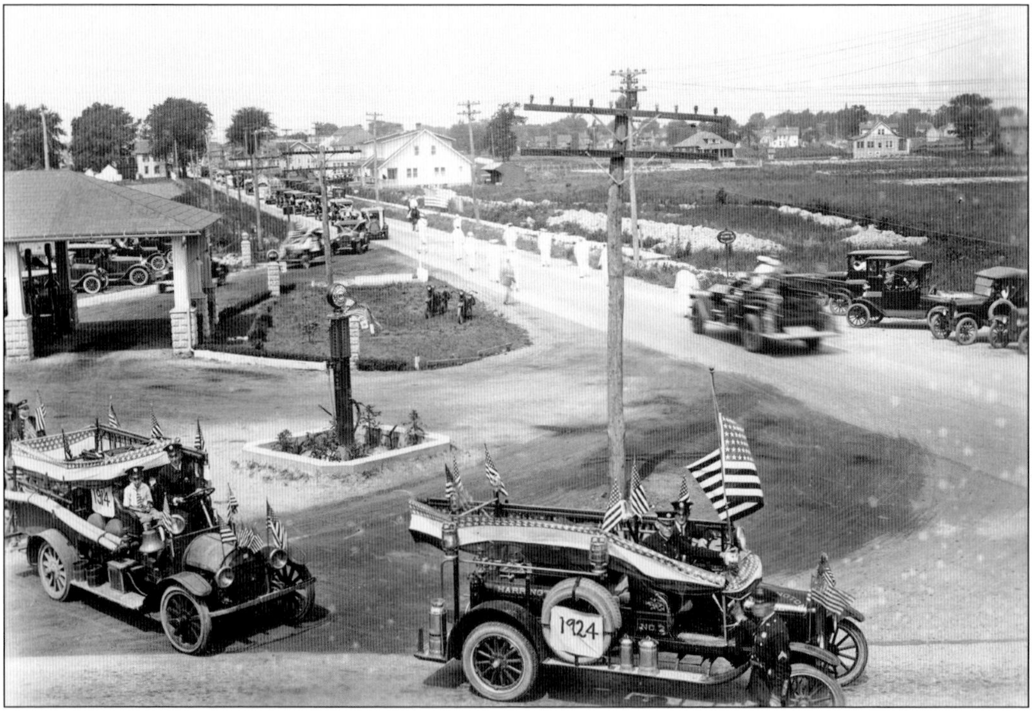

On January 27, 1919, the fire company reorganized, adopting a new constitution and bylaws. Membership began to climb. The fire company became a symbol of town pride, and the company held an annual parade through the streets of Harrington showing its appreciation to the citizens it protected. (Courtesy of the Delaware Public Archives.)

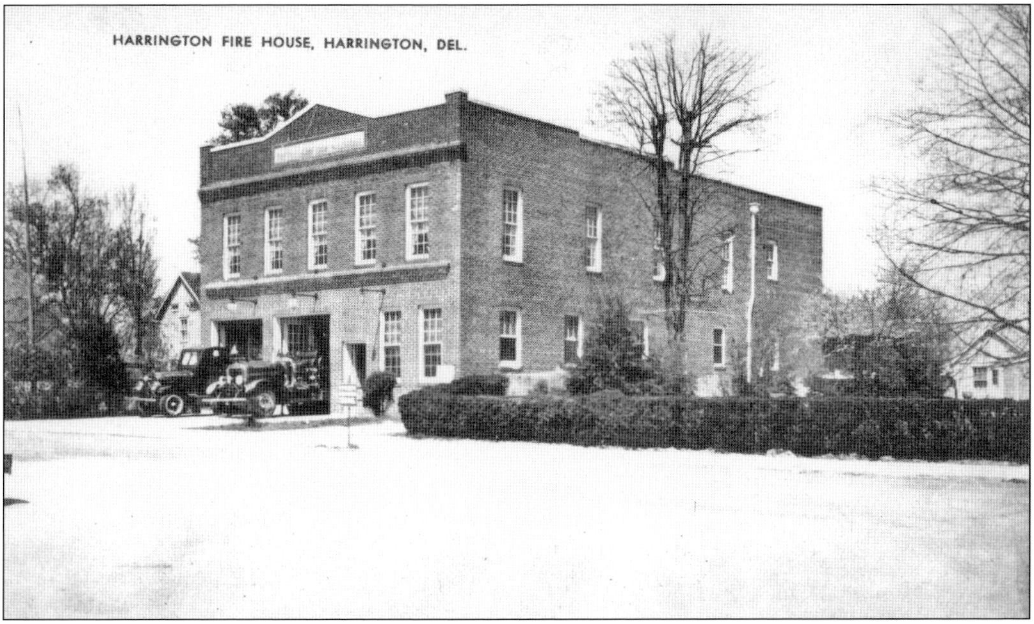

A new, modern fire house was built in the 1930s. Designed to house the two engines the department owned, by the 1960s it was home to four fire trucks and an ambulance. The fire company began to provide ambulance service to the town in 1953; before that, house calls were the method by which most received care, and trips to the hospital were in the cars of family or friends.

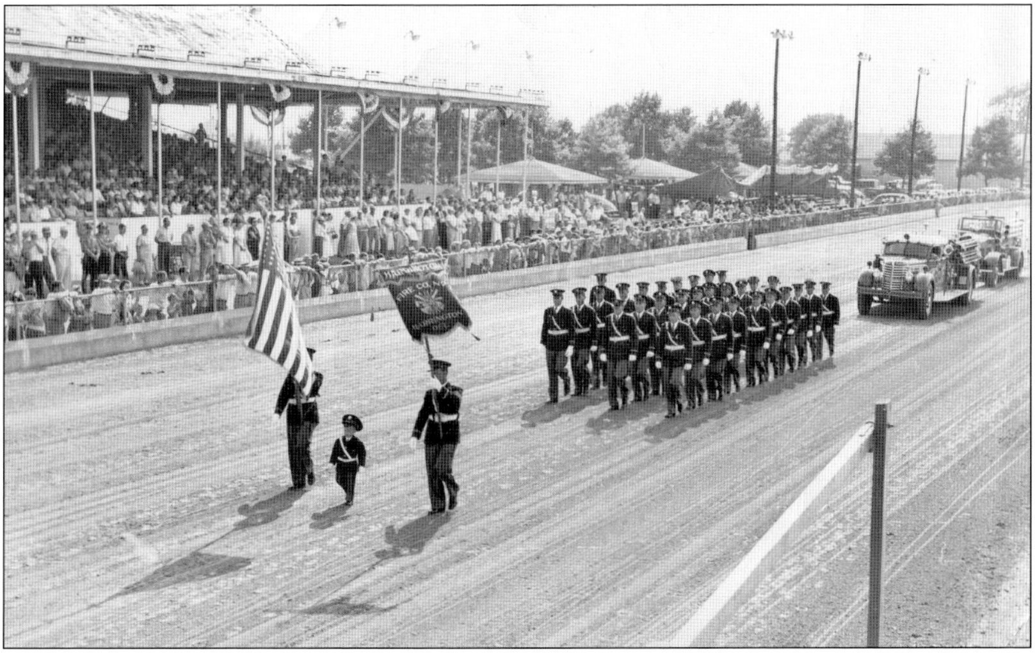

The Harrington Fire Company continued to serve the community not only as volunteer firemen but also in the cherished role as the ambassadors for the city. The fire company marched in parades all over the area, frequently bringing home multiple trophies and prizes. Pictured here during one of their annual parades at the fairgrounds in the mid-1940s, this dedicated group made Harrington proud.

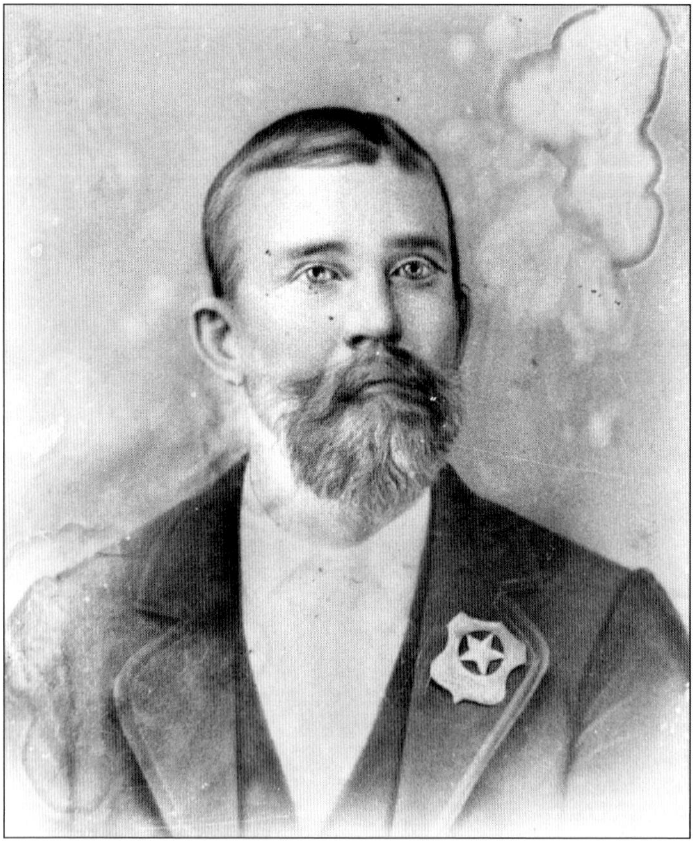

John Wesley Paris was the first constable in the town of Harrington. He also doubled as the lamplighter, since the streetlamps were gas fired. With his son Fred at his side, he lit the lamps each night, extinguished them each morning, and cleaned the lamp glass. The Parises owned a small black horse that was also a part of the team. Fred would climb up on the horse's back and light the lamp, and as soon as he sat down, the horse would gallop to the next light and stop without any directions. In 1946, the Harrington Police Department purchased its first motorized police car. Pictured below is the new vehicle with Patrolman Frank Morgan.

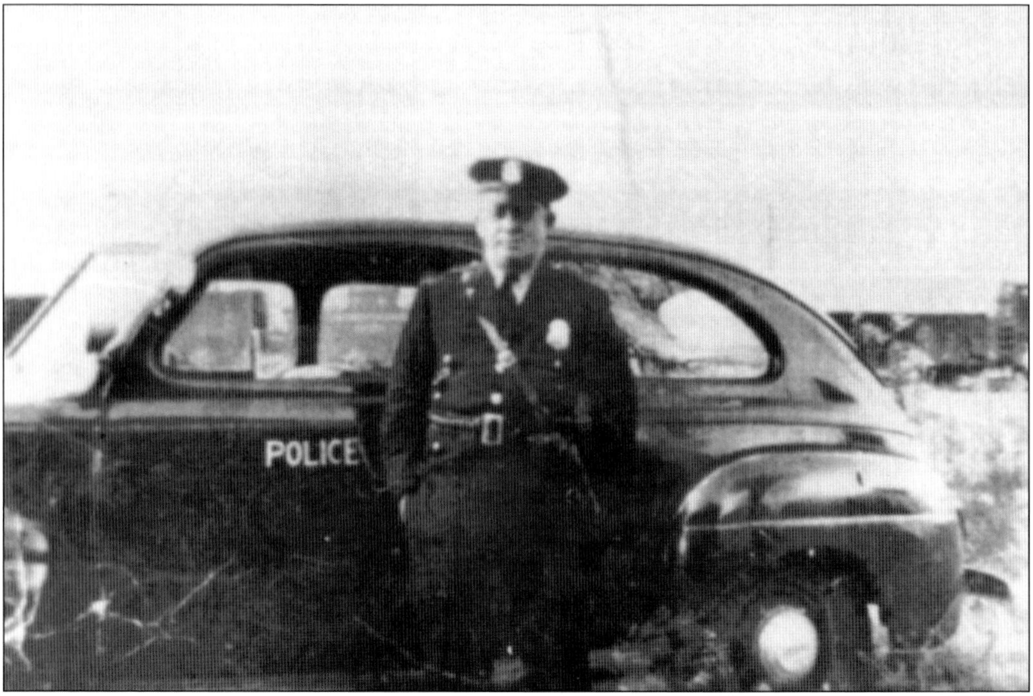

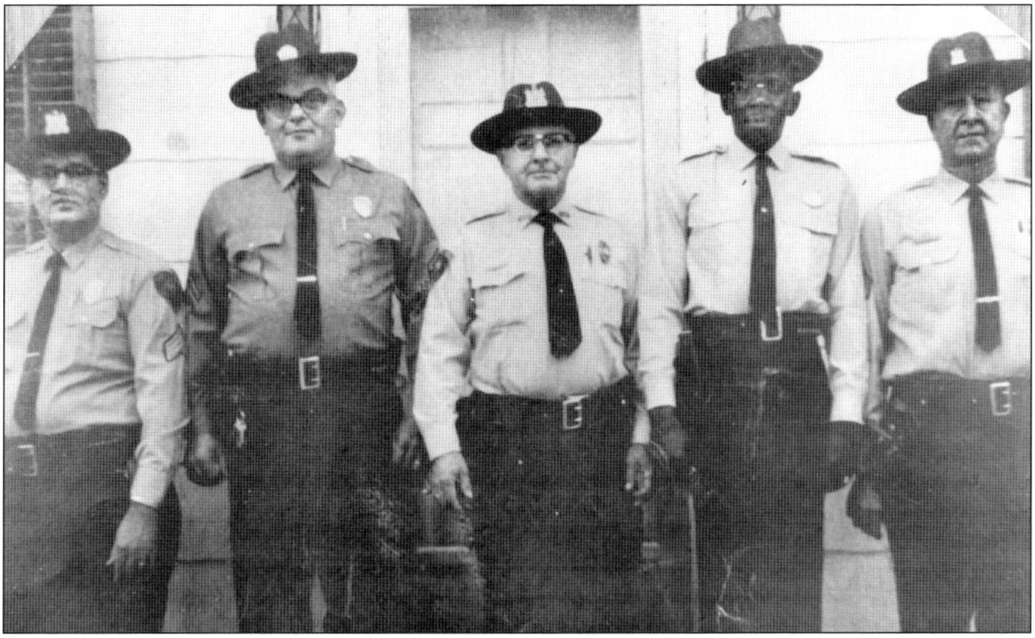

In 1964, the police department was under the direction of Chief Franklin Rogers (center). The department now provided 24-hour coverage to the citizens. Harrington was one of the first towns in the state to employ a black police officer, in the early 1960s.

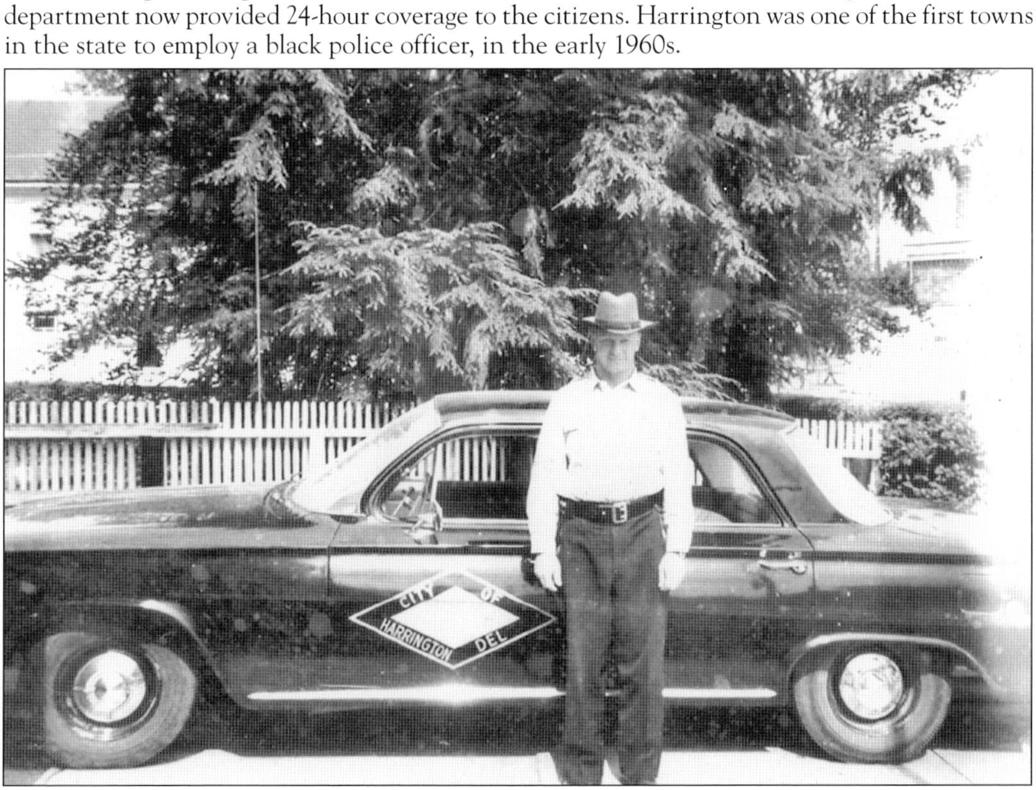

By the 1970s, the department was under the direction of Chief Dave Peterson. Chief Peterson doubled as the head of the city's water and sewer department. When the chief retired from the police force in 1978, he continued to serve with the water department for another decade.

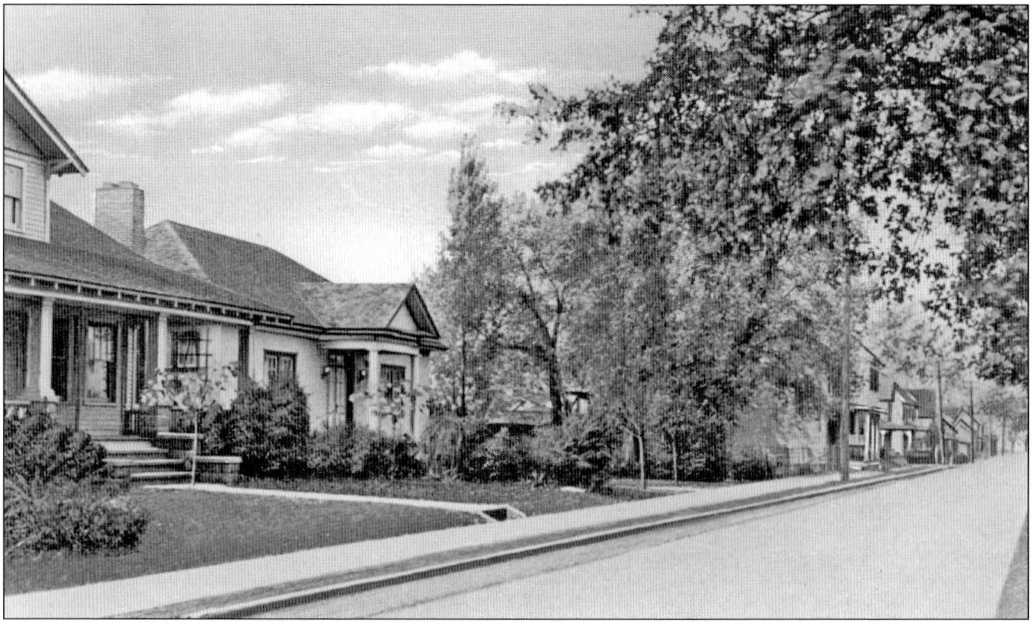

The New Century Club was founded on April 9, 1909, by a group of women looking to raise money to beautify the city. They installed two water fountains and set about planting trees and flower gardens to enhance the city's appeal. In 1921, it purchased the building pictured above for a clubhouse. For decades, this dedicated group worked to improve the aesthetics of the city. In 1959, it gathered to celebrate its golden anniversary. During the American bicentennial, the club partnered with the city to plant trees around town. (Above, courtesy of the Delaware Public Archives.)

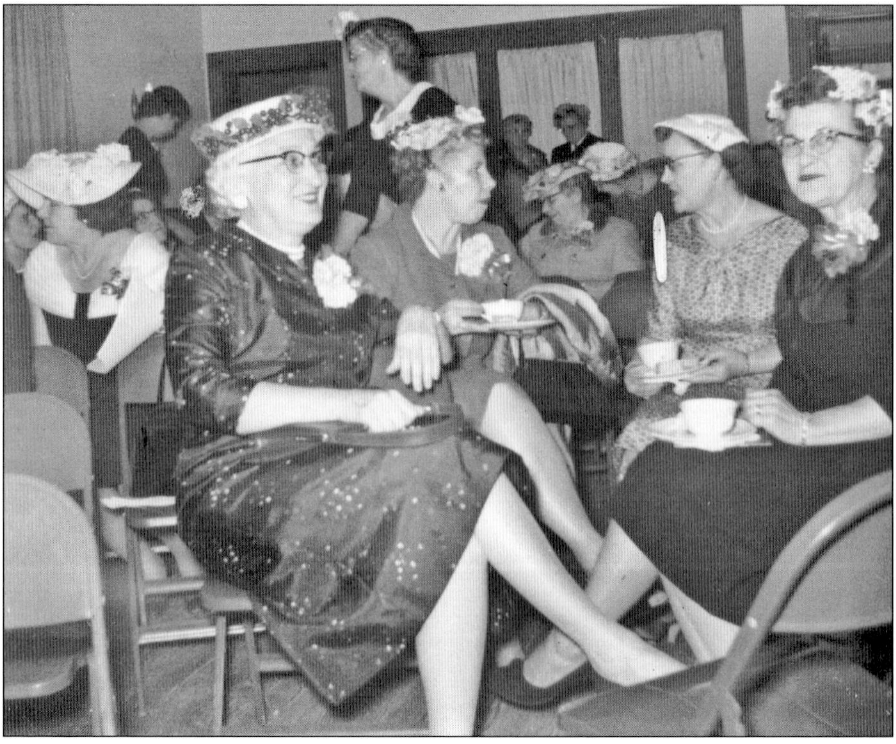

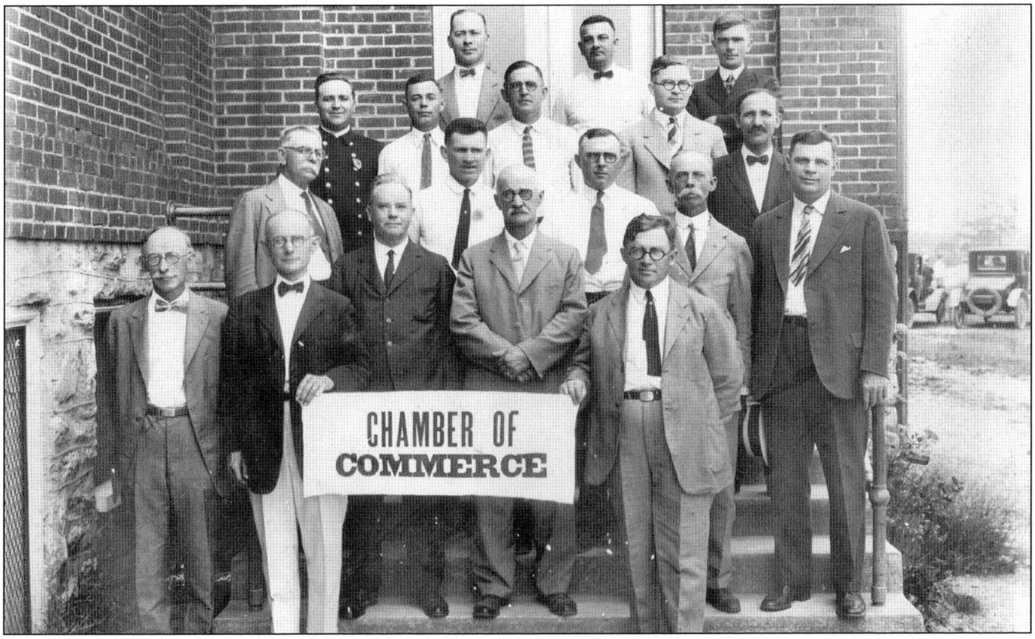

The Harrington Chamber of Commerce was founded in 1928. The group of men promoted businesses and business opportunities in the Harrington area. From left to right are (first row) John Sheldrake, Garrett Harrington, and Wilbur Jacobs; (second row) Rev. George Morris, Mayor D.E. Sawtelle, S.O. Bailey, and Frank B. Smith; (third row) Frank White, Luther Johnson, Fred Wilson, and Rev. Ed Collins; (fourth row) Harry Tee, Fred Greenly, Will Sharp, and Ernest Raughley; (fifth row) Dr. William T. Chipman, Warren T. Moore, and James Cahall.

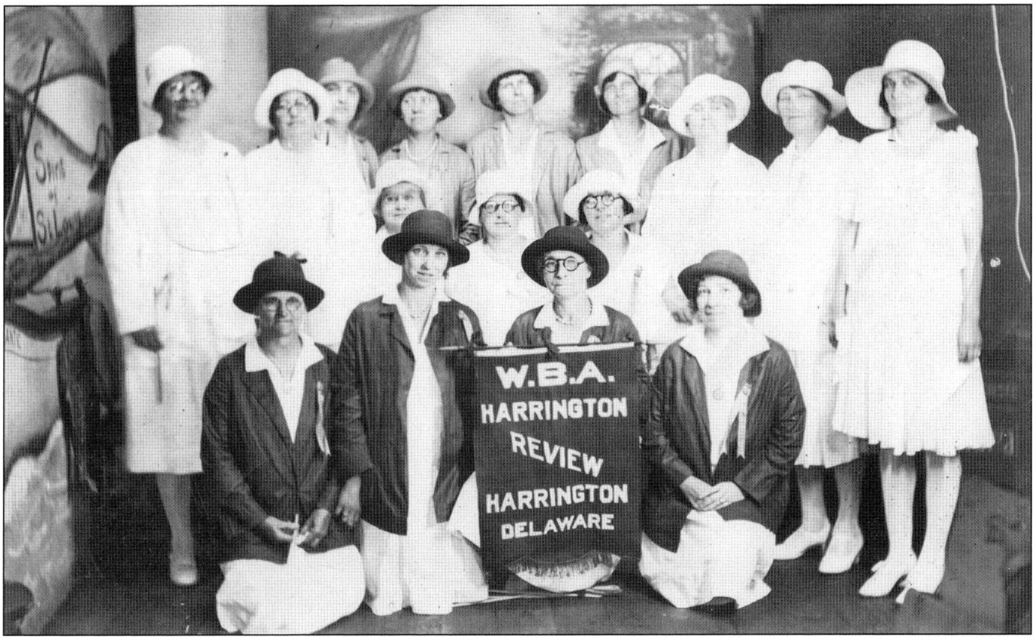

Harrington also boasted the Women's Business Association. This group was founded for women who either owned businesses or were in positions of stature within businesses in the city. This group promoted fair wages and opportunities for all women in the workforce as early as the 1930s.

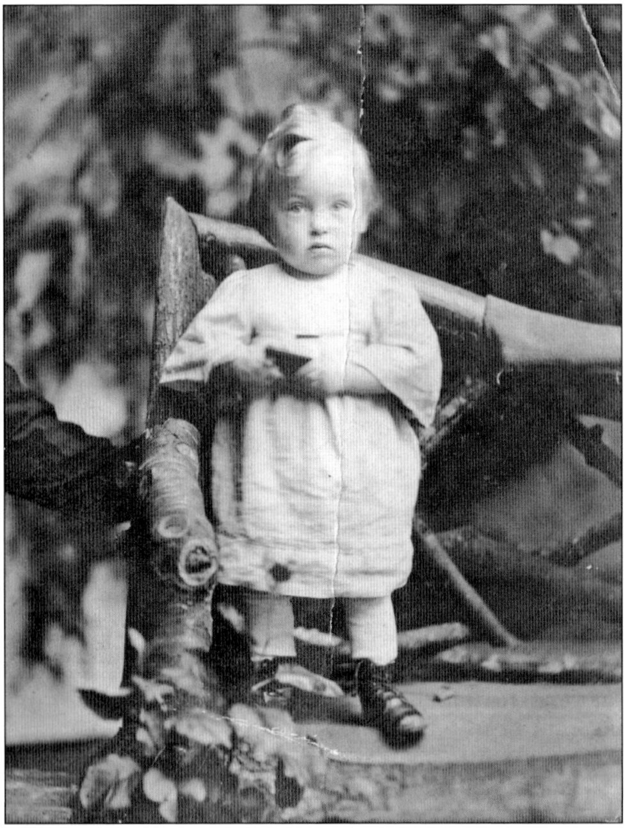

Heroes come in all shapes and sizes, but each begins as a small child. John Mitchell Butler was born on June 23, 1918, on the family farm near the country crossroads of Andrewsville, Delaware, just outside of Harrington. As a young man, John got his pilot's license, purchased his own plane, and enjoyed flying as often as possible.

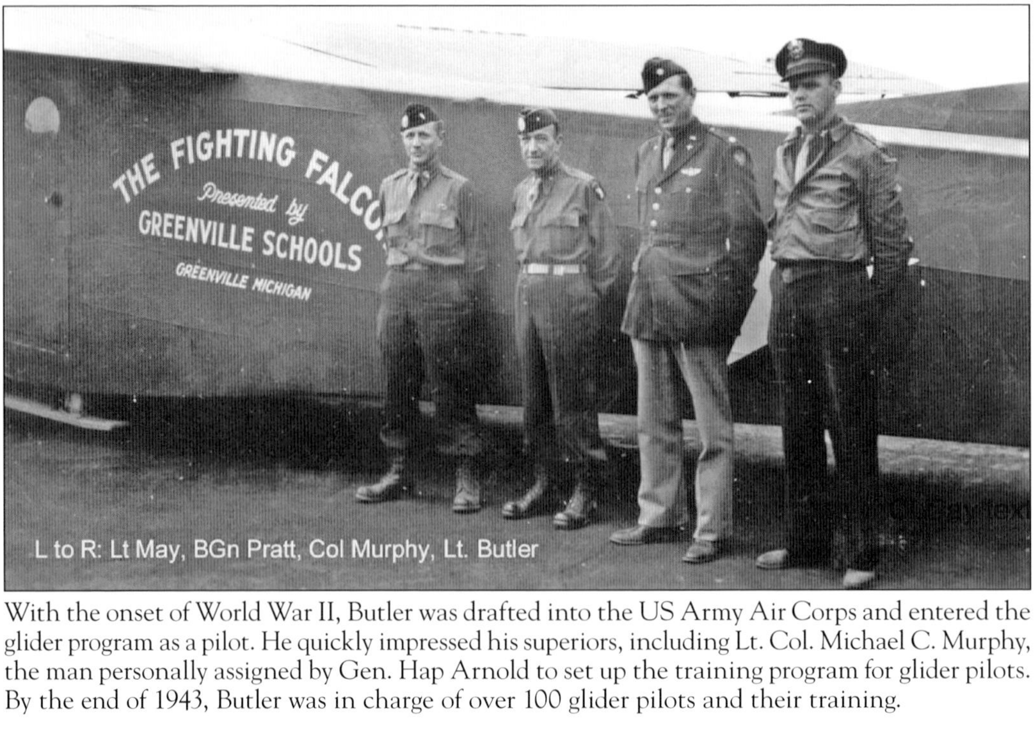

L to R: Lt May, BGn Pratt, Col Murphy, Lt. Butler

With the onset of World War II, Butler was drafted into the US Army Air Corps and entered the glider program as a pilot. He quickly impressed his superiors, including Lt. Col. Michael C. Murphy, the man personally assigned by Gen. Hap Arnold to set up the training program for glider pilots. By the end of 1943, Butler was in charge of over 100 glider pilots and their training.

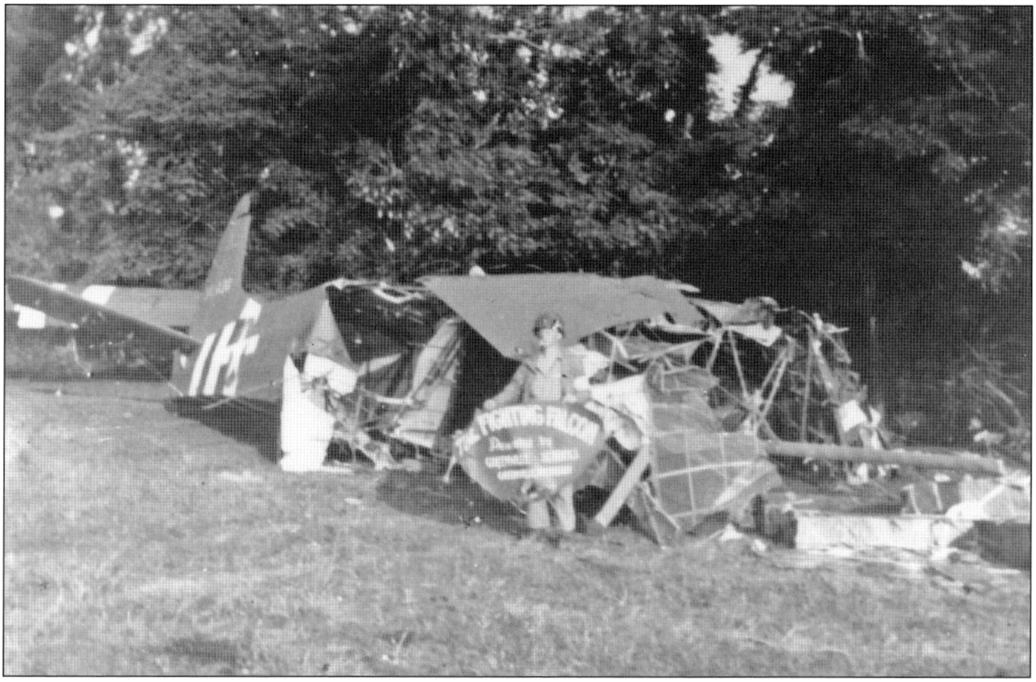

Butler and Murphy were transferred to Europe to prepare for D-Day. They again impressed their commanders, so these two pilots were placed in charge of all glider operations for the Normandy invasion. During preparations, Murphy asked Butler if he would fly with him on D-Day. Butler agreed, and the two were assigned glider position 1 in a glider named the *Fighting Falcon*, funded fully by a group of schoolchildren from Michigan. They transported Brig. Gen. Don Pratt, the second in command of the 101st Airborne Division, and his aide, Lt. John L. May. Landing at just after 4:00 a.m. on June 6, 1944, the glider crashed, killing Pratt and Butler. Murphy suffered severe injuries but survived. May suffered only minor injuries. When Butler's body was returned home in 1948, he was given a funeral befitting a fallen hero.

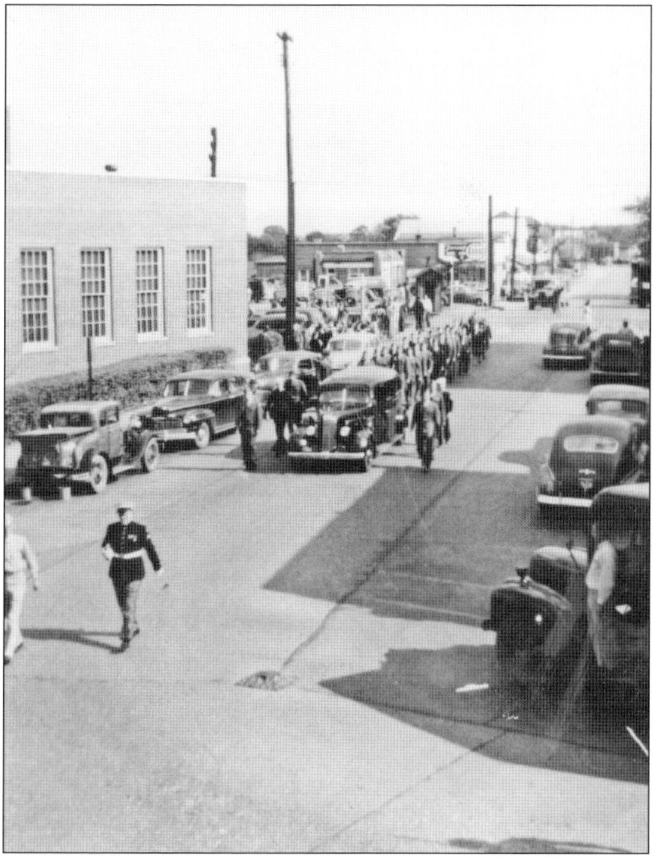

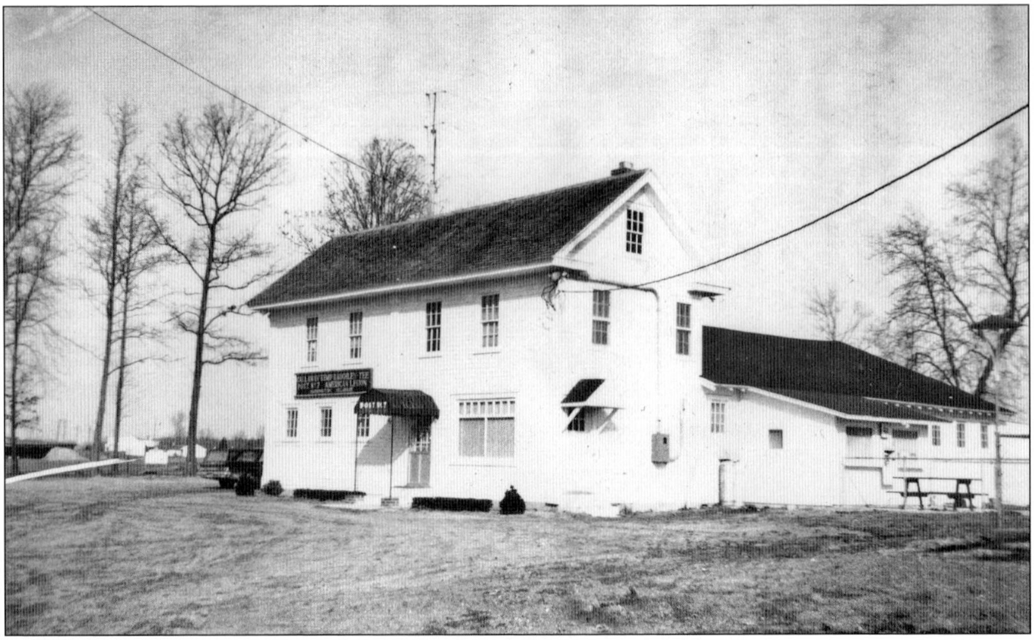

The American Legion Post Callaway, Kemp, Raughley, Tee No. 7 was founded in October 1919 with 16 members. The officers were Capt. Dr. Joseph Bringhurst, commander; Lt. John Kern, vice commander; Earl Sylvester, adjutant; Horace Riley, finance officer; and Coursey Langrell, chaplain. Early meetings were held at the firehouse and the local bank. In 1948, the building in this photograph was constructed.

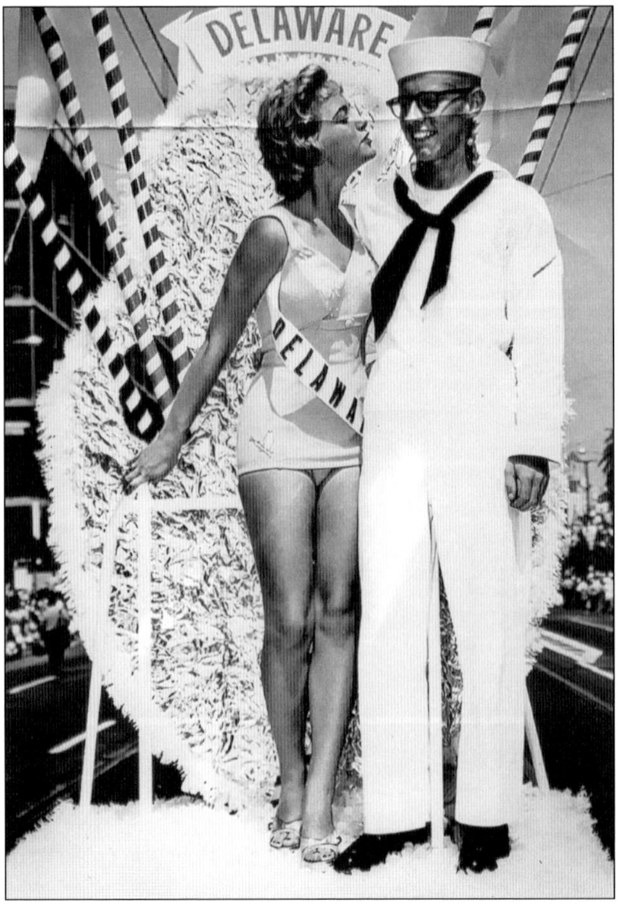

Harrington was honored to have three women represent the town and the state in the Miss America pageant. Pictured here is Linda Humes, Miss Delaware 1959. The photograph shows her and an unidentified lucky sailor riding on the float used during the Miss America pageant.

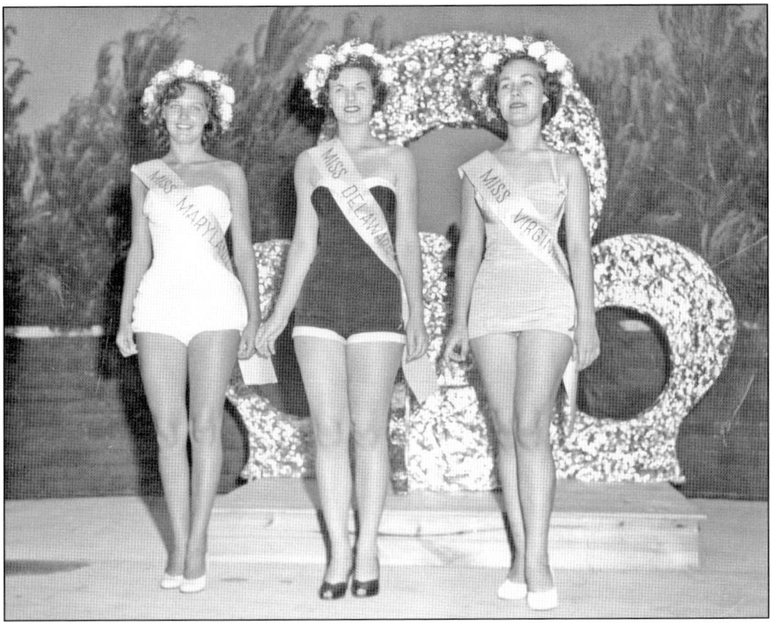

In 1953, Barbara Smith was the beauty queen from Harrington selected to represent Delaware. She is pictured participating in the Chicken Festival, held each year in a different town on the Delmarva Peninsula to celebrate the poultry industry that had become such a profitable business for farmers of the area. (Courtesy of the Delaware Public Archives.)

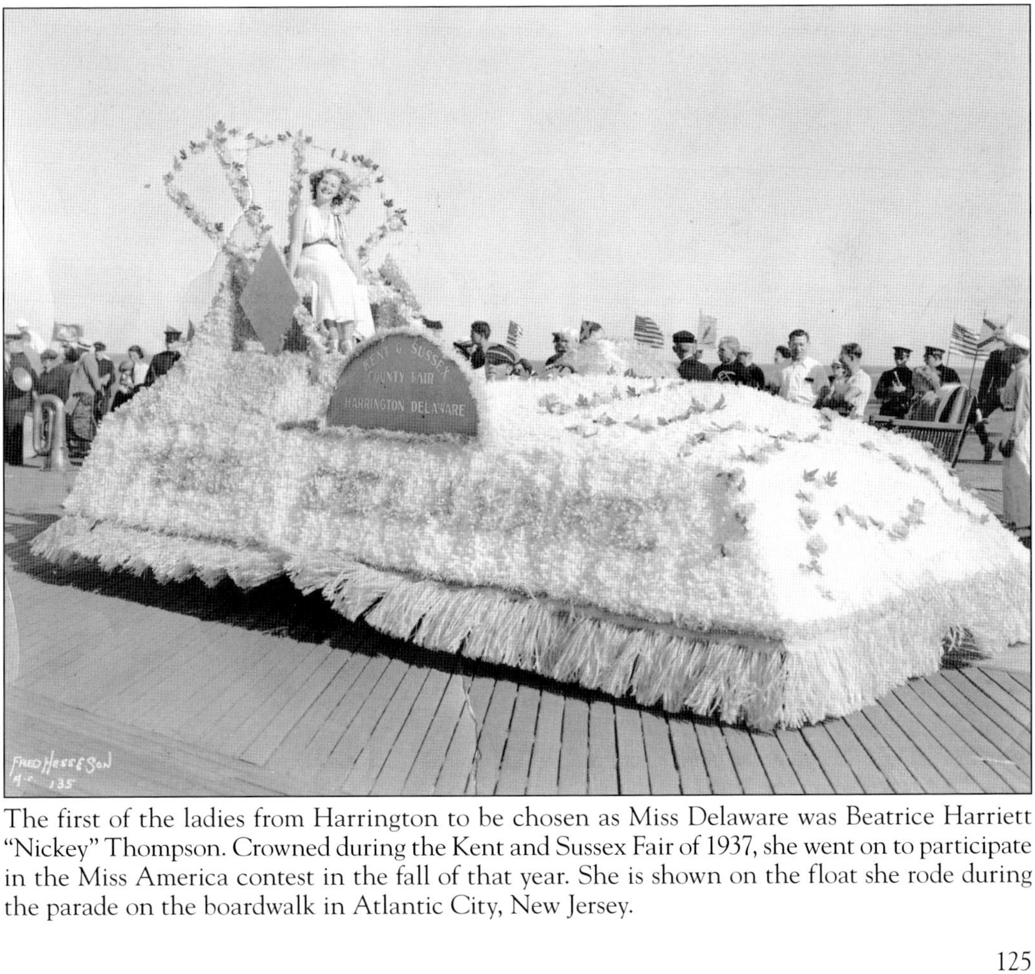

The first of the ladies from Harrington to be chosen as Miss Delaware was Beatrice Harriett "Nickey" Thompson. Crowned during the Kent and Sussex Fair of 1937, she went on to participate in the Miss America contest in the fall of that year. She is shown on the float she rode during the parade on the boardwalk in Atlantic City, New Jersey.

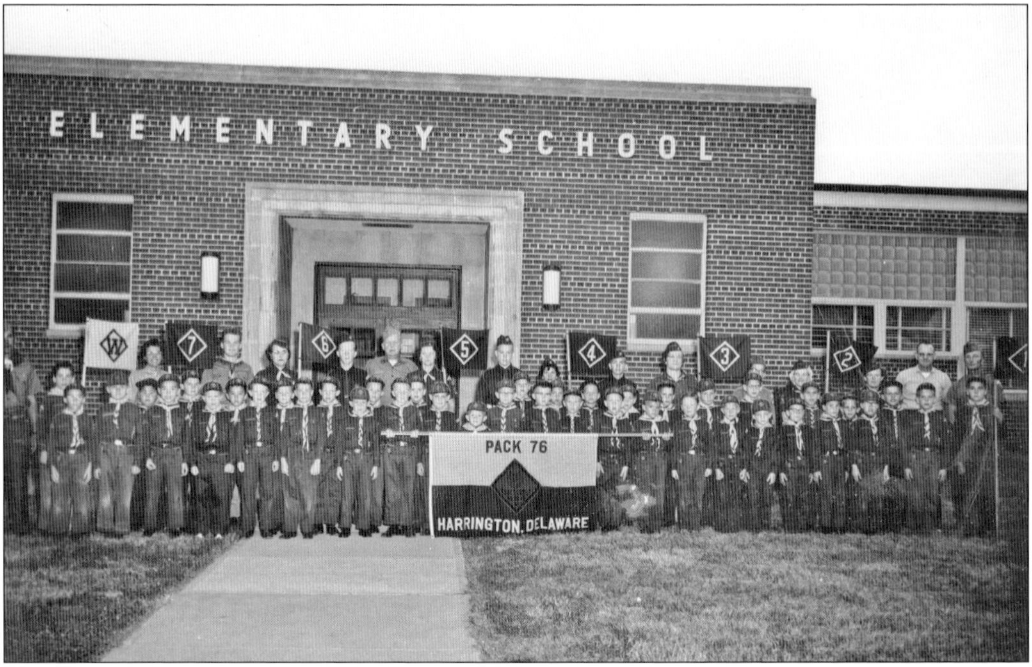

Boy Scout Troop 76 was founded in 1926, and meetings were held in the elementary school. J.C. Messner was the first leader of the organization. Shown here in the 1950s, the organization now had seven Cub Scout dens, one Webelo den, and one Boy Scout troop. The boys performed community service and activities to earn their badges.

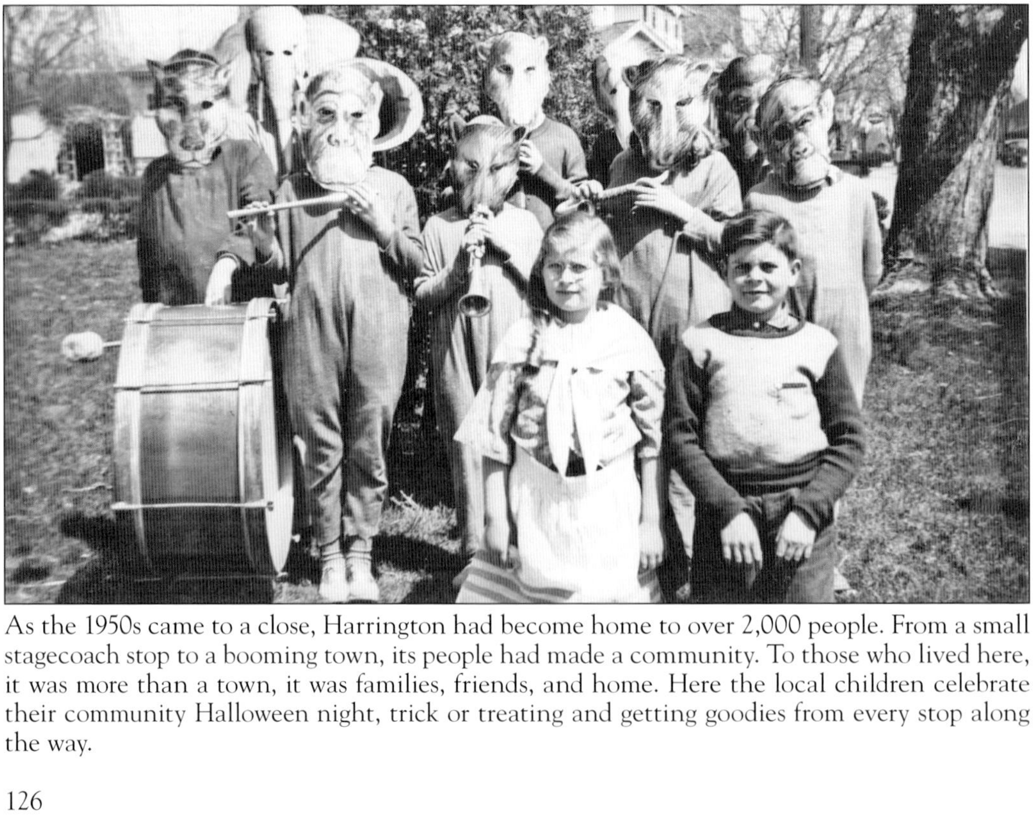

As the 1950s came to a close, Harrington had become home to over 2,000 people. From a small stagecoach stop to a booming town, its people had made a community. To those who lived here, it was more than a town, it was families, friends, and home. Here the local children celebrate their community Halloween night, trick or treating and getting goodies from every stop along the way.

About the Greater Harrington Historical Society

The Greater Harrington Historical Society is 40 years old and still thriving. Not surprisingly, it began in one of Harrington's best known places, Burton's Sports Shop and Soda Fountain. Maybe it was the history surrounding them, maybe they saw a need, but whatever their motivation, the founders set out to preserve the history of the area they knew as their home. Slowly they reached out, mostly by word of mouth and articles in the town's newspaper, to the citizens of the town and the small crossroads in the countryside. The first museum barely filled a small room. A few showcases displaying items from the area were the first attempt by the group to preserve the town's history. Little did any of them dream that the group they began would amass a collection now numbering over 50,000 items. From a small room, they expanded to the first museum. While rescuing the history of the area, they also rescued a small red church, one of the oldest structures still standing in the town. Restoring the church to serve as their first home brought more members and more artifacts. The Harrington High School Alumni donated a large collection to the museum, once again filling the building they owned. Fortunately, the citizens saw the need to expand the museum again to save their history. They acquired property next to the church and constructed an annex to hold more artifacts. One of those artifacts was the soda fountain around which the first discussions to create the society were held. It was completely renovated in 2018 by Derek Hart of Norfolk, Virginia, so it once again dispenses old-time sodas, allowing today's citizens to enjoy the history that began it all. To make sure the town always remembers it roots, the historical society also purchased the railroad signal tower along with a 1925 caboose, and restored both to their original state. Plans had been made to destroy these items until the group stepped in to preserve them, allowing future generations to witness firsthand the items that helped shape the city. The group continues to seek out new items and ever expanding means to display the history of the area. The author's royalties from the sales of this book will go toward a building fund to once again expand the museum, providing interpretive displays and a new archives room that will allow visitors to research and read about the rich history of Harrington.

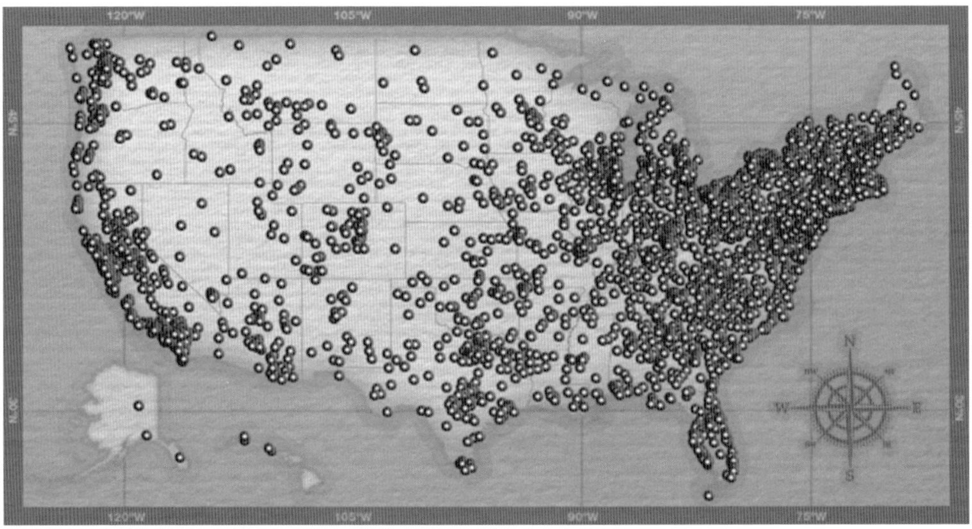

Consistent with our mission to preserve history on a local level, this book was printed in South Carolina on American-made paper and manufactured entirely in the United States. Products carrying the accredited Forest Stewardship Council (FSC) label are printed on 100 percent FSC-certified paper.

MADE IN THE USA